The Oglethorpe Plan

The Oglethorpe Plan

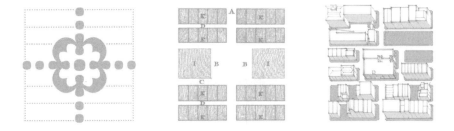

Enlightenment Design in Savannah and Beyond

Thomas D. Wilson

University of Virginia Press   *Charlottesville and London*

University of Virginia Press
© 2012 by the Rector and Visitors of the University of Virginia
All rights reserved
Printed in the United States of America on acid-free paper
First published 2012

9 8 7 6 5 4 3 2 1

LIBRARY OF CONGRESS CATALOGING-IN-PUBLICATION DATA
   Wilson, Thomas D., 1947–
     The Oglethorpe Plan : Enlightenment Design in Savannah and Beyond /
   Thomas D. Wilson.
     p. cm.
     Includes bibliographical references and index.
     ISBN 978-0-8139-3290-3 (cloth : alk. paper)
       1. City planning—Georgia—Savannah. 2. Oglethorpe, James Edward, 1696–1785.
   3. City planning—Social aspects. 4. Civic improvement. I. Title.
   HT168.S28W55 2012
   307.1'21609758724—dc23

                                                                    2012002590

Illustrations not otherwise credited are by the author.

Contents

List of Illustrations   vi

Preface   ix

Prologue: Historical Context   1

1. The Plan for a Model Colony   37

2. The Plan for an Ideal City   63

3. Implementation of the Plan   101

4. The Plan Today   134

5. The Future of the Plan   159

Epilogue: Enlightenment Legacy   189

Appendix A   Chronology of the British Enlightenment,
Oglethorpe's Life, and the Planning and Founding of Georgia   209

Appendix B   Biographical Profiles   214

Notes   219

Bibliography   233

Index   245

Illustrations

Tables

1. Purposes for establishing the Georgia Colony   53
2. Hierarchy of regional plan elements   70
3. Structure of the regional plan   71
4. Savannah regional plan specifications   83
5. Ward element dimensions in feet, cubits, and ells   87
6. Chronology of the settlement of Georgia   103

Figures

1. The Oglethorpe family tree   5
2. The royal houses and the Oglethorpe family   6
3. Events and political alliances during the economic revolution (1688–1756)   18
4. *A Scene from The Beggar's Opera*   33
5. *A Harlot's Progress*   35
6. *Bambridge on Trial for Murder*   39
7. Idealized depiction of Georgia Colony   64
8. Peter Gordon map of Savannah, 1734   66
9. Map of Savannah County   67
10. Plan of Zamosc   75
11. Plan of Timgad   77
12. Map of Chatham County, 1873   80
13. Completed six-ward plan for Savannah, 1770   82
14. Conceptual regional plan of Savannah   84
15. Savannah regional map, to 1798   85
16. Ward design specifications   87

17. McKinnon map, 1798   94
18. The Georgia Trustees   107
19. Map of the Georgia Colony and part of Carolina, 1741   110
20. Urban residential character   136
21. Urban commercial character   136
22. National Historic Landmark District   138
23. Historic wards and squares of Savannah   139
24. Map of the city of Savannah, 1856   142
25. Restoration of Decker Ward   145
26. Ellis Square parking garage   146
27. Ellis Square restored   146
28. Civic Master Plan, East Riverfront   147
29. Savannah and the original grid   152
30. Plan of New Ebenezer   154
31a. Plan of Darien, 1806   155
31b. Plan of Darien, ward design, 1788   155
32. Pedestrian connectivity   183
33. Shared space   183
34. Focused redevelopment   184
35. Multiple opportunities for entrepreneurship   184

Preface

In Savannah one hears constant references to the Oglethorpe Plan. The name has acquired a certain magic that conjures up a sense of continuity in the city's history yet also a sense of relevance that transcends time. Deep reverence for the plan is also found among historians, urban designers, and town planners, who count it among the world's great city plans. Yet the term *Oglethorpe Plan* remains obscure, with many connotations but no precise delineation.

The core purpose of this book is to define the Oglethorpe Plan in terms of its original intent and then to demonstrate that facets of the plan remain relevant today. One only needs to visit Savannah to see that a portion of the plan remains remarkably intact and adaptable to modern conditions, yet little of the plan has been deconstructed and reapplied elsewhere. It follows that the intended result of this investigation is to stimulate thought about how a brilliant plan, born in the Enlightenment, can be brought to light and put to use outside of its historic preserve in Savannah.

Quotations from Oglethorpe and his contemporaries are used extensively in establishing the historical context of the plan. The lack of standardization in the English language during Oglethorpe's time, however, is such that the original style could easily become a distraction for a modern reader. Therefore, quotations and excerpts from primary source material, such as minutes and letters, are often modified with modern spelling and grammar.

Dates are less frequently modernized. England used the Julian calendar until 1752, when it switched to the modern Gregorian calendar. Thus all original records related to the conception, founding, and early settlement of Georgia used the old calendar. The formal entity authorized by royal charter to found the colony, the Trustees for Establishing the Colony of Georgia in America, thus began the New Year on April 1. Some later editions of their records clarify the dates between January 1 and March 31 by referencing both years; thus the first anniversary meeting of the Trustees is often recorded as March 15, 1732/33. An eleven-day difference in the calendars is generally left uncorrected, except where new dates are commonly cited, as in the founding of Georgia, which was on February 1, 1732, under the old calendar and is corrected to February 12, 1733, for the new calendar. Where clarification is required, a Julian calendar date is noted by the convention Old Style (O.S.) and a Gregorian calendar date is noted as New Style (N.S.).

Many people and organizations over the course of years of research have informed and inspired the content of this work. At the University of Virginia Press Boyd Zenner provided wise counsel at critical times and escorted the book project to completion; Angie Hogan and Mark Mones added much to the book's improvement during its later stages. George Roupe, as copy editor, greatly improved the final product.

Colleagues at the Chatham County–Savannah Metropolitan Planning Commission provided vital support. Milton Newton, executive director when the project was conceived, established the productive and creative environment necessary to begin the work. Beth Reiter, historic preservation officer, now retired, was among the few who understood the deep structure of the Oglethorpe Plan. Sarah Ward, historic preservation officer, offered invaluable assistance. Alan Bray and Courtland Hyser of the Comprehensive Planning Division provided insights into the relationship between the historic plan and modern challenges such as gentrification and critiqued early manuscripts. Mike Weiner with the City of Savannah Engineering Department and David Anderson with Chatham County Engineering Department assisted in locating important materials.

Libraries and museums provided essential support. Appreciation is due to staff of the Hargrett Rare Documents Library of the University of Georgia, particularly Mary Linnemann and Chuck Barber, who were consistently helpful in locating critical material. Glenda Anderson with the Savannah City Research Library facilitated the discovery of an early map that supported new conclusions about the plan for Savannah, and Luciana Spracher, the city archivist, ably located other necessary resources. The staff at the library of the Georgia Historical Society in Savannah assisted many times in navigating through their extensive holdings. The Beaufort

County Library facilitated interlibrary loans; special thanks to reference librarian Stacey Edmonds. Candy Lowe, director of the Massey School Museum for Architecture and History, also provided essential support.

Teri Norris collaborated on graphic concepts and created several illustrations that appear in the book; she also provided insightful comments on various draft chapters. Several other people offered invaluable advice as the manuscript matured into this book. Professor Kenneth C. Martis of West Virginia University read the entire first draft and offered insightful and detailed comments. Dr. Imre Quastler, professor emeritus of San Diego State University, read early draft material and provided continual support. Professor Barry Haack of George Mason University offered encouragement and professional advice. Valerie Webb and Elizabeth Doerr of GeoEye provided satellite images for analysis purposes. Andrew Haack of the U.S. Geological Survey provided technical assistance with aerial and space imagery. Patrick Shay of GMS Architects and Planners in Savannah offered comments and support through several early drafts. Christian Sottile, of Sottile & Sottile Urban Design, provided an insightful and detailed review of chapter 4. Others providing invaluable support were Dr. Clark Alexander of Skidaway Institute of Oceanography; Buddy Sullivan with the Sapelo Island National Estuarine Research Reserve; Thomas Erwin; and Dr. G. M. Jeffery, an authority on tropical diseases. Elizabeth Emslie, American Institute of Certified Planners, personified a theme of the book on a daily basis through her work as a planner with humanistic values, and her mother, my wife Susan Townsend, never wavered in her support.

Advances in the field of planning, as in most endeavors, generally occur through the gradual accrual of knowledge. Advances in planning also occur through challenges to existing practices and paradigms, "planning by provocation" as it might be called. This work intends to fall as much in the latter category as the former, particularly in presenting an argument by historical example that humanism should be the organizing principle of the profession. The speculations, interpretations, and conclusions about the Oglethorpe Plan, which attempt to support that argument, are the author's, and thus any flaws of reasoning that may be discovered are attributable solely to him.

The Oglethorpe Plan

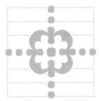

Historical Context

James Edward Oglethorpe is known today principally for three accomplishments. He was a prison reformer, chairing a parliamentary committee that investigated conditions in three debtors' prisons. He was the founder of the Georgia Colony, inspired to act on behalf of the working poor, especially those released from prison as a result of his efforts. And he was the town planner who created the unique ward design now enshrined in the Savannah National Historic Landmark District.

Most of the literature on these accomplishments portrays them in static terms: Oglethorpe's committee led to the release of thousands of inmates and marginally improved prison conditions, but a complete overhaul of the system would not come for another fifty years. His founding of the Georgia Colony was a utopian scheme that dissolved after twenty years of futile effort. His design of Savannah's wards is revered as a masterpiece of planning yet rarely applied by the planners who praise it.

This static portrayal of Oglethorpe's role in history and his relevance today underestimates his contributions to social reform, political theory, and town planning. The present study provides an alternate interpretation, deconstructing the Oglethorpe Plan to portray Oglethorpe as a more dynamic influence in history. While the focus is on Oglethorpe's contribution to town planning, the scope is necessarily wide because the plan he conceived for Georgia was both broad and deep. The plan provided a template for town and regional development coupled with a system of social equity, all of which rested on a humanistic political philosophy. It was that philosophy that led the historian Phinizy Spalding to describe Oglethorpe in more fluid terms than do most authorities on Georgia history, placing him among the American founders, comparing him with Thomas Jefferson, and characterizing him as a man of the Enlightenment.[1]

Many of the principles embedded in the Oglethorpe Plan are as relevant today as the humanistic principles articulated at the dawn of the American Revolution. Yet urban planners, although deeply appreciative of Oglethorpe's plan for Savannah, have fallen short of recognizing the larger framework of his planning model, particularly as it relates to the problem of fostering social equity through physical design—a problem too often addressed only superficially in the planning and design professions. Close examination reveals that Oglethorpe's principles of integrated town planning can be widely applied rather than confined to the living museum of a revered historic district.

The focus on Oglethorpe, therefore, is essentially empirical more than biographical, historical, or philosophical. Oglethorpe synthesized a comprehensive body of ideas and practices, aspects of which demonstrably have modern applications. Most important, his integrative and humanistic approach to planning is one that planners should study as they increasingly embrace the intersection of physical design, the natural environment, and human ecology. Additionally, it will be shown that functional elements of the Oglethorpe Plan offer enhancements and alternatives to current practices.

Oglethorpe's greatest legacy may well be the Savannah plan, which contains the genetic code of Enlightenment humanism. The Enlightenment is particularly relevant today as planning and design professions search for a means to place humanism at the core of a new planning paradigm. Enlightenment humanism may be defined as a social philosophy that emphasizes basic human fulfillment and seeks to achieve social equity through rational methods of solving human problems.[2]

The Oglethorpe Plan was meant to be a path to a model society, one that would circumvent political upheaval and bloodshed. The argument that Oglethorpe intended to create a model society on the nation's frontier is speculative, since he never went on record with a specific statement to that effect. However, this book builds on the work of historians and biographers by triangulating Oglethorpe's position from the many initiatives he undertook, from those with whom he associated, and from the intellectual traditions he followed.

James Edward Oglethorpe was more than an intriguing figure in history. His social reform initiatives and the Georgia colony were vital pieces in the progression of the Enlightenment. His integrated approach to planning the Georgia colony suggests a better model for planning at various levels today. And his often-cited yet poorly understood design of Savannah, preserved in a renowned historic district yet responding to the needs of a modern city, is even more relevant today than it was in 1733.

A Plan Framed by the Ideals of the Enlightenment

The Oglethorpe Plan, a portrait of the Enlightenment, yielded the only colony that embodied all of the major themes of the age, including science, humanism, diversity, and secularism. The last of the thirteen colonies, Georgia would become the first to embody the principles later embraced by the Founders. Remnants of Oglethorpe's portrait of the Enlightenment exist today, and they reveal the vibrancy of ideas behind its conception. The fact that those remnants were preserved for so long and the portrait is now being partially restored invites exploration of its enduring qualities.

At the heart of Oglethorpe's comprehensive and multifaceted plan there was a vision of social equity and civic virtue. The mechanisms supporting that vision, including yeoman governance, equitable land allocation, stable land tenure, prohibition of slavery, and secular administration, were among the ideas debated with the establishment of Georgia and refined later in the century by the American Founders. The historical context in which the Oglethorpe Plan was conceived must be understood to fully appreciate its structure.

Oglethorpe was born in the aftermath of the Glorious Revolution, an abrupt turning point in British history that also marked the beginning of the Enlightenment. The revolution was followed by wide-ranging material advancements and intense debate about whether those advancements created social stability. The dynamic new age, with all of its opportunities and challenges, was the context in which Oglethorpe's character and purpose in life developed. His plan for a new colony, the Oglethorpe Plan, would synthesize promising elements of the new age with proven elements of British tradition and Roman civilization. His purpose for establishing the colony, at its core, was to create a model for reviving Britain's rural values and the traditional role played by the gentry under Stuart regimes, a role that he viewed as essential to a stable and beneficent society.

An assessment of influences on Oglethorpe's life and his plan for the Georgia Colony must therefore begin with family. As members of the gentry, the landowning class below the nobility, the Oglethorpes believed it was their duty not only to serve the nation's royalty, which they had done for generations, but also to support and represent working-class citizenry who depended on them for their livelihood. The sense of duty to the worthy people who worked the land would become a guiding principle for Oglethorpe throughout his life.[3]

The Oglethorpe Family and the House of Stuart

The lives and fates of the Oglethorpes and the house of Stuart became increasingly intertwined over the course of the seventeenth century and well into the eighteenth century. The Oglethorpe family tree and the family's relationship with the Stuarts are illustrated in figure 1 and figure 2.

The reign of the house of Stuart in Great Britain began with James I in 1603, following the death of Queen Elizabeth, the last monarch of the house of Tudor. The only child of Mary, Queen of Scots, James had been prepared by advisors in Elizabeth's ministry to succeed her. During his reign, he authorized a new translation of the Christian Bible (the King James Version) and expounded a new doctrine of divine right, which asserted that a monarch derives authority from God and not from the people. The balance of governmental powers finely tuned under Queen Elizabeth began to shift toward the monarchy under James.

James was succeeded in 1625 by his son, Charles I, who placed increased emphasis on the doctrine of divine right and sought to vest near-absolute power in the monarchy. Charles's relationship with Parliament deteriorated irreversibly when he eased restrictions on Catholics, thereby threatening the authority of the Church of England. His rule became progressively more tyrannical, leading to the English Civil War, which began in 1642. The fighting paused in 1648 when Charles was captured, brought to trial, and sentenced to death. James Oglethorpe's grandfather, Sutton Oglethorpe, who commanded loyalist forces, was imprisoned and heavily fined by the republican government of Oliver Cromwell.[4]

In 1660, Parliament ended the republican experiment, which had become dictatorial, and restored the monarchy under Charles II. Following the Restoration, as this event is known, the Oglethorpe family fortunes were again on the rise. Lands confiscated from Sutton Oglethorpe during the Commonwealth period were returned. New lands were later awarded by the king to Oglethorpe's father, Theophilus, an army captain, for defeating Scottish rebels in 1679. Subsequent services to the king led to additional rewards and promotions.[5]

Theophilus was quartered on the Thames River next to the royal palace when he met Eleanor Wall, an employee of the royal household. The

FIGURE 1 The Oglethorpe family tree

Sir Theophilus Oglethorpe
(1650–1702)
Born in Bramham, Yorkshire
Raised Protestant

Lady Eleanor (Ellen) Wall Oglethorpe
(1662–1732)
Born in Tipperary, Ireland
Raised Catholic

Lewis (1681–1704)
Never married; served as MP for Haslemere (1702–4); died in Europe from combat wounds

Theophilus Jr. (1682–1737)
Never married; worked for East India Company; MP for Haslemere (1708–13); made Baron Oglethorpe by James III

Anne Henrietta, baptized An Harath (1683–1756)
Never married; made Countess of Oglethorpe by James III; lived at Westbrook and later moved to France

Eleanor (1684–1775)
Lived in France from 1689; married the Marquis de Mezieres; had seven children; descendants include members of royal families throughout Europe

Luisa Mary (Molly) (1693–?)
Married the Marquis de Bersompierre; lived in France and then in Spain, where she held a post in the royal court

Sutton (1693)
Molly's twin
Died in infancy

James (1689–1690)
Died at age one

Frances Charlotte (Fanny) (1695–?)
Married the Marquis des Marches of Piedmont; had at least one son; lived in France until she became lady-in-waiting to the queen of Savoy and Sicily ca. 1726

James Edward
(Dec. 22, 1696–June 30, 1785)
Founder of Georgia
Married Elizabeth Wright, 1744; had no children; resided with Elizabeth at her estate in Cranham and their town house in London

Sources: Ettinger, *Imperial Idealist*, chapter 1; Roberts, "Notable Kin"; Hill, *Oglethorpe Ladies*, chapter 1. (Hill identifies a child named Charles born in 1686 who died in infancy.)

FIGURE 2   The royal houses and the Oglethorpe family
(dates indicate the reign of each monarch)

HOUSE OF STUART

James I (1603–25)
Son of Mary Queen of Scots

Charles I (1625–49)
Son of James I
Executed during the English
Civil War

**Commonwealth of
England,** 1649–58

Charles II (1660–85)
Son of Charles I

James II (1685–89)
Son of Charles II
Exiled by the Glorious Revolution

William and Mary
William III (1689–1702)
Mary II (1689–94)
Daughter of James II

Anne (1702–14)
Daughter of James II
Last Stuart monarch

James III (b. 1688, d. 1766)
James Francis Edward Stuart
"The Old Pretender"
Son of James II

James Francis Edward Stuart
(b. 1720, d. 1788)
"Bonnie Prince Charlie"
or "The Young Pretender"
Son of James III

HOUSE OF HANOVER

George I (1714–27)
Great-grandson of James I

George II (1727–60)
Eponym of Georgia Colony

George III (1760–1820)
Urged by Oglethorpe to avoid the
American Revolution

OGLETHORPE FAMILY

Sutton
Grandfather of James Edward Oglethorpe
Loyal to Charles I

Theophilus and Eleanor
Parents of James Edward Oglethorpe
Served Charles II and James II;
Eleanor also served James III

**Siblings of
James Edward Oglethorpe**
Loyal to James II and James III

James Edward Oglethorpe
Publicly loyal to the ruling
house of Hanover

couple married in 1680, and the first of nine children arrived the following year (see figure 1). Three boys and four girls would survive infancy to make their mark on the world. The last was James Edward, or Jamie as he was known to family.[6]

During Charles's reign, Theophilus rose to the rank of colonel, and Eleanor expanded her influence within the royal household. In February 1685, as Charles lay on his deathbed, Theophilus guarded one door while Eleanor stood by another, admitting a Catholic priest to administer last rites. Charles, unlike his father, had suppressed his Catholic sympathies and his inclination toward a strong monarchy during much of his reign, thereby maintaining the support of Parliament. However, his brother, James Stuart, who took the throne as James II, was openly Catholic.[7]

The young Oglethorpe couple became increasingly influential during the first year of James's reign. Eleanor was granted the title of Lady Oglethorpe and became an advisor on domestic matters. Sir Theophilus, recently knighted, became a trusted advisor on state security. Their influence was so highly valued by James that he rewarded them with land in London, attached to the palace compound, on which to build a house. Previous land grants had made them wealthy, and they were already counted among the gentry and nobility who could be asked to lend money to the royal coffers. Capping a remarkably successful year, Sir Theophilus was elected to Parliament, beginning a legislative tradition that would continue with his sons Lewis, Theophilus junior, and James for a period of nearly seventy years.[8]

The Oglethorpes would soon suffer a dramatic reversal of fortune. James II had reigned for less than four years when the Protestant oligarchy, composed of nobility, gentry, and clergy acting through Parliament, initiated his overthrow. Openly Catholic and actively seeking greater religious tolerance toward his faith, James had evoked the specter of Bloody Mary, who forcibly restored Catholicism as the state religion in the previous century. When a Catholic son was born to James in June 1688, the threat of Catholic succession, coupled with the Stuart appetite for a strong monarchy, became intolerable. Parliament invoked ancient Anglo-Saxon law vesting it with authority to determine who would be king. A nearly bloodless revolution followed.[9]

Historic Turning Point: The Glorious Revolution (1688–89)

The coup d'état ousting James II, which soon became known as the Glorious Revolution, was plotted jointly with Holland, also a Protestant nation with a tradition of parliamentary government. Holland's elected leader, William of Orange, and his wife, Mary, agreed to take the throne in Britain once James II was removed. Mary, as the Protestant daughter of James II, was seen as a legitimate successor, while William, a grandson of Charles I, was also of Stuart lineage. By preserving the monarchy for the house of Stuart, Parliament softened the tenor of the revolution.[10]

The invasion plan worked out with Dutch authorities was implemented in November 1688. Holland assembled a massive invasion force, while Parliament marshaled most of the British army and navy for coordinated action. Dutch forces reached England on November 15. English forces loyal to James II, some of whom were led by Theophilus Oglethorpe, offered weak resistance. James II attempted to negotiate a resolution but was offered only Dutch protection to leave the country.

In a desperate move to avert his overthrow, James II sent Lady Oglethorpe to the archbishop of Canterbury with the royal seal as a sign of commitment to preserving the authority of the Church of England. The gesture was rejected by Parliament. The deposed king fled to France on December 22, with protection from anti-Catholic rioters arranged by William. William and Mary were crowned as joint reigning monarchs in what would become the only shared sovereignty in British history.[11]

The era that followed brought fundamental change to the country. William and Mary not only secured the preeminent status of the Church of England and the constitutional monarchy, but they brought with them Dutch traditions of religious and intellectual freedom and Dutch institutions of centralized trade and banking. The new alliance with Holland, with its 100,000-man army and the third largest fleet in Europe, also contributed to mutual security. Britain was on its way to becoming the greatest power in Europe, both economically and militarily.[12]

The dynamic new era brought about by the Glorious Revolution would shape the life of James Edward Oglethorpe as a man of the eighteenth century, even as his family remained immersed in seventeenth-century political intrigue. The new, more stable era was characterized by a radically altered political landscape, expansion of the British Empire, scientific advancement, increased literary and artistic achievement, and the dilemma of greater prosperity coupled with increased human misery. It was a milieu that would eventually impel Oglethorpe toward the New World with a plan to build on the era's promising foundation while restoring vital elements of the nation's agrarian traditions.

The Oglethorpes and the Jacobites

Eleanor and Theophilus Oglethorpe remained loyal to James after he fled to exile in France, where he had a strong ally in Louis XIV. Spain and the papal states also supported James and recognized him as the legitimate monarch of England, Scotland, and Ireland. The exiled king established court at Saint-Germain-en-Laye near Louis's court at the Palace of Versailles, and remained there until his death in 1702.[13]

Eleanor followed James to France, disguised as an old medicine seller, hiding the royal seal and other valuables on her person. Theophilus refused an offer to serve under William and Mary but continued to reside at Westbrook Manor, the family estate forty miles southwest of London. Eleanor and her eldest daughter, Anne, returned to Westbrook, where they continued to serve as couriers, spies, and advisors to James II and later to his son and successor, James III, known in England as the Old Pretender. They remained in the service of James III even as he relocated several times, eventually settling in Rome.[14]

Those who remained loyal to the exiled Stuarts became known as Jacobites, a name derived from *Jacobus,* the Latin form of James. The Jacobite label was one that would stay with the Oglethorpe family, although James Oglethorpe himself would adroitly function outside its compass through much of his life. Whether he was a true Jacobite at heart is a matter of legitimate conjecture. However, whether he was or not, it is clear that he had a larger purpose in life. The Jacobite cause, in any case, was a defining influence in his life.

Sir Theophilus regained a seat in Parliament for Haslemere in 1698 and resumed a normal life for the first time in ten years. He swore allegiance to King William and buried himself in parliamentary committee work until his defeat in the election of November 1701. He died five months later at the age of fifty-one. Theophilus's eldest son, Lewis, was elected to his seat in Parliament but relinquished it after one term to serve in the British army in Europe during the War of the Spanish Succession, where he died in battle. Theophilus junior was later elected to the Haslemere seat in Parliament, serving until 1713.[15]

Lady Oglethorpe, known as Old Fury for her temperament, became increasingly influential with king and court when in France and was at the epicenter of Jacobite conspiracy when in England. The power of her daughters was enhanced by their liaisons and marriages. Her eldest daughter, Anne, known as Young Fury, began an affair with Secretary of State Robert Harley (1661–1724) in 1704. Sisters Eleanor, Molly, and Fanny Oglethorpe, who had become acculturated in France, pursued their dedication to the Jacobite cause in part by becoming influential among the French nobility (see figure 1). Before she married into French nobility, a myth developed that Fanny was a mistress of the Old Pretender, which led some to refer to her as "Queen Oglethorpe." Another popular myth held that James Oglethorpe, who preceded James Edward and died in infancy, was really James III, switched at birth when the true heir to the throne died.[16]

Theophilus junior, following defeat for reelection to Parliament in 1713, left England permanently for Europe. Having never acquired the level of influence enjoyed by his mother or sisters, he lobbied advisors to James III unsuccessfully for a diplomatic position. Although James III was disinclined to view him as useful, the loyalty of the Oglethorpe family deserved to be rewarded, and the Old Pretender was persuaded in 1717 to award one of the few Jacobite peerages to Theophilus junior, making him Theophilus, Baron Oglethorpe of Oglethorpe; the peerage could be passed to his direct heirs or to James Edward, his only surviving brother.[17]

Following the death of William in 1702, Mary's sister, Anne Stuart, became queen. Anne, like Mary, was a half sister of James III. Although Anne was a devout Protestant, an absence of enmity between her and James left many in Parliament uneasy. Jacobites, on the other hand, held out hope that she would one day be succeeded by James, who was twenty-three years younger. Anne's ministers Robert Harley and Henry St. John Lord Bolingbroke (1678–1751) communicated with the court in exile and discussed the possibility of restoring James to the throne. Eleanor Oglethorpe, who gained influence with Queen Anne, and her daughter Anne (Harley's mistress) were among those who facilitated their communications.[18]

James Oglethorpe was five years old when Anne became queen. Her twelve-year reign spanned the formative years of his primary- and secondary-school education. The cautious, relatively balanced reign of Queen Anne would be an important early influence on James Oglethorpe and would eventually help to position him as a reformer rather than a Jacobite plotter or a new-era radical. He would become less concerned than the rest of his family about restoration of the house of Stuart and increasingly concerned, instead, with the accrual of power and wealth in cities and the effect of that trend on the lives of ordinary people.

Influences at Oxford and in Europe

When Oglethorpe completed his schooling, part of which was at Eton, Eleanor wrote to Oxford to secure his entrance to the university. He was enrolled in Corpus Christi College, which had a Jacobite tradition, in July 1714. Although he studied there less than two years, his education in classical antiquity had a lasting influence on his life and engaged him intellectually with contemporary interest in ancient Greek and Roman times, a defining characteristic of the period that would become known as the Age of Enlightenment. Eleanor undoubtedly hoped to prepare James for a future role as a Jacobite leader when she sent him to Corpus Christi; however, his classical studies exposed him to a broader sweep of history, leading him to look more to prospects of a future age than contemporary political alignments.

Queen Anne died suddenly in August 1714, shortly after Oglethorpe enrolled at Corpus Christi. In spite of British law providing for succession to the house of Hanover, Jacobites maneuvered for a Stuart succession by James III. Whigs, led by a group known as the Junto, acted quickly and effectively to secure succession for George Louis (Georg Ludwig in German), elector of Hanover. The new monarch was unobtrusively brought to England and proclaimed George I, King of Great Britain and Ireland. George was not fluent in English and not entirely comfortable with his new subjects. However, he melded with the Protestant oligarchy and complied with the goal of the Whigs to maintain a balanced government with a strong Parliament.

In 1715 the Whigs won a majority in parliamentary elections, and the Tory leadership faced a time of decision. Bolingbroke and the Duke of Ormonde, both notable influences in Oglethorpe's life, fled to France and placed themselves in the service of James III, while other Protestant Tory leaders remained in England to face the new regime. Robert Harley was one of those who remained in England, only to be impeached and imprisoned.

Bolingbroke became James's secretary of state but was soon disaffected. He communicated secretly with English officials but was discovered and dismissed. Ever adaptable, he shifted to other interests such as philosophy and literature, establishing a circle of intellectuals in Paris who, for a time, examined and debated politics from outside the halls of power. The exchange of political ideas in Bolingbroke's Paris circle, which included

Voltaire and Montesquieu, would later influence humanistic thought in England, France, and America.[19]

George I, who was having difficulty adjusting to life in England, was not well received by the populace. The Jacobites knew they could not dislodge him through Parliament but felt they might have sufficient popular support to do so through an insurrection. In September 1715, a Scottish Jacobite force led by the Earl of Mar captured Perth in Scotland. The rebellion, known as "The Fifteen," faltered when other forces failed to make gains and as coup leaders elsewhere in Britain were arrested by the government. James III, the Old Pretender, arrived near Perth in December only to find his forces in retreat. He briefly set up court but soon abandoned the adventure and returned to France.

Oglethorpe was unaccountably absent from Corpus Christi for three months in 1715 during the Jacobite rebellion. If he participated in the rebellion or was poised to do so, it was kept secret. There was no clear evidence of overt collusion on his part with the Jacobites or participation in any of their overthrow attempts. However, given Eleanor Oglethorpe's manipulation skills, it seems likely that she positioned her son to participate in a successful revolution or to remain in the shadows in the event of its failure.[20]

In January 1716, early in the reign of George I, Oglethorpe left Corpus Christi to attend a military academy in Paris, after which he joined the army of the Holy Roman emperor as an aide to Prince Eugene of Savoy. He saw action against the Turks and fought in the Siege of Belgrade in 1717. He served with distinction during the bloody battle and earned the respect of senior officers.[21]

Oglethorpe's exposure to Prince Eugene and his circle of erudite advisors further intensified his interest in classical antiquity, notably Roman military strategy and colonial settlement planning. Roman history took on deeper meaning as he marched with Eugene's army through Roman ruins from Petrovaradin to Timisoara en route to Belgrade. Empirical knowledge of Roman settlement patterns acquired in Europe would augment Oglethorpe's classical studies at Oxford and form the basis of his later concepts of town and regional planning.[22]

After serving under Eugene, Oglethorpe visited his sisters in France and his brother in Italy. The visit with Theophilus junior in Turin in October 1717 may have left an enduring impression. While there, he was exposed to a town plan with a remarkable resemblance to the later design of Savannah discussed in chapter 2. At year-end Oglethorpe and his older brother met again, this time in Rome. From there, they traveled to Urbino, where Theophilus arranged for his younger brother to be introduced to the Old Pretender (not actually so "old" at age twenty-nine). The Duke of Mar, who was then in Urbino with the Old Pretender, wrote that the king "was well pleased with him, and I believe Jamie no less with him." However, the experience may have confirmed an impression that the Jacobite cause was futile.[23]

Later in life, Oglethorpe described his youthful experience in Europe as one that brought him in contact with the most powerful men of the Continent: "Even from my childhood I made it my business to see all the great men of my time from Lewis the 14th and Victor Amadeus, two kings, and the truly great Prince Eugene down to the poor spirited, coviteous Duke of Marlborough, and good King John of Portugal."[24]

Oglethorpe returned to England in late 1718 and reenrolled at Corpus Christi, completing the equivalent of two years of study. While he did not finish a program of studies for the bachelor's degree, he was awarded the degree of master of arts in July 1731 in recognition of a long-standing affiliation with the college and notable philanthropic accomplishments. While at Oxford, Oglethorpe would begin to assemble a circle of friends and associates that he would later draw from in planning the Georgia colony. He would also begin building a sizable library that reflected a life-long interest in history and political philosophy. When he left Oxford, he had a promising career ahead, and there is no convincing evidence of further involvement with the Jacobite cause, although he would be accused of complicity.[25]

Oglethorpe returned to Westbrook Manor in 1719, prepared to establish himself as a respected figure in Haslemere. He intended, upon attaining the eligible age of twenty-five, to stand for the seat in Parliament previously held by his father and brothers. While living at the family estate, he attended to practical business and local affairs, even as mother Eleanor and sister Anne transported Jacobite conspirators into the home through the secret tunnel from town, continuing their efforts on behalf of the Stuart cause.[26]

Election to Parliament and Commitment to Reform

In 1721, upon reaching the age of eligibility to serve in Parliament, Oglethorpe was elected to the House of Commons. He took office in the 1722 session, entering government as a Tory in a period of political stability and

Whig dominance. It was a time of peace, prosperity, economic growth, literary achievement, and scientific advancement. Oglethorpe intended to contribute to the momentum of the time.

Two incidents, however, marred Oglethorpe's entry into public life and left an enduring mark on him. In the first incident, the *Daily Journal* (London) reported that he encountered an opposition candidate during his campaign for office, had words, then drew his sword and injured his opponent. Oglethorpe wrote a lengthy response to the *Daily Journal,* asserting that his opponent had drawn on him first and that he only then subdued his opponent and a companion. Within a month of the election, in a far more serious incident, Oglethorpe once again drew his sword in an angry encounter, this time killing a man. According to the *Daily Journal,* the incident took place in a "Night-House of evil Repute" after Oglethorpe, "overcome with Wine," accused another patron of stealing a piece of gold. Oglethorpe was arrested this time but spent little time in jail, perhaps as a result of a plea of self-defense. The sobering experience may well have influenced him to become a reformer.[27]

Such an unfortunate entry into public life coupled with a Jacobite heritage made for a cool reception by colleagues in Parliament. Nevertheless, Oglethorpe soon established himself as an articulate voice on matters of principle and substance. His first speech on the floor of the House of Commons was in defense of Francis Atterbury, bishop of Rochester, who stood accused of aiding a Jacobite restoration plot. Oglethorpe had already exhibited skill in taking a balanced approach to potentially polarizing issues, but this speech would be a defining moment. In the speech, which addressed a proposal to banish the bishop from England, he minimized the significance of the exiled court of James III as "a company of silly fellows" while pragmatically suggesting that Atterbury could cause more trouble abroad than under watchful eyes at home. The speech failed as a defense of Atterbury, who was banished from the country, but it succeeded in distancing Oglethorpe from the Jacobite cause and establishing him as a thoughtful voice of moderation. In other actions he further distanced himself from the Jacobite label by aligning himself politically with Sir William Wyndham, a respected Tory, and advocating a strong national defense.[28]

Over the next several years, Oglethorpe diligently served on various Parliamentary committees dealing with business regulation, road improvements, naturalization of foreigners, and numerous other practical matters. The issues of greatest concern to him, however, were those that dealt with humanitarian causes. In 1728, in what would become a lifelong concern, he advocated reform of conscription of naval seamen. Conscription was done by press-gangs that forced men between the ages of eighteen and fifty-five into servitude on warships. The injustice was made worse when conscripted seamen were released from service with inadequate resources to reestablish themselves in society. He documented these injustices and recommended reforms in a tract entitled *The Sailor's Advocate*.[29]

Oglethorpe's visibility and reputation ascended to a higher level in 1729 when he was appointed to chair a new committee to inquire "into the State of the Gaols of this Kingdom." The course of this initiative, which led directly to the plan for the Georgia colony, is taken up in chapter 1.[30]

The Economic Revolution

Preconditions for a powerful new urban economy followed the Great Plague and the Great Fire of 1666 when the rebuilding of London improved its resistance to disaster, making it safer to permanently reside there. A mercantile class that was oriented to the city and had no ties to the country grew rapidly. By living in the city, close to their businesses, merchants kept their enterprises thriving and growing. In contrast, the nobility and gentry in the country, who came to the city for business matters or for its cultural offerings, experienced an erosion of power and influence. The stage was set for a political realignment that would place Oglethorpe in a milieu quite different from that of his Jacobite parents and older siblings.

The expansion of city commerce and trade ventures accelerated after the Glorious Revolution, bringing about a period of economic revolution. When William and Mary ascended to power, they introduced sophisticated Dutch banking and trade institutions to England. Those institutions would quickly take root and precipitate fundamental changes to the economy. One of the first Dutch-inspired institutions created early in the reign of William and Mary was the Bank of England. Established in 1694, it provided a centralized system of government finance. Prior to that, England had no formal mechanism for long-term borrowing. It relied on ad hoc short-term borrowing, the sale of estates, and similar methods of raising revenue to finance domestic operations and expensive wars abroad. The Bank of England created a depository for investors buying stock in government-related trading corporations, including the East India Company, the Royal African Company, and the new South Sea Company.[31]

A thriving stock exchange developed during the 1690s in conjunction with the Bank of England. Many features of modern stock markets, including licensing and regulation, can be traced back to this period. Other developments contributing to the economic revolution included the registration of land titles (which helped to attract wealthy new citizens to Britain), equitable division of estates, codification of mercantile law, establishment of mercantile courts, expansion and better regulation of credit, provision of marine and fire insurance, and improvements to infrastructure such as the deepening of harbors. Administrative advancements of the period included the development of actuarial science as a basis for the new insurance industry and a government accounting system that maintained records of revenues and expenditures.[32]

The increased concentration of mercantile power in London after the Glorious Revolution created synergies that induced a dramatic expansion in a wide range of enterprises. The city became an international center of banking and investment. The insurance industry became established as an essential component of the free market. The diamond trade expanded dramatically when import and export duties were removed in 1733, the same year Oglethorpe founded the Georgia Colony.[33]

Scientific advancement was another component of the new economy. England, again following the Dutch model, saw science as a partner to mercantile growth. The Royal Society for the Improvement of Natural Knowledge, founded in 1660, attracted prominent men of wide-ranging interests, including several Georgia Trustees (and Oglethorpe at a later stage in life).

Religious tolerance and multiculturalism characteristic of Dutch society were also elements of the new economy. William and Mary were obligated by their agreement with Parliament to secure the prominence of the Church of England and to place new restrictions on Catholics. However, they did so in the least repressive manner possible, while reducing religious tensions in general. Furthermore, they understood that tolerance was essential for attracting the expertise from other countries necessary to foster robust trade and commerce.

Those who supported the new economy and its Dutch-inspired institutions pointed to the ability of the nation to obtain credit cheaply and reliably. Where in the past the government had to finance operations through loans from wealthy nobility and increased taxes on the landed gentry, it now had credit institutions—the Bank of England and the stock market—that assembled funds from a broader base of investors, thereby creating a large new reservoir of funds for public finance. As a result, the nation was able to stabilize revenues and expenditures, adequately finance its military in time of war, and expand trade, with the benefit of producing more tax revenue and economic growth at the same time. This capability soon set England apart from other European states that continued to rely on traditional borrowing mechanisms or did not have the volume of trade to produce the quantity of revenue required to be a dominant power.

Tension between rural and urban interests intensified when high yields from the stock market diverted money from land investment, making it difficult to obtain mortgage financing and to improve land. Tories feared that the men of finance and commerce would become the lords of traditional landowners. Not only had the rural gentry seen increased taxes on their land, principally to finance wars they did not always support, but the difficulty of borrowing left them unable to maintain their estates without selling off property. The flush accounts of urban business magnates were used to acquire rural estates and rent them back to the gentry, making them tenants of the newly rich. The impact of the economic revolution on Oglethorpe's political milieu is illustrated in figure 3.[34]

Critics of the new era missed an opportunity for structural change during a major financial crisis, the South Sea Bubble of 1720. The South Sea Company was established in 1711 for the purpose of developing trade in South American markets, which had long been dominated by Spain and Portugal. The company proved to be more of a financing entity, however, than one that actually developed trade. It wildly oversold stock, resulting in a frenzy of speculative buying that reached a peak in the summer of 1720. At the same time, the Bank of England offered loans on its own stock that contributed to general credit inflation. The financial bubble burst, hurting thousands of investors including many of the nation's most prominent citizens.[35]

The effects of the bubble rippled through Europe, damaging the economies of several nations. In September 1720, the bubble contributed to the collapse of the French Mississippi Company, a venture planned and initially financed by Oglethorpe's sister Eleanor and her French husband. Like the South Sea Company it had been largely a paper venture. Unlike the South Sea Company, however, the Mississippi Company intended to acquire and settle land between the Mississippi River and the Atlantic Coast. The scheme lacked detailed planning for the establishment and defense of new towns in the colony. Such a glaring deficiency would have been noticed by Oglethorpe, by then well versed in Roman colonial planning, an observation that may have influenced him to take greater care, a decade later, in planning his own colonial venture.[36]

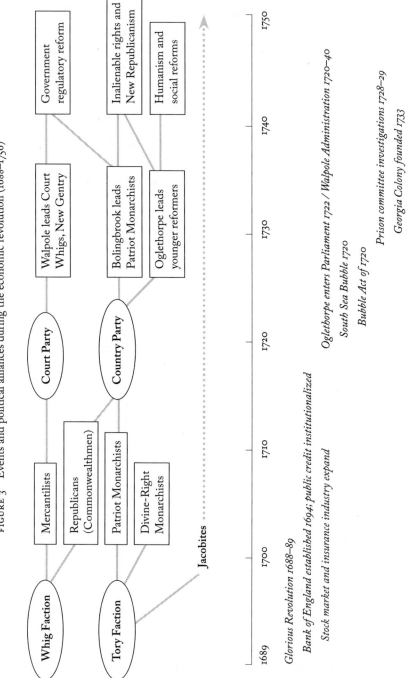

FIGURE 3 Events and political alliances during the economic revolution (1688–1756)

Whig Faction

Mercantilists

Republicans (Commonwealthmen)

Court Party

Walpole leads Court Whigs, New Gentry

Government regulatory reform

Tory Faction

Patriot Monarchists

Divine-Right Monarchists

Country Party

Bolingbrook leads Patriot Monarchists

Oglethorpe leads younger reformers

Inalienable rights and New Republicanism

Humanism and social reforms

Jacobites

1689   1700   1710   1720   1730   1740   1750

Glorious Revolution 1688–89

Bank of England established 1694; public credit institutionalized

Stock market and insurance industry expand

Oglethorpe enters Parliament 1722 / Walpole Administration 1720–40

South Sea Bubble 1720

Bubble Act of 1720

Prison committee investigations 1728–29

Georgia Colony founded 1733

With Bolingbroke in exile and Tories in disarray, the Whig party purged itself of those responsible for the South Sea Bubble and restored confidence in the financial system. Robert Walpole, as first lord of the Treasury and leader of the House of Commons, acquired power equivalent to that of prime minister (a post that did not yet formally exist). Under his leadership, the Whig party completed a transformation from seventeenth-century republicanism to eighteenth-century mercantile nationalism.

The new Whig power structure ran the government ministries; increased the size of the bureaucracy, bloating it with loyalists; and formed a political machine that influenced the outcome of elections in favor of ministry candidates. All of the initiatives undertaken by Oglethorpe as a member of Parliament—changes to the practice of conscription of sailors, prison reforms, establishment of the Georgia colony—required Walpole's support. Although a Tory frustrated with the direction the Whigs were taking the nation, Oglethorpe exhibited sufficient respect for Whig authority to function effectively within the Walpole government.[37]

A New Political Landscape

The opposition Tory faction, which traditionally supported a strong monarchy, largely realigned itself to advocate country-based republicanism. Where once the Whigs had been known as the *country party*, representing traditional rural interests, they now became the *court party*, representing an alliance of government and city interests (the term "court" in this context referred to government ministries and the monarch's council). The new political dichotomy reflected the realignment of interests from a land-based social and economic hierarchy to a more fluid urban society and its financial institutions such as credit markets. The political realignment was completed at precisely the time Oglethorpe began planning the Georgia colony.[38]

For the country party of the seventeenth century, the term "country" meant "nation," and its adherents held that the nation's ancient constitution vested power broadly with the people, who were represented by Parliament. Country party leaders such as the 1st Earl of Shaftesbury opposed an accumulation of power by the court, believing that it violated the principle of balanced government established by the nation's ancient constitution. By the turn of the century, the country party political model was embraced by a range of theorists opposed to a "hydra-headed monster" that included a standing army, political placements, pensions, excise, high taxation, national debt, and long sessions of Parliament (exposing members to corrupting influences), all of which tilted constitutionally balanced government in favor of the court.[39]

The country party alliance of Oglethorpe's milieu opposed not only the "hydra-headed monster" of court power but also the associated power residing with the urban gentry who dominated the nation's financial and commercial sectors. The country party of this new era, led within Parliament by William Wyndham and William Pulteney, thus acquired a more distinct rural-urban axis. Outside Parliament, Bolingbroke led a more radical faction of the country party opposition. They argued that the transfer of power from rural landowners to urban moneyed men amounted to a transfer of rule from natural leaders of communities to selfish special interests. Oglethorpe and other humanitarian reformists also worried that the migration of rural population to urban areas, where industrious people who labored on the land would be subject to corrupting influences and left to fend for themselves by the new urban gentry made up of merchants and traders.

Country party theorists of the eighteenth century such as Oglethorpe and Bolingbroke built on the work of their predecessors in looking to the seventeenth-century political philosopher James Harrington (1611–1677) for a conceptual foundation. Harrington adapted classical theory of the rise and fall of states and applied it to the British context. In discussing its application in Georgia, the historian Sylvia Fries describes "the Harringtonian formula for a durable commonwealth" as "an equitable distribution of land among a population of independent freehold proprietors with safeguards against the conversion of land into a marketable commodity, and the protection of liberties within the setting of imperial expansion through the maintenance of a citizen army." The experimental Georgia colony would become, in Fries's words, "what England had been in the days of her 'ancient constitution.'"[40]

Oglethorpe's political philosophy, unlike that of Bolingbroke, is not explicitly stated in the form of lengthy writings. The conclusion that Oglethorpe pursued a vision derived in part from the philosophy of Harrington is based on an assessment of his publicly stated goals (which were usually targeted to a broad audience), privately stated principles (mainly in letters), and statements by his surrogates (at times in sermons before meetings). The conclusion is also supported by the works of Harrington and his philosophical predecessors held in Oglethorpe's library, works that were widely discussed by intellectuals of the time.[41]

Two parallel radical concepts of reform emerged from country party opposition to urban political power and the corruption, injustice, and poverty that were perceived to accompany it. The first concept, conceived by Oglethorpe and his circle of confidants, determined that the economic system perpetuated by the court party could not be structurally altered and reformed from within. Oglethorpe knew from his Jacobite family's experience that it was nearly impossible to replace an entrenched government and its institutions through revolution. Change would need to come from outside, and America provided a blank slate where a more just system could be established on a renewing frontier. The other radical concept of reform articulated by Bolingbroke sought to return the nation's government to its original constitutional principles through an inspired future monarch, a Patriot King. Such a leader would return the agrarian gentry to a position of leadership and restore the balance of powers in government that had preserved national integrity for centuries.[42]

The two men's circles overlapped to some extent, but Oglethorpe made sure that his circle appeared moderate. The Georgia Colony had strong prospects for bipartisan support, provided it offered specific benefits to those in power; to participate in Bolingbroke's circle or to engage him in the colonial design, even remotely, would have constituted a threat to the Whig government and made any argument about its benefits appear as a ruse. Nevertheless, Oglethorpe understood that he and Bolingbroke were ideological compatriots, and it is plausible that he foresaw a time when their separate plans would fuse into a single national purpose.

Oglethorpe's circle consisted of respected philanthropists, scientists and academics, and reform-minded members of Parliament. The Oxford historian Thomas Carte, a Jacobite, described Oglethorpe as influencing "twenty-five or thirty young members of the house, that were wavering between the court and the country interest." The circle is described in more detail in chapter 1, in the context of the theoretical foundation for the Oglethorpe Plan.[43]

The radical aspects of Oglethorpe's plan for the Georgia Colony resided deep under its ostensible purposes. The practical benefits of the colony were articulated in great detail through promotional tracts and magazine articles. Representations to the king and queen emphasized philanthropy and national defense. Discussions with Walpole and mercantilists emphasized new trade opportunities. The colony would appeal to those who sought revolutionary change, but such a utopian appeal would spread through subtle suggestions and private conversations.

Oglethorpe's reform efforts in Parliament had given him a sense of urgency. London was an increasingly dangerous city, with poverty and misery far worse than at earlier times in British history. High unemployment rates induced the formation of an underground economy, exacerbated by the British navy's practice of discharging sailors on the streets of London and other cities. Cheap gin became widely available after 1720, and alcoholism was rampant. Public facilities for the ill and destitute were almost nonexistent. Prisons were overcrowded, and conditions were deteriorating.[44]

Unemployment and diminished opportunity were not limited to the unskilled. Many persons with specialized skills were subject to unpredictable terms of credit and therefore unable to maintain small businesses as tradesmen. Oglethorpe's friend Robert Castell, imprisoned for debt incurred in self-publishing his *Villas of the Ancients*, was a prime example. In the country, estate owners provided employment for willing workers; hard work was rewarded with meager but predictable wages, and a supportive social network cared for those in need. In the city, the rewards of hard work were often undermined by creditors and frauds that often led to poverty or debtors' prison.[45]

Oglethorpe's ally in Parliament, John Percival (1683–1748), who would soon become the Earl of Egmont, expressed the country party view of urban vices in a conversation with Queen Caroline in April 1732:

> We talked of the vices of the age, and she thought the world as good as it was formerly. I said it ought to be so, considering what a good example we had before us, but there were fashionable vices that reigned more one age than another, as cheating and over-reaching our neighbor does now more than ever, occasioned by riches, trade, and the great increase of the city, for populous towns have more roguery than little ones, for here men may hide it, but when men lived more in the country, as in former times, there was not that knowledge how to cheat, neither the temptation, nor the opportunity given. "May be," replied the Queen, "you are for reducing people to poverty to make them honest." "Not so," replied I, "but great wealth occasions luxury, and luxury extravagance, and extravagance want, and want knavery."[46]

In developing provocative reformist strategies, Bolingbroke and Oglethorpe both arguably contributed more to the eighteenth century and its defining paradigm, the Enlightenment, than is generally recognized. Bolingbroke's contribution has been underestimated because, as a politician, he failed to lead the country party to power, and as an intellectual leader he failed to carry his vision of national renewal to a successful conclusion. His contribution took the less acclaimed form of a strong current of thought influencing the American and French revolutions. Similarly, Oglethorpe's contribution has been underestimated because his humanistic initiatives failed to achieve dramatic success, and his underlying vision for the Georgia Colony never completely materialized. His contribution took the less visible form of a current of conviction that strongly influenced later achievements in human rights, notably the abolitionist movement (see the epilogue to the present volume).

The Enlightenment

When Oglethorpe returned from the Continent at the age of twenty-two, he was prepared to set aside the Stuart cause and become a leader for the new age. He found the stimulation required to complete the transformation in the vibrant London intellectual scene of the 1720s. The city had firmly established itself as a center of scientific achievement, philosophical investigation, and creative expression. London was leading a new European renaissance, the Age of Enlightenment, and Oglethorpe's emerging intellectual pursuits would be sculpted into final form by that milieu.[47]

The Enlightenment was a period of intellectual advancement that took inspiration from the new scientific paradigm and its crowning achievement, the discovery of mathematical laws governing the natural world. In parallel with the success of scientific advancement, philosophers developed empirical models for the acquisition of knowledge and argued that spiritual knowledge was accessible through reason. Artists, designers, and writers adopted formal styles that emulated the precision of natural laws. Humanism emerged as a defining property of the Enlightenment, inspired by the proposition that man was capable of understanding and improving his world. Humanism would close the Enlightenment as profoundly as science began it, culminating in the American and French revolutions and the birth of modern democracy.

Voltaire, an icon of the Enlightenment and contemporary of Oglethorpe, famously said that writing history is playing a trick on the dead. Describing the Enlightenment as having a beginning, a peak, or an end is one such trick. Nevertheless, the Glorious Revolution of 1688–89 stands out as a defining event marking the beginning of the age. The French Revolution in 1789 similarly stands out as an end point. Between these dates, the arc of the Enlightenment differed among countries. In Britain,

Enlightenment creativity arguably reached peak intensity during the 1720s, at the time Oglethorpe entered Parliament and became a noted reformer.

The Enlightenment can be seen as having developed over three periods. In the first, new ideals about human rights and the power of reason became widely accepted. In the second, those new ideals were acted upon within the framework of established government and religious institutions. In the third, established institutions were overturned and replaced with new institutions founded on the ideals of the earlier periods. Oglethorpe's role in the Enlightenment is discussed in terms of this perspective.

The Early British Enlightenment

The defining features of the British Enlightenment were largely framed at its inception by three men. Isaac Newton (1643–1727) demonstrated that *natural laws* governed the universe and that all such laws could be revealed by rational inquiry and inductive reasoning. John Locke (1632–1704) applied inductive reasoning to philosophy and argued that liberty was an entitlement derived from *natural* rights, similar to Newton's natural laws. Anthony Ashley Cooper, the 3rd Earl of Shaftesbury (1671–1713), brilliantly synthesized the work of Newton and Locke, etching the contours of a new philosophical paradigm into the thought patterns of an era, adding to it a potent new moral philosophy. Oglethorpe's plan for the Georgia Colony took form within that context.

Locke was close to Anthony Ashley Cooper, the 1st Earl of Shaftesbury, and wrote the constitutions for the Carolina colony, founded by Shaftesbury and seven other lords proprietors. Shaftesbury would formulate the "Grand Modell" for British colonial planning, a design that Oglethorpe would later improve upon. Oglethorpe would be influenced by later generations of Shaftesburys as well. Shaftesbury's grandson, Anthony Ashley Cooper, the 3rd Earl of Shaftesbury, who was mentored by Locke, framed the science and philosophy of Newton and Locke in a comprehensive manner. His *Characteristicks of Men, Manners, Opinions, Times* was one of the most influential books of the Enlightenment and the second most reprinted book in England during the eighteenth century. The 3rd Earl's son, Anthony Ashley Cooper, the 4th Earl of Shaftesbury, was close to Percival and Oglethorpe and at their invitation became one of the Trustees administering the Georgia Colony.[48]

The influence of the three framers of the British Enlightenment on the Oglethorpe Plan can be seen in its integration of design precision and humanism. Additionally, Shaftesbury articulated a new moral philosophy and stoicism that would shape Oglethorpe's milieu. He argued that morality linked harmony, order, and proportion with beauty. This sense of moral life as an elegant composition was a guiding influence on Oglethorpe as he forged the plan for Georgia. Shaftesbury's stoic philosophy, moreover, reinforced the later country party political philosophy that centered on work, service, and community.

Freemasonry provided an accessible institutional framework for the philosophy of the early Enlightenment. The establishment of the United Grand Lodge of England in 1717 transformed the ancient society's orientation from one that was "operative," or applied, to one that was "speculative," or symbolic, a transformation that was codified in *The Constitutions of the Free-Masons*, published in 1723. John Desaguliers, a protégé of Newton and a grand master, insured that freemasonry codified reverence for a harmonious universe governed by natural laws. In the estimation of the historian Margaret Jacob, freemasonry had the potential at this juncture to become a new religion. Oglethorpe, Trustees George Heathcote and Stephen Hales, and advisors Hans Sloane and John Pine were Freemasons.[49]

The creative arts during this period were in an incipient stage of development preceding a great takeoff in the 1720s. Talented writers were often hired by the government to write tracts in support of its initiatives. Daniel Defoe (1659–1731) and Jonathan Swift (1667–1745) were among the government writers who would later become prominent. As one authority on the period has written, "The connection between political theory and utopian fiction is to some extent a necessary one. The 'great tradition' in political philosophy has ... not only factual or descriptive accounts of political institutions and activities, but also recommendations about the ideal ends of political activity—the dimension of ideology."[50]

Bolingbroke formed the Scriblerus Club in 1712, a literary circle that was critical of the explosion of hack writing of the time. The circle included Swift, Alexander Pope, and John Gay, all of whom would become prominent in the 1720s. Other members were John Arbuthnot, Thomas Parnell, and Robert Harley. The group remained active into the 1740s. Swift served as an advisor to Queen Anne with Eleanor Oglethorpe and then briefly worked for the Whig ministry before becoming a Tory. The club was dedicated to the fictional Martin Scriblerus, a persona the writers employed in their critique of contemporary literature. Most of those in the club became associated with the country party, in opposition to Walpole's court party.

The Middle British Enlightenment

An intellectually vibrant and creative atmosphere emerged in London during the 1720s, beginning a second period of the British Enlightenment. The environment attracted intellectuals from the Continent, some of whom would later influence the American and French Revolutions. Notable among them were Voltaire (1694–1778) and Baron de Montesquieu (1689–1755), both of whom lived in London in the late 1720s. They had befriended Bolingbroke during his years in France and became part of his circle in London. The London intellectual scene during this period constituted Oglethorpe's milieu as he pursued social reforms and planned the Georgia Colony.[51]

During the middle Enlightenment, Shaftesbury's work was taken up by the philosopher Francis Hutcheson (1694–1746) in a series of essays published between 1725 and 1728. Hutcheson built on that work at the University of Glasgow, where he brought together intellects such as David Hume (1711–1776) and Adam Smith (1723–1790) to found the Scottish Enlightenment. Hutcheson's concepts of "invisible union," "inalienable rights," and "posterity's liberty and happiness" merged with Locke's philosophy of social contract and the natural right to "life, liberty, and estate" to find expression in the American Declaration of Independence.[52]

George Berkeley (1685–1753) may have had a more direct influence on the Oglethorpe Plan. A philosopher and cleric mentored by Percival, he may have met Oglethorpe in Turin as early as 1716. In any event, as will be discussed in chapter 1, Berkeley, Percival, and Oglethorpe discussed the plan for the Georgia colony at least once in 1730 and perhaps subsequently.

Berkeley, John Locke, and David Hume are now considered the founders of a school of philosophy known as British empiricism. Berkeley ventured into astonishing new philosophical territory by recasting Locke's empiricism in a new mold, the theory of *immaterialism*. To Berkeley, matter was a construct of the mind, an immaterial world of God's design. He encapsulated the theory of immaterialism in the famous phrase *esse est percipi* (existence is perception). Moreover, time, like matter, had no independent reality and existed only as a succession of ideas in the mind.

The significance of Berkeley's empiricism to Oglethorpe rests in its role as part of the dominant intellectual paradigm of the era. In formulating the plan for the Georgia Colony, Oglethorpe applied a largely inductive approach, assessing latitude, climate, and geopolitical situation, among other factors, and then argued the case for the colony as if making a presentation to the Royal Society. Berkeley's willingness to question basic assumptions about the nature of human beings and their relationship to the universe, even the very existence of matter, was characteristic of the Enlightenment. Oglethorpe, who had direct links with Berkeley and Locke, walked onto the stage of British politics with the same boldness, sensing that change based on the emerging ideals of the time was inevitable.

Theology was also questioned during the middle Enlightenment. It was theorized that religious institutions had lost their way during the Middle Ages, as classical Greek and Roman achievements had been distorted or lost over the centuries. True Christianity, it was argued, had been displaced by ignorance and self-perpetuating priestcraft. The church had transformed God into a human image, a perversion of religion that would be corrected in a new era grounded in reason.

For the Enlightenment thinker, the harmonious universe discovered by Newton reflected God's true nature. God was not engaged in petty human drama but infused through the universe with higher purpose. Man possessed the God-given gift of reason, providing him with the ability to pursue knowledge of God's world and the intent behind his design. It was consequently a duty of man to emulate the beauty and order of creation in worldly endeavors. Religious dogma would no longer confine man, opening a new era of reason, peace, humanism, and sustained progress.

Oglethorpe's view on religion, like his view on government, was cloaked in ambiguity. If he challenged established belief, he would be marginalized by the Whig oligarchy, undermining his reform agenda. His private beliefs, however, can be surmised from his family history, his circle of confidants, and his organizational affiliations. From those connections, it appears likely that Oglethorpe's religious beliefs were progressive, in conformity with Enlightenment values of reason and tolerance, but not to the extent of challenging the legitimacy of the established church. It appears that it was his intent to limit the influence of religion in the Georgia Colony to education and moral instruction, while excluding it from policy making and administration.

Deism emerged in the 1720s as a compelling alternative to organized religion and was a potent influence in Oglethorpe's milieu. Deists maintained that God provided man with a route to all knowledge, including religious knowledge, through reason rather than through answers to prayer, revelation, or miracles. Shaftesbury, considered a deist by some, described a universe of "mutual dependence, the relation of one thing to another; the sun to the earth; the earth to the planets to the sun; the order, symmetry, regularity, union, and coherence of the whole." Through a *universal* "Divine architecture" the "Deity is present with all things, knows all things, and is provident over all." Deism undoubtedly influenced Oglethorpe, although not to the extent it would later influence the American Founders.[53]

Radical deism, which criticized nearly every aspect of Christianity, constituted a mortal threat to the established church. Writers such as John Toland (1670–1722) were singled out by Christian theologians for special criticism. In *Christianity Not Mysterious* (1696), Toland argued that knowledge of God is accessible through common sense and reason rather than revelation and faith. He was forced to flee the country and live in exile for several years after publishing his ideas.

While there is no evidence Oglethorpe subscribed to Toland's ideas, he was exposed to them through multiple channels. Prince Eugene's advisors, Bolingbroke, and John Pine are all linked to Toland while he was in exile in Holland. It was there that a movement described by the historian Margaret Jacob as the "Radical Enlightenment" took form. Oglethorpe and Toland may have also encountered each other in London through their Masonic affiliation or through Robert Harley, Anne Oglethorpe's intimate friend, who secretly retained Toland's services as a writer.[54]

Such connections are intriguing and merit investigation by historians. However, where Toland indisputably attracted Oglethorpe's attention was as editor of the works of James Harrington, a major resource in Oglethorpe's formulation of the design of the Georgia Colony, and as an articulate advocate for Harrington's gentry utopia. Toland's *Anglia Libera* (1701) and *State Anatomy* (1717) updated Harrington's republicanism for the eighteenth century and merged it with country party ideology, bridging the politics of the 1st Earl of Shaftesbury with that of Oglethorpe's milieu. Oglethorpe conceivably saw himself as a discreet protégé of Toland and Bolingbroke in reformulating Harrington's republicanism for the new century, although it would have been political suicide to publicly admit to such associations.[55]

The reaction to Toland and other deists can be seen in Handel's *Messiah*. George Frederic Handel (1685–1759), who emigrated from Germany to England in 1712, contributed to the advancement of religious and secular music in a manner that strikingly paralleled the era's paradigm-shifting achievements in science and philosophy. Handel's most productive period, spanning the 1720s and 1730s, coincided with Oglethorpe's reformist period as a member of Parliament.[56]

In composing *Messiah* Handel collaborated with Anglican theologians who were troubled by the threat of both Judaism and deism, both of which denied the divinity of Christ. Old and New Testaments were brought into alignment by prophesying, then recognizing, the true Messiah, validating Christianity over Judaism. The powerfully triumphant quality of *Messiah* was created to inspire and reinvigorate Christians in the face of growing interest in deism, attacks on revealed religion, and the subversive influence of Judaism.[57]

Oglethorpe, who had unbounded intellectual curiosity, avoided becoming entangled in such debates as he conceived the plan for the Georgia colony. By doing so, he was able to draw substantial support for its philanthropic goals from evangelical Christians. The Georgia colonial model thereby set a precedent for secular governance in America.

To complete the picture of Oglethorpe's milieu in the middle Enlightenment, the influence of the creative arts must be noted. The arts flourished during the period, in part by becoming intertwined with science, philosophy, and politics. New styles of painting emerged, a new age of English literature took form as book and periodical sales soared, and the performing arts attained a new height of popularity. In the creative arts, as in science and philosophy, classical Greek and Roman traditions were a potent influence.

William Hogarth (1697–1764), who painted the portrait of the prison committee, emerged as the first English artist of note. He was a master of political satire, attacking social problems that intersected with Oglethorpe's reform agenda. The convergence of Oglethorpe's reform initiatives and Hogarth's depictions of social injustice in the middle Enlightenment made a strong impression on British society and set the stage for revolutionary change in the late eighteenth century.

John Pine (1690–1756), the accomplished designer-engraver retained by Oglethorpe and the Trustees of the Georgia Colony, was a close friend of Hogarth. Oglethorpe may have been introduced to Pine by Hogarth during the prison investigations, but in any event they were acquainted by 1730, when he was retained to create the first conceptual settlement plan of the Georgia Colony (see chapter 2). Pine may have been involved at a deeper level in conceptualizing the colony. He studied engraving in Holland with the publisher Bernard Picart, who was associated with the Radical Enlightenment described in the earlier discussion of deism. Those associated with the movement sought more fundamental changes to society than the political establishment could easily bear. Pine's early exposure to radical ideas, his friendship with Hogarth, his use of ancient symbolism and Newtonian order to define Masonic imagery, and the later involvement his son, the artist Robert Edge Pine, with the American Revolution suggest that he may have been in Oglethorpe's inner circle. Pine is believed to be the first black Freemason, although his ancestry is undocumented.[58]

One of the great tensions of the Enlightenment was the contrast of geometric formalism and natural randomness seen in the respective styles of Pine and Hogarth. Classical formalism is also found in the work of the 3rd Earl of Burlington and his protégé, William Kent. Burlington studied classical and Renaissance architecture in Italy in 1719, taking away an appreciation of the designs of Andrea Palladio (1508–1580). He subsequently promoted the application of Palladian architecture in England. Burlington, Kent, and Oglethorpe's friend Robert Castell established Palladian architecture and classical landscapes as a dominant theme in England's rural landscape. Their influence also brought increased attention to Vitruvius and classical design. Oglethorpe's exposure to classical design in virtually every field of study led him to examine Vitruvian principles when he began planning settlement patterns for the Georgia Colony.[59]

Classical formalism melded with social commentary in the work of such literary figures as Swift and Pope, both of whom became quite prominent in the 1720s, beginning an era that became known as the Augustan Age of English literature (a name derived from George I, whose given name was George Augustus, but which drew cachet from the Golden Age of Augustus Caesar). The Augustan Age spanned the 1720s and 1730s and reached a creative peak in 1728, the same year Oglethorpe began his investigation of prisons.[60]

Authors of the Augustan Age explored the science and metaphysics of Newton, the moral philosophy and deism of Shaftesbury, and the epistemology and political theory of Locke. They also aligned themselves on either side of the country-court political divide of the era. Those who took the country party position expressed deep concern about the nation's future and lamented the decline of yeoman farmers and landed gentry, excoriated the self-interest and greed of the new mercantile gentry, and defended the nation's traditional values. At the other end of the political spectrum advocates for Walpole's Whig oligarchy and the new mercantile era portrayed the old nobility and gentry as decadent and unable to build a new, dynamic nation, while extolling the enterprising minds of the rising mercantile class. They saw the Whig government (the court party) as facilitators of an expanding empire that offered upward mobility to more of its citizens.

Jonathan Swift became a potent advocate of country party philosophy, arguing that "possessors of the soil," the landed gentry and nobility, were motivated by and ethic of public service, whereas men of commerce and finance were ill suited for public service because they were motivated by self-interest. He believed in the wisdom of the British constitution with its balance of powers and endorsed Bolingbroke's thesis that a tyrannical government should be brought down by a Patriot King if it betrayed the original principles under which it was established and thereby enslaved its citizens. Swift's *Gulliver's Travels* (1726), one of the most powerful social satires ever written, was an expression of his political philosophy. His satirical poem "Helter Skelter," published in 1731, reflected his skeptical attitude toward attorneys. The following year, Oglethorpe and the Georgia Trustees resolved to keep attorneys out of the new colony.[61]

Alexander Pope, one of the most quoted writers in the history of English literature, was a lifelong friend of Swift and a member of Bolingbroke's circle. He was also a friend of Oglethorpe, whose philanthropy he admired and immortalized in these lines:

One, driven by strong benevolence of soul,
Shall fly, like Oglethorpe, from pole to pole:
Is known alone to that Directing Power,
Who forms the genius in the natal hour;
(Pope, *Horace Imitated,* in *Major Works,* 2:276–79)

The memorialization of Oglethorpe by Pope and other Augustans established him as an icon of humanism, an image that would endure to the Age of Johnson (see epilogue). A Catholic, Pope's Jacobite leanings were evident in his writing. As a poet, he had license to express his views more freely than others. His work reflected the influences of Newton and Shaftesbury, portraying harmony in God and nature. In *An Essay on Man,* published in 1733, Pope wrote in great detail about natural law, beauty, and humanism. His interest in natural law led him to an appreciation of natural landscapes, which stood in contrast to the views of many Newtonians and Freemasons, who often extended their affinity for geometric regularity to the landscape around them. His philosophy of design consonant with nature later established him as a pioneer in creating the discipline of landscape architecture, and his concept of genius loci, the "genius of the place," remains a fundamental tenet in that discipline. In "An Epistle to Richard Boyle, Earl of Burlington" (1731), Pope wrote, "let nature Never be forgot" and advised to "Consult the genius of the place in all."[62]

Criticism of the Walpole oligarchy by Pope and Swift reached a peak between 1726 and 1732, contributing indirectly to public support for Oglethorpe's reform initiatives. A decade later Swift and Pope lost hope that the ship of state would right itself through the existing political process. They saw Bolingbroke's concept of a Patriot King as the only opportunity to restore true republican principles of the Glorious Revolution. Pope set the concept of a reform-minded Patriot King to verse in 1740.[63]

Bolingbroke was a philosopher and writer as much as he was a politician. Banned from serving in Parliament after an interlude with the Pretender's government in exile, he launched *The Craftsman* in December 1726 as a voice for country ideology. William Pulteney, a Whig member of Parliament but an outspoken critic of Walpole's court party, was among the frequent anonymous contributors, as were Swift and Pope. It was in *The Craftsman* that Bolingbroke began a series of essays, entitled "A Dissertation on Parties," that articulated his concept of an opposition party as it is known in modern times. It was also in *The Craftsman* that Bolingbroke developed his theory of national renewal.[64]

Bolingbroke's positions on nearly every issue were closely aligned with those of Oglethorpe, but they could not be seen as allies. Nevertheless, the political playing field upon which Oglethorpe maneuvered during the 1720s and 1730s was largely of Bolingbroke's design. It was not until much later in his life that Oglethorpe would be comfortable speaking appreciatively of Bolingbroke.

The writer John Gay (1685–1732) and the poet James Thomson (1700–1748) were also prominent in Oglethorpe's formative milieu. Gay's *The Beggar's Opera* (1728) opened as Parliament debated prison reform and appointed Oglethorpe to chair a committee to investigate the matter. Scene 5 of the *Opera*, set at Newgate Prison, is captured in the painting by Hogarth (figure 4). The daughters of a corrupt warden and a lawyer plead with their respective fathers to free the man they both believed to be their husband. The popular play's critique of the inequities in British society paralleled criticisms in *Gulliver's Travels*, thereby enhancing Oglethorpe's status as a social reformer.

Thomson, influenced by the moral philosophy and deism of Shaftesbury, became the first English humanitarian poet and was responsible for beginning an ethical movement in the genre. His first major work, *Seasons*, composed as a quartet between 1726 and 1730, contained references to Oglethorpe's prison reform committee and the Georgia Colony, both

FIGURE 4 *A Scene from The Beggar's Opera.* The 1731 painting by Hogarth depicts the final, dramatic scene in Newgate Prison, where the principal character, a condemned highwayman by the name of Captain Macheath, is fought over by Lucy Lockit and Polly Peachum, characters who both believe they are married to him. The women are pleading with their fathers, a corrupt prison warden and a lawyer, to free him. (The Tate Museum)

mentioned as his references to philanthropy increased. In *Liberty: A Poem,* dedicated to Frederick, Prince of Wales, Bolingbroke's hoped-for Patriot King, Thomson praised Oglethorpe much as Pope had done, with emphasis on relief for persecuted Europeans.[65]

Daniel Defoe (1660–1731) shared a literary social conscience with country party writers, but he rejoiced in the new age, whereas Swift hated it, Bolingbroke opposed it, and Oglethorpe sought to reform it. Defoe's novels demonstrated a form of triumph over adversity. In *Robinson Crusoe* (1719), Crusoe is left shipwrecked on a wild, ungoverned island, but he eventually overcomes threats to his survival through a Lockean contract with the island's inhabitants. To Defoe the new age produced a new class of people who were responsible for building a great new nation, a view diametrically opposite that of most Augustan writers and the country party. Defoe described the upwardly mobile commercial class as displacing rural gentry and nobility, who were mired in a backward, agrarian economy.[66]

Newspapers and magazines were another vector for political ideology and increasingly a source of information on classical antiquity, philosophy, science, literature, business, and world cultures. Most, such as *The Craftsman,* had a political slant, but many simply reflected the intellectual interests of the British Enlightenment. *The Gentleman's Magazine,* founded in 1731, the first periodical to call itself a "magazine," published numerous accounts of Oglethorpe's activities, including letters written by Oglethorpe, accounts of others about Oglethorpe, and updates of the development of the Georgia Colony between 1733 and 1744. The *London Magazine* was established in 1732, with support from Walpole, to advance the Whig perspective.

The themes found in literature, played on the stage, or seen in contemporary art were potent forms of social criticism that served to reinforce Oglethorpe's resolve and add status to his work as he probed prison abuses and formulated a vision for a New World colony. In the creative arts, no one paralleled Oglethorpe's critical analysis of society more than Hogarth, who produced numerous works exposing corruption and injustice. In *A Harlot's Progress,* Hogarth illustrates a central problem that concerned Oglethorpe throughout his life, that of the erosion of rural society, which he believed caused a migration to cities. Hogarth depicted a young woman (the "harlot") arriving from the country and immediately being recruited into prostitution, as seen in figure 5; the painting was one of six completed in 1731 and engraved for wide distribution the following year. Loss of virtuous rural society was a concern that ran through Oglethorpe's life, as demonstrated by his interest in Oliver Goldsmith's poem *The Deserted Village* (1770), discussed in the epilogue.

Oglethorpe pursued his investigations with parliamentary decorum, without overtly playing to public sentiments heightened by the literary community. To the extent that he used the new media of expression to advance his own agenda, he did so by publishing nonpolitical tracts and magazine articles. While he attracted the notice of Pope, Thomson, and other acclaimed writers, he avoided an appearance of collaborating with critics of the ministry. In walking that thin line, he was able to create a vision for a new colony with wide appeal. Part of his public relations strategy was to suppress the revolutionary core of his vision for the colony, while emphasizing its philanthropic purposes.

FIGURE 5 *A Harlot's Progress.* In this first of a series of plates engraved by Hogarth in 1732, Hogarth illustrates the corrupting influences of the city on young people moving to London from the country. Here, a young Moll Hackabout is welcomed to the city by an older woman who leads her into a career of prostitution. (The Tate Museum)

The Later British Enlightenment

The Enlightenment saw a progression of philosophical thought paralleled by and increasingly linked to bold actions, one of which was Oglethorpe's plan for the Georgia Colony. While the colony was short lived, debate about its underlying principles flowed into the wider stream of progressive and ultimately successful reform movements and revolutions of the later Enlightenment. As the writings of Locke, Shaftesbury, Voltaire, Bolingbroke, Hutcheson, and others produced revolutionary ideas, the reform initiatives advanced by Oglethorpe were kept alive in Augustan literature and London's intellectual circles. While the Georgia Colony did not become the vector of change envisioned by Oglethorpe, the ideas behind it lived on to influence the later Enlightenment.

Oglethorpe may therefore be seen as a transformational figure in the middle Enlightenment, one who did not write about political philosophy but attempted to effect it. His efforts to end three great injustices—

impressment of sailors, systemic corruption in the prison system, and slavery—were ultimately successful. His effort to identify and solve the underlying causes of poverty and social disintegration may have been quixotic from some perspectives, yet he assembled a set of formidable tools forged to build a model colony. Those tools would succeed in individual parts, and some would survive to the present as highly regarded design concepts. The physical legacy of the Oglethorpe Plan, visible and vibrant in Savannah today, constitutes the principal subject of the following five chapters. Oglethorpe's place in the Enlightenment is taken up in the epilogue, where it is shown that he maintained a constancy of humanistic values and pursuits through the age.

The Plan for a Model Colony

It is widely believed that James Oglethorpe conceived the Georgia Colony as a refuge for debtors and then secured support for the colony by promoting its geopolitical and mercantile value. Oglethorpe, however, had an even more fundamental purpose in mind for the colony, a purpose that remains little understood today because it was unstated at the time. That core purpose was to create a utopian agrarian society that would preserve and nourish fundamental principles of the British nation, principles that Oglethorpe believed were being eroded by urbanization and social disintegration. The colony was to become a model based on tenets of country party political philosophy.[1]

The Oglethorpe Plan, therefore, comprised not only a set of tactics aimed at specific social, economic, and national security challenges but also a set of strategies aimed at creating a better society in the New World. The tactical objectives of the plan, which were both pragmatic and evangelical, were endorsed by the king, Parliament, the Church of England, and various private benefactors. The strategic goals of the plan, formulated quietly by Oglethorpe and close confidants, were, in contrast, elaborate and idealistic.[2]

Oglethorpe incorporated this diverse array of purposes for the Georgia Colony into a single framework much like a modern strategic plan. The plan contained an implicit vision, a set of goals and guiding principles, and detailed implementation mechanisms and strategies. This chapter discusses the genesis, theoretical framework, and structure of the Oglethorpe Plan. The structure is then deconstructed into goals and strategies identified primarily from materials written between 1730 and 1732, when planning for the colony took place. Chapter 2 then deconstructs the celebrated town plan for Savannah and the regional settlement plan of which it was a part, showing how physical design supported a grander humanitarian vision.

The Genesis of the Plan

On February 25, 1729, Oglethorpe was appointed chair of a committee of the House of Commons to investigate conditions in the nation's prisons. The committee was to focus on debtors' prisons, a lingering problem that others had previously attempted to address. Oglethorpe had become acutely interested in prison conditions following the death of a friend, Robert Castell, in the notorious Fleet Prison. Castell had incurred debt when he self-published *The Villas of the Ancients Illustrated* in 1728, a book that richly depicted plans of classical Roman villas. The cost of publishing the book was not recovered through sales, and Castell, unable to pay his creditors, was sent to prison.

London's prisons were brutal places. Even though they were state owned and subject to regulation, they operated as private, profit-making concerns. Debtors under English law had no protected status, and creditors could have them arrested and imprisoned. The enrichment of prison officials through bribery infected a large segment of the justice system that included elected officials and magistrates. Nearly all aspects of life in a debtors' prison were controlled by a prisoner's ability to pay fees. As a result of fees, the original debt became more difficult to repay, leading to protracted terms of imprisonment. Wardens held many prisoners in nearby detention facilities, called "sponging houses," where they had free reign.

Oglethorpe's ninety-six-member parliamentary committee, which contained a core of perhaps twenty dedicated members, produced three reports focusing exclusively on debtors' prisons. The first report was on Fleet Prison, where Castell had died in a smallpox-infested sponging house. It focused on Warden Thomas Bambridge, accused of assuming "Unwarrantable and Arbitrary Power," and on the lack of judicial oversight. William Hogarth, a contemporary of Oglethorpe and a social satirist, as discussed in the prologue, was also an advocate of prison reform. Hogarth's father, like Oglethorpe's friend Robert Castell had been imprisoned for indebtedness resulting from publishing ventures, leading the painter to become acutely aware of the need for prison reform. Hogarth painted a scene in which the prison committee questioned warden Bambridge in the presence of an abused prisoner (figure 6).

FIGURE 6 *Bambridge on Trial for Murder by a Committee of the House of Commons,*
William Hogarth (1729). At Fleet Prison, a prisoner begs for mercy, trembling in fear of
the warden, standing at left, next to Oglethorpe, who is seated. (The Tate Museum)

Oglethorpe and his committee went on to present reports to Parliament on Marshalsea Prison and King's Bench Prison. The committee was shocked to find conditions at Marshalsea even worse than at Fleet. As many as fifty prisoners were locked into a cell of sixteen square feet and forced to remain there for long periods and relieve themselves in the cell. Prisoners' wives were sexually assaulted when they visited. One prisoner had been kept with corpses so long that he reported, "Vermin devoured the Flesh from their Faces, . . . the Eyes out of the Heads of the Carcasses, which were bloated, putrified, and turned green." At King's Bench Prison the committee found imperfect but nevertheless acceptable conditions. The committee's final report was issued in May 1730.[3]

The House of Commons voted unanimously to prosecute Bambridge and William Acton, warden of Marshalsea Prison, among others. The entrenched penal system fought back. Parliament was persuaded to drop the charges against the warden at Marshalsea and the recommendations for reform. Even Bambridge was acquitted on appeal. Success was limited to replacement of a few officials and the release of prisoners. Acton, although acquitted, was kept in prison, forcing him to appeal to Oglethorpe for release. Oglethorpe responded that it was not within his authority to do so, but added that "were I prosecutor, I should desire the prisoner might be released; not that I think him innocent, but that every Englishman, let him be never so unjustly acquitted, hath, by the Habeas Corpus Act, on his acquittal a right to be discharged." The response is an important illustration of the value Oglethorpe placed on British constitutional traditions.[4]

Oglethorpe's experience with the prison committee would intensify his interest in social reform while also increasing his sense of the limitations inherent in purely political solutions. The experience would also assemble a group of men who shared a concern about social reform and who saw the need for a greater role for private philanthropy as well as regulatory reform in resolving social problems. This group would later form the nucleus of the Trustees for the Establishment of the Colony of Georgia in America.

In the winter of 1729–30, as Oglethorpe considered another round of investigations, he also contemplated a new initiative: establishment of a colony that would offer freed prisoners a new chance in life. While the experience with the prison committee had taught him that achieving systemic change through formal channels was virtually impossible, the New World was a blank slate in need of settlers, where struggling people might have a second chance in life. It was also a place where structural reforms could be instituted without interference from entrenched power and corrupt officials. Moreover, if such reforms succeeded abroad, they might serve as useful examples in the homeland.[5]

Oglethorpe found sufficient support among his circle of reformers to pursue founding a new colony, and he abruptly set aside prison reform in mid-1730. Urban problems such as debtor imprisonment, unemployment, crime, alcoholism, and prostitution (illustrated vividly by Hogarth in figure 5) would require new-model solutions, and the colony would be a blank slate for the initiative. The founding principles for such a colony would reinstitute traditional British agrarian values in a setting where they could be protected and cultivated.

The Associates of Dr. Bray as a Vehicle for Reform

Oglethorpe found a suitable vehicle to implement a humanistic agenda, and ultimately for establishment of the Georgia Colony, in the work of Rev. Thomas Bray (1658–1730), a philanthropist with an interest in prison reform and a dedication to alleviating the "intellectual poverty of colonial

America." Bray had formed three organizations with missions in the colonies: the Associates of Dr. Bray, the Society for Promoting Christian Knowledge (SPCK), and the Society for the Propagation of the Gospel in Foreign Parts (SPG). The latter two institutions have survived to the present day as charitable organizations.[6]

The Associates of Dr. Bray administered a bequest dedicated specifically to educating and converting slaves in the British colonies to the Christian faith. Oglethorpe met with Bray in December 1729 to propose widening the mission of the group to include supporting a new colony. Bray endorsed the proposal and permitted Oglethorpe to expand the Associates with as many additional members as would be necessary to carry out the new mission. Bray, who was seriously ill, signed a legal transference of authority in January 1730 designating Oglethorpe and other Associates as trustees of the expanded organization. Of more than thirty nominations in the document for "Trustees and Associates," twenty-one accepted and became active participants; three others were added shortly thereafter (see appendix B).[7]

Bray died soon after expanding his organization, which Oglethorpe and the other trustees then renamed the Associates of the Late Dr. Bray; their first meeting of record took place on March 21, 1730. By associating himself with the Bray organization, Oglethorpe grounded his reform agenda in mainstream religious philanthropy and in doing so further distanced himself from the radical country party element led by Lord Bolingbroke (discussed in the prologue). The association with Bray enabled Oglethorpe to portray himself as a man of character in the tradition of the gentry and one who had the interest of the people at heart.[8]

Oglethorpe was drawn to Bray not only for his reformism and philanthropic stature but also because of the latter's earlier involvement in a colonial effort initiated by Thomas Coram, a wealthy merchant and noted philanthropist in his own right. Coram had previously attempted to establish the colony of Georgeia, which was to be founded on humanistic principles. Georgeia would have served as a buffer colony between Maine and Nova Scotia, prohibited distilled spirits, and placed limits on land ownership, features that Oglethorpe would endorse for the colony of Georgia. It was undoubtedly reassuring to Bray, when he neared the end of his life, to have formidable men like Oglethorpe and Coram join forces to continue his work and enlarge its scope.[9]

Once the Associates were expanded to carry out the new mission, Oglethorpe set about meeting with key people who he believed would politically and financially support the plan. On February 13, 1730, Ogle-thorpe met with John Percival, one of the original Associates of Dr. Bray and a member of the prison committee, to discuss funding prospects. Oglethorpe described the colony as beginning with "a hundred miserable wretches" let out of prison as a result of their reform efforts; it would be thoughtfully regulated, it would be a buffer colony protecting "our posses-sions against the French and Indians of those parts," and it would "promote our manufactures" to the benefit of the nation. Percival was impressed with the details of the proposal and agreed to support it.[10]

Oglethorpe must have discussed the specifics of the plan with several other confidants around the same time. However, there is almost no record of such meetings and no reference to them in Percival's diary, a rich source of information about the colony. An exception is found in a meeting with George Berkeley, the cleric and eminent philosopher, at Percival's residence in January 1732.

Berkeley was an advocate for education in America who until recently had pursued a plan to establish a college in Bermuda to provide education and promote Christian values throughout the New World. In the meet-ing, Percival appealed to Berkeley to fold his effort into the Georgia plan, since it had a similar philanthropic mission and educational goals. Berke-ley appears to have tacitly endorsed the plan while declining to transfer private donations he had received, preferring instead to donate those funds to a new college in Connecticut (which later became Yale University) that "came nearest his own plan."[11]

Berkeley and Percival were very close, and over the course of numerous meetings in 1731 and 1732 they must have discussed the principles under-lying the Georgia Colony and perhaps even details related to the design of its settlements. The two men shared an interest in classical design, as revealed in correspondence between 1713 and 1720, when Berkeley traveled extensively throughout Italy. Berkeley and Oglethorpe may have had their own earlier interaction on design principles, since they appear to have met in Turin in 1716 or 1717, an encounter that led the planning historian John Reps to speculate that the design of the Piazza Carlina in that city may have become the template for the Savannah plan.[12]

Whether or not Berkeley contributed design concepts to the Ogle-thorpe Plan is a matter of conjecture. It is known that Berkeley had a strong humanistic interest in the New World, which is reflected in his efforts to establish a college in Bermuda. Percival was one of his stron-gest supporters in the venture, offering both encouragement and advocacy.

However, Berkeley returned to Ireland in 1733 and had no further involvement with the Connecticut college or with the Georgia Colony. His legacy of supporting education in the New World was eventually recognized by two prominent universities. Yale University named a residential college in his honor, and the trustees of the University of California named the site of their first campus after him.[13]

Percival committed himself fully to Oglethorpe's plan for the Georgia Colony once Berkeley withdrew his plan for the college in Bermuda. Trusted by the king and queen and respected by Walpole, he was able to secure support for the colonial plan. Without his advocacy, it is questionable whether the colony would have been chartered. Percival was named in the charter as the first president of the Trustees for the Establishment of the Colony of Georgia in America.

Percival visited Oglethorpe on April 1, 1730, and discussed details of the colonial plan for three hours. Oglethorpe urged moving forward promptly on the "project of sending a colony of poor and honest industrious debtors to the West Indies [i.e., America]." He informed Percival of estimates that ten thousand debtors had been released from prison as a result of their work the previous year, and many were immigrating to Prussia in search of employment. The proposed colony in America would productively re-employ talented citizens for the betterment of Britain, without a drain of capable people to other countries.[14]

At a meeting of the Associates on July 1, 1730, Oglethorpe reported that Sir Joseph Jekyll, master of the rolls, issued a final decree recognizing the Associates as a formal body. Jekyll conveyed his admiration for their work and offered his full support. Following a number of organizational actions, including commitments of mutual support for the SPG and SPCK, the Associates agreed to seek a grant of land in America "that such poor Persons may be transported thither, who shall be willing to go beyond the Seas for their better Maintainance [to be under the Direction and Management of this Society], and that Mr Oglethorpe, and such other Persons of this Society, whom he shall desire for his Assistance do take Care of the same."[15]

The Associates met again on July 30, 1730, to review a draft petition to King George for a grant of land "Southward of Carolina." The petition was approved and forwarded to the king; it was read by the Privy Council on September 17, 1730, and referred to committee. Crafting the final details of the charter for the colony of Georgia, including identification of the western boundary, led to further delays; however, by January 1732 all concerns were resolved. On April 21, 1732, George II signed the charter, although it was not transmitted from the government to the petitioners until June 20. At that point, the Associates of the Late Dr. Thomas Bray officially became the Trustees for Establishing the Colony of Georgia in America.[16]

The historian John Doyle characterized the Georgia Colony as the first "systematic and organized effort" to alleviate poverty, and he anointed Oglethorpe "the founder of modern philanthropy."[17]

The Trustees for Establishing the Colony of Georgia in America

The charter incorporating the Georgia Trustees identified an initial group of twenty members, all of whom were Associates of the Late Dr. Bray. It provided for a Common Council with executive powers to conduct the business of the corporation and oversee administration of the colony and for annual meetings to be held on the third Thursday in March, on which occasion new Trustees could be elected. John Percival was named president of the corporation. The first meeting of the Trustees after receiving the charter took place on July 20, 1732, at Palace Court, Old Palace Yard.[18]

The first purpose of the colony as stated in the charter was resettlement of the king's subjects who "through misfortune and want of employment" might "gain a comfortable subsistence for themselves and families." The charter asserted further that the colony would benefit the kingdom by increasing trade, protecting South Carolina from Indian attack, and securing the frontier with Florida. To emphasize the charitable purpose of the colony, Trustees were prohibited from receiving any profit or benefit from their position, including any grant of land in the colony.[19]

The authority of the Trustees extended for a period of twenty-one years, during which time they were granted power to "prepare laws, statutes, and ordinances" necessary to govern the colony, provided they were consistent with the laws of England. They were further empowered to establish courts, survey and inspect lands, maintain official records, collect fees, regulate crop plantings, train and govern a militia, erect forts, fortify towns, and enact martial law. Land grants and leases were limited to a maximum of five hundred acres, although the standard grant for Trust-supported colonists was set at fifty acres by the Trustees.[20]

The charter described the boundaries of the colony as lying between the Savannah River on the north and the Altamaha River, near the frontier with Spanish Florida, on the south. Its western boundary extended from the headwaters of those rivers to the "South Seas," thereby challenging the French, who were colonizing the Mississippi River basin.[21]

Colonists would have "a liberty of conscience allowed in the worship of God." Persons born in the colony would enjoy full rights of citizens of the Kingdom of Great Britain. These two provisions of the charter were particularly significant, since it was clear at the time the charter was drafted that many of the colonists would be fleeing religious intolerance in Europe. However, the provision for religious freedom (intended primarily for Protestant sects) also enabled the Trustees to administer the colony in a largely secular manner.[22]

The Trustees instituted a well-organized campaign for government and private support as soon as they knew the charter would be approved. Parliament declined to grant funds in 1732; however, the Bank of England, the East India Company, and private donors provided encouraging support during the first year. A broad base of financial and popular support was created by commissioning hundreds of church ministers and other respected people to collect subscriptions to the colonial venture, emphasizing its philanthropic and evangelical purposes. Prospects for a parliamentary grant and continuing private support allowed the Trustees to schedule the first embarkation of settlers for November. Subsequent funding of the colony is discussed in chapter 3.

The Trustees advertised their intent to establish a new colony in newspapers and other popular periodicals. In July 1732, Oglethorpe wrote an unattributed article for the *Daily Journal* that drew extensively from a 110-page unpublished tract he had authored while the charter was pending approval, entitled *Some Account of the Design of the Trustees for Establishing Colonys in America*. He drew from the same source again in preparing a compilation of supportive tracts from various authors, entitled *Select Tracts Relating to the Colonies*, printed in November 1732, and *New and Accurate Account of the Provinces of South-Carolina and Georgia*, published in December 1732. A short version of Oglethorpe's *Some Account* was prepared by Benjamin Martyn for the Trustees later in 1732 under the similar title *Some Account of the Designs of the Trustees for Establishing the Colony of Georgia in America*.[23]

Church ministers and parish administrators encouraged families supported by charity to apply to the Trustees for an opportunity to settle in Georgia. Word spread quickly, and the Trustees were soon interviewing candidates. The Trustees met with all applicants to ascertain their circumstances and their willingness to face the rigors of a frontier colony for the prospect of a better life. Many were rejected as unsuitable, often because they were "able to live though poorly in England." Those who were selected signed an agreement to the terms offered by the Trust. They would be granted land and supported by the public store until their farms became productive. In return they agreed to be subject to regulation of land tenure and requirements to clear, fence, and cultivate their land within a specified period of years.

Prospective colonists were briefed on requirements of the charter, terms of land ownership, and various duties and regulations. Martyn listed the following regulations in *Some Account:*

First, they are to be obedient to their directors.

Second, they are to assist each other and by joint endeavors fortify such place as their chief commander shall think proper to establish their town in.

Thirdly, they are by joint endeavors to build houses for themselves and cultivate and sow lands for their next year's provision.

Fourthly, after that is done, the houses that are built and the land that is cultivated are to be divided amongst themselves, each man to have a house and twenty acres of land to himself and to his heirs male forever. Each man is to pay for his house and land one day's labor in the week, which labor is to be employed in the service of the public.

Fifthly, all persons that have three children alive at the same time shall during the time of their three childrens being alive be exempted from the rent of labor.

Sixthly, all persons above sixty years of age shall be exempt from labor.

Seventhly, no person shall leave the country in two years without license obtained, which shall not be refused anyone who will repay to the commander in chief the expense which the Trustees have been at on his account.

Eighthly, all persons that go are themselves and families to be free and no labor taxes, tythes nor money under any pretense whatsoever is to be exacted from them save only the above-mentioned labor, which is to be the rent of their lands, the produce of which labor is to be laid out for the support of the colony in time of war, sickness or famine and for the sending over more poor families to increase it.

Lastly, all males from seventeen years of age to forty-five shall be obliged to take up arms in defense of the colony and shall be exercised for that purpose.

The names of colonists selected by the Trustees were published in the newspapers so that anyone with outstanding debts or obligations could be identified before they sailed.[24]

On October 18, 1732, Thomas Coram informed Percival (who had missed a meeting) that the Trustees "had concluded to send a small number of persons over, and that Mr. Oglethorpe resolved to go with them." Percival, typically cautious, expressed concern that it was premature; however, he was pleased that Oglethorpe would lead the settlers and fill the needed role of "governor," although no such position formally existed. Oglethorpe would serve in various capacities as leader of the colony for over ten years. During that time he would return to England twice, primarily to resolve concerns of the Trustees, to appeal to Parliament for additional support, and (on his second visit) to obtain command of a regiment for colonial defense.[25]

The Trustees' Vision for the Colony

The purposes for establishing the new colony were described in more detail in early promotional documents than in the charter. While the purposes stated in the promotional documents were consistent with the charter, the promotional documents contained lengthy references to visionaries and political theorists, suggesting that idealism rather than pragmatism drove the plan for the colony. The theory that Oglethorpe and his circle were pursuing a secret agenda is particularly compelling in view of references to Niccolò Machiavelli (1469–1527) writing about the role of colonies in the Roman Empire, coupled with references to agrarian law.[26]

By citing Machiavelli, Oglethorpe led the reader not only to a certain interpretation of history but also to the political philosophy of James Harrington. Harrington applied Machiavelli's theories (in turn derived from classical sources) to Britain in his principal work, *The Commonwealth of Oceana* (1656), in which he envisioned an agrarian utopia. Harrington's philosophy was widely read within the country party, as noted earlier, and its prescription for land ownership appears to have influenced the Oglethorpe Plan. Oglethorpe and his circle of confidants developed an integrated, multilayered plan to ensure perpetuation of equality and opportunity beyond the founding of the colony. The plan expanded upon Harrington by elevating the land-working class to a land-owning class of small farmers. The agrarian system envisioned for the colony was outlined in various documents, excerpts from which are quoted below:

The Diary of Viscount Percival, afterwards Earl of Egmont (from 1730). Percival maintained a detailed diary, a practice acquired from his father, of all aspects of his life. Entries from the 1730s contain thorough accounts of both private discussions about the colony and (from 1732) the proceedings of the Georgia Trustees. The earliest entry related to the purposes of the colony is dated February 13, 1730. In the excerpt, Percival paraphrases the purpose of the colony as stated to him by Oglethorpe: "To procure a quantity of acres either from the government or by gift or purchase in the West Indies [i.e., the Americas] and to plant thereon a hundred miserable wretches who, being let out of jail by the last year's act, are now starving about the town for want of employment; . . . that in time they with their families would increase so fast as to become a security and defence of our possessions . . . employed in cultivating the flax and hemp which, being allowed to make into yarn, would be returned to . . . greatly promote our manufacturing.[27]

Some Account of the Design of the Trustees for Establishing Colonys in America (1730–31). Oglethorpe wrote *Some Account*, but it was never published by the Trustees. Instead, they directed Benjamin Martyn to prepare a shorter and less controversial version for publication in 1732. Oglethorpe argued that colonization based on ancient Greek and Roman practices is an essential dynamic of a nation, relieving it of excess population, refreshing its resources, and renewing its energy on the frontier. In this passage he describes those who would benefit from opportunity in the new colony: "Many poor Familys are reduced to the utmost necessity by inevitable misfortunes. As Tradesmen who have suffered losses, Artificers and Manufacturers of such branches of Trade as are decayed or overstocked, Fathers of numerous Familys by Sickness thrown behind hand so as they cannot retrieve it, Laboring men who having served in the Army . . . when discharged are rendered by disuse incapable of returning to their former Occupations. Many by too much good nature to rescue others have undone themselves. The Prisons were full of these who were bound for others or ingaged in Law Suits."[28]

"An Appeal for the Georgia Colony" (1732). In an anonymous article in the *Daily Journal* on July 29, 1732, attributed to Oglethorpe, the philanthropy of Christianity and classical civilization are portrayed as inspirations for the colony. The article contains one of the few references made publicly of a utopian design based on agrarian law. The concepts of liberty and freedom of religion arose here to gestate through the middle Enlightenment and emerge as Jeffersonian democracy. The article also contains Oglethorpe's first public condemnation of slavery: "Trustees intend . . . to relieve the Prisoner, to give Bread to the Hungry, Clothes to the Naked, Liberty of Religion to the Oppressed . . . ; to rescue the. . . Youth; . . . and of these to form well-regulated Towns, . . . to instruct them in how to raise . . . good things which make Life comfortable; . . . under such Laws as tend to make them virtuous. . . . If they give Liberty of Religion, establish the People free, fix an Agrarian Law, prohibit . . . that abominable and destructive Custom of Slavery, . . . they go upon the glorious Maxims of Liberty and Virtue . . . more advantageous to Britain than the Conquest of a Kingdom."[29] In later life Oglethorpe would become a catalyst in forming the abolitionist movement (see epilogue).

Select Tracts Relating to the Colonies (1732). Oglethorpe is the probable editor of these tracts, published in London on November 7, 1732. The publication consisted of selections from the works of Sir Francis Bacon, Machiavelli, John DeWitt, William Penn, and Sir Josiah Child. Oglethorpe's intent was in part to counter a prevailing belief that the people of Britain (even the poor) were an asset that should not be removed to the colonies. It also reflects Oglethorpe's belief that Britain's colonial enterprise would prosper if modeled after those of ancient Greece and Rome. Citing Bacon: "Gard'ners, Plowmen, Labourers, Smiths, Cooks, and Bakers" should populate the colony rather than "wicked condemned Men" who "will ever live like Rogues, and not fall to work, but be lazy, and do mischief." Citing Machiavelli: it was the practice of great kingdoms of ancient times "to establish Colonies and build new Towns and Cities" for "Agriculture and Defence." Religion, Machiavelli maintained, "produced good Laws, good Laws good Fortune, and good Fortune a good End. . . . Take away Religion, and take away the Foundation of Government."[30]

A New and Accurate Account of the Provinces of South-Carolina and Georgia (1732). This substantial tract by Oglethorpe was published in December 1732 and was likely assembled from *Some Account*. His primary argument was that the colony furthered national interest and should be supported with government funds and policies. He provided a lengthy description of the physical geography of the region, its geopolitical significance, and its mercantile potential. However, he also made an appeal for relieving the able poor: "Let us in the mean Time cast our Eyes on the Multitude of unfortunate People in the Kingdom of reputable Families, and of liberal, or at least, [hon]est repute[b]le Education: Some undone by Guardians, some by Law-Suits, some by Accidents in Commerce, some by Stocks and Bubbles, and some by Suretyship. . . . What various Misfortunes may reduce the Rich, the Industrious, to the Danger of a Prison, to a moral Certainty of Starving!"[31]

The name the Trustees appear to have adopted for the new system was "agrarian equality," possibly derived from the term "agrarian equal" found in Harrington's *Oceana*. The term, however, is used only once in Oglethorpe's writings. In a letter to the Trustees dated July 4, 1739, he wrote that changes they were considering would allow "uniting of lots and destroying the Agrarian Equality one of the first principles on which you set out." Francis Moore, who served as Oglethorpe's secretary in the colony, used similar language four years earlier when he wrote that "the first regulation of the Trustees was a strict Agrarian law" to avoid various "inconveniences" and to prevent "the rich monopolizing the country." Another use of the term is found in a sermon to the Trustees by Rev. Philip Bearcroft, a student of classical antiquity, in which he anticipated that the Georgia colonists would be led to "a virtuous Frugality, under the happy Influence of this Agrarian Law."[32]

While all of those who became Georgia Trustees shared Oglethorpe's basic philanthropic agenda, it is likely that only Percival and a few others thoroughly understood or subscribed to the larger vision of a model (or utopian) colony. Oglethorpe's inner circle initially included Percival, John Burton, and among others perhaps Thomas Coram. Percival was an original member of the Bray Associates and a member of the prison committee, and for several years he had been an advocate for the plans of his friend George Berkeley to establish a college to train educators for the New World. Percival mentored Berkeley and was the first to read many of his brilliant philosophical concepts. Having grappled with Berkeley's famous dictum, *esse est percipi* (existence is perception), Percival would not have been difficult to cautiously embrace the secret philosophy underlying Oglethorpe's colonial plan. Burton was a theologian and classical scholar who became close to Oglethorpe at Oxford's Corpus Christi College.

Thomas Coram, noted earlier for having proposed the colony of Georgeia, was initially in close consultation with Oglethorpe, but they later became adversaries over the restrictive land inheritance provisions of agrarian equality.

Others consulted by Oglethorpe in formulating the plan, who may have become part of his inner circle, were members of Parliament recruited two years earlier for the Bray Associates. They included George Heathcote, Rogers Holland, Robert Hucks, John Laroche, Robert More, Stephen Hales, Thomas Tower, and John White. Heathcote, Holland, and Laroche, like Oglethorpe, were Freemasons, a notable affiliation discussed further in the epilogue.

Anthony Ashley Cooper, the 4th Earl of Shaftesbury, elected to the Trust in 1733, may have been another like-minded framer, given the politically radical persuasions in his family tradition, especially the widely read Newtonian philosophy of his father. Shaftesbury, still in his twenties, republished his father's influential book, *Characteristics of Men, Manners, Opinions, Times,* which, in part, harmonized the science of Isaac Newton with the empiricism and humanism of John Locke. Young Shaftesbury wrote a new introduction to the popular work the same year he became a Georgia Trustee.[33]

While Oglethorpe brought most of his circle of intellectual acquaintances into the Bray Associates, and then the Georgia Trustees, there were others he called upon to assist in formulating the plan for the colony. Among those confidants, three stand out as likely participants in planning the details of the colony. John Pine, an engraver and cartographer, captured the fundamental elements of the physical plan for the town of Savannah and the colony in his engraving for *Some Account of the Trustees Design,* the Trustees' tract on their design for Georgia penned by Benjamin Martyn. Sir Hans Sloane, a member of the Royal Society, conceived of the colony as an opportunity for practical botanical experimentation and assisted in funding a botanist. Sir Joseph Jekyll, a senior judge and member of Parliament, provided a link to both intellectual and political circles with dissenting, secularist views and was a strong advocate for the colony. There may have been other confidants who shared Oglethorpe's political philosophy, but as care was taken to avoid an appearance of radical idealism, such linkages were never documented.[34]

The Trustees wasted no time in implementing their plan, and immediately proceeded to interview prospective colonists, initially seeking one hundred to establish the colony. They did not, however, select the "miserable wretches" from the streets of London as Oglethorpe originally described the colonists to Egmont. Instead, many of those they selected were skilled tradesmen who were unable to make a decent living in England. Their intent may have been to establish order in the colony with more able colonists before introducing unskilled poor people in the mix. In any case, they knew the success of the colony would depend to a great extent on the character and capabilities of the colonists.

The Trustees painted an attractive picture of the new colony for prospective colonists, but they also made it clear that a new social order would be put into effect and strictly enforced. They were providing industrious but misfortunate people with a second opportunity, and hard work would be required to create an environment in which they could thrive without corrupting urban influences. Colonists would be assigned to "well regulated towns" integrated with the surrounding countryside. They would be granted a lot in town for a home, another lot just outside town for a kitchen garden, and a larger lot beyond that for a farm. Their property would have to be cleared, fenced, and planted in accordance with a predetermined schedule. They would be supported by the Trust until they became self-sufficient.[35]

Motives for establishing the colony varied among the Trustees, a reality that was initially smoothed over by Oglethorpe. Many Trustees, some of whom were among the clergy, viewed the colony as an extension of the evangelical philanthropy of the Bray Associates. They saw themselves working in conjunction with SPCK and SPG to convert Indians and enslaved Africans to Christianity, to provide Christian education in the New World, and above all to provide a place of renewed opportunity and Christian instruction for Britain's worthy poor and Europe's persecuted Protestants. Oglethorpe and his circle of utopians either shared or indulged those motives but were driven by a more secular philanthropy and an ambitious vision of Georgia as a model for a new society. There were other philanthropists, constituting a third group, who appear to have shared Oglethorpe's political and humanistic philosophy, but who were more adamantly secularist. Whig pragmatists recruited by Oglethorpe to the Trust for their financial and political influence constituted a fourth group. Of these, most were more concerned about commerce and trade than religious or secular philanthropy; however, some were discovered to be "ministry men," who were essentially informants for Walpole, who was never a strong supporter of the colony. The various motivations of the Trustees are summarized in table 1.

	Principal trustee factions			
Purpose	Oglethorpe's circle	Anglican philanthropists	Secular/ dissenter philanthropists	Ministry and commerce pragmatists
Charity				
Relief for urban poor	P	P	P	S
Relief for persecuted European Protestants	S	P	S	S
Evangelism				
Religion instruction and education for colonists	S	P	—	S
Conversion and instruction of slaves and Indians	S	P	—	S
Pragmatism				
Stabilization of the southern frontier	P	S	S	P
Increased trade and commerce	S	S	S	P
Humanism				
Secular philanthropy	P	—	P	—
Expression of Enlightenment moral philosophy	P	—	P	—
Political philosophy				
Establishment of a model society	P	—	S	—
Restoration of traditional values	P	—	—	—

Key: P = primary concern, S = secondary concern

Philosophical differences among these constituent groups later bubbled to the surface under the strain of administering the colony. Accommodating those differences, resolving occasional disputes arising from them, and presenting a unified message to benefactors and Parliament would prove to be a constant struggle. Oglethorpe provided the glue that initially bonded the Trustees together in common purpose, but the longer he remained in Georgia, the weaker the bond became.[36]

For a time, Percival was well positioned to assume Oglethorpe's leadership role. He was president of the Trust, highly regarded by all, and by nature cautious and a capable mediator. He was politically neutral and indisputably evangelical yet sympathetic to country party philosophy and more at ease with secular humanists than his religious colleagues. However, Percival lacked Oglethorpe's intensity, and he lost influence with the ministry after a falling out with Walpole, who had sabotaged his son's bid for election to Parliament. Percival's leadership of the Trust was necessary to maintain cohesiveness, but it proved insufficient to prevent factionalism.

The first serious dispute among the Trustees arose when James Vernon expressed concern about the secularist faction to Percival in March 1734, identifying George Heathcote, John White, Thomas Tower, Robert Hucks, and Robert More as the offending parties. Vernon also accused the Trust secretary, Benjamin Martyn, of leading these gentlemen. Percival, who held Vernon in high regard, wrote in his diary, "I perceive a division growing up among the trustees of Georgia, which I must labour to stifle, or our affairs will go on very heavily."[37]

It deeply troubled Percival "to see so little concern for the religious concerns of the Colony" and noted that if he and Vernon were to "lose our point next meeting" they would "be obliged to protest." Vernon was even prepared to resign from the Trust, but Percival "begged him not to do it till Mr. Oglethorpe should be returned to England, for it would be a great shock and discouragement to him to see himself deserted by those who hitherto had shown the greatest zeal and been of most advantage to the success of the Colony." Ultimately unappeased on this issue and other matters, Hucks, More, and White resigned from the Common Council (but remained Trustees) effective at the anniversary meeting in 1737.[38]

Percival wrote at length in his diary about the division between the religious and secular Trustees, making a list of each group. He feared the secularist Trustees, who had acquired a reputation in Parliament as "averse to anything that bears relation to the Church," were "designing to have no Church establishment in Georgia." Their actions, he worried, would bring "suspicion on us as enemies to the present Constitution in Church and estate." Later he would be informed by trust accountant William Verelst that twelve Trustees, the secularists and others, met for dinner and agreed to moderate their position for the sake of the colony and to avoid "disgusting so many gentlemen as were for this thing, and who applied themselves with so much zeal for the service of the Colony." Percival noted, however, that White and More had not attended a meeting since the matter of religious policy came up, and Laroche, Shaftesbury, Hucks, and Heathcote had attended only infrequently. The "handsomely and respectfully drawn" resignations of More and White from the Common Council were soon received. The two secularists, however, remained in support of the colony, which they were "fully persuaded was one of the most useful and noble designs that could have been thought of."[39]

The remainder of this chapter examines the vision, guiding principles, and implementation strategies of the plan. The politically complex and philosophically fertile milieu in which the Oglethorpe Plan was conceived and implemented is explored further in the epilogue.

The Strategic Plan for the Colony

In a sermon at the first anniversary meeting of the Trustees in 1733, John Burton preached that Georgia was not only a charitable colony but one of an entirely new kind, where colonists would "seem in a literal sense to begin the world again." Colonists would leave behind an Old World system that offered little opportunity, and they would become part of a new society that would reward hard work and personal virtue. Burton's description sounded very much like the concept of rebirth of first principles, or *ridurre ai principii*, found in the writings of Machiavelli, whose works were viewed in a positive light at the time. The concept had considerable cachet during the early Enlightenment and was well known to Oglethorpe. As articulated by Bolingbroke, the concept evolved into a theme of country party philosophy. It called for a return to "original principles" of the constitutional monarchy, most importantly a return to balanced government stabilized by vigorous agrarian representation.[40]

While Oglethorpe and Bolingbroke both sought a return to the traditional principles of the ancient constitution, it is unlikely (however compelling the thesis may be) that the two men and their respective circles were engaged in a secret, concerted effort to precipitate political change, one from within the nation and the other from without. However, individual Trustees with ties to Bolingbroke may have been attracted to the colonial enterprise as a form of external, or frontier, *ridurre ai principii*. Arthur Bedford was chaplain to the Prince of Wales, Bolingbroke's designated agent of *ridurre ai principii*. Trustees Heathcote, Holland, Hucks, Laroche, More, and White were also active in opposition to the court party of Walpole and potentially aligned in some way with Bolingbroke. William Wyndham, leader of Tory and country party factions in Parliament and a friend of both Oglethorpe and Bolingbroke, may have indirectly bridged their like-minded plans.

Whether or not Oglethorpe and his circle intended ultimately to reform British society through a return to agrarian social order and original principles in the New World is a matter of conjecture. The circumstantial evidence suggests they did, but the assertion is difficult to prove. It is clear that Oglethorpe's plan for the Georgia Colony reflected a concern about the dramatic shift of power from country to city, from freeholders to financiers, from farmers to traders, and the magnification of inequality that resulted. Oglethorpe must have been looking for structural solutions, as argued earlier, and he would not have been put off by the enormous challenge of pursuing them.

Aside from any possible underlying utopian or revolutionary intent, the vision for Georgia shared by Oglethorpe and the Trustees had three broad goals, all stated in the charter. First, and of greatest importance to nearly all of the Trustees, was the philanthropic mission of relief for those suffering poverty or religious persecution. Second, of greatest importance to the government, was the strategic significance of establishing a colony in the geopolitical void between British, Spanish, and French spheres of influence. Third, of greatest concern to mercantile interests, was the opportunity to create (and protect) new trade opportunities. The Trustees recognized that placing emphasis on the first would be necessary for broad public appeal, while an emphasis on the second and third goals would be necessary to obtain the political and financial support that would make the colony a reality.

Statements of purpose for the Georgia Colony can be found in promotional materials and records of the Trustees, as seen in the excerpts quoted above. The primary purpose for establishing the Georgia Colony, according to all published accounts, was to provide relief and new opportunity not only for debtors (the initial motivation) but for many others who had suffered life's misfortunes. Even where Oglethorpe described the mercantile or geopolitical benefits of the colony, he consistently returned to the humanitarian mission. In *An Appeal for the Georgia Colony* he described the practical benefit of trade, but then diminished its importance by saying, "The Profit and Gain that will arise from this Design, if it is well executed, is the meanest Motive; therefore I shall not dwell upon that."[41]

Clearly, however, relief for the poor and misfortunate was inextricably linked in Oglethorpe's mind to "original principles" as understood through the lens of country party philosophy. Not only was it a matter of duty and honor to aid such people, but it was a means of rebuilding national character. Oglethorpe's reading of Machiavelli appears to have taken him beyond the concept of *ridurre ai principii* to that of *translatio virtutis*, the migration of civic virtue to fertile frontiers. However, Oglethorpe did not cite either concept in his lengthy version of *Some Account*. Clearly, he needed to avoid an association with Bolingbroke's prescription for regime change, but he also needed to avoid invoking *translatio virtutis*, thereby suggesting that the homeland was becoming corrupted.

Oglethorpe also avoided citing James Harrington, again to distance himself from any suggestion of radicalism. The controversial theory that distribution of power should be proportional to the distribution of land found in *Oceana* may have inspired the system of agrarian equality, but limitations enacted by the Trustees were justified as a pragmatic means of protecting the colony's small farmers and as a mechanism for populating the colony at a density ideal for defensive purposes. The reference to "agrarian law" in *An Appeal for the Georgia Colony* is the only instance where Oglethorpe personally seems to invoke Harrington, although as noted earlier the term "agrarian law" was used by two of his associates.[42]

Oglethorpe returned to Machiavelli for specific elements for the design of a colony derived from Roman experience. Four specific elements vital to the design of a colony were identified by Machiavelli. *Density* should establish a "commodious Distribution of the People ... living regularly and in Order," neither too sparsely nor too densely populated, "making them indigent and poor." Machiavelli also noted the importance of density to defense, which for Oglethorpe became a critical element in the design of Savannah and other towns. *Religion*, Machiavelli asserted, was at the heart of a stable society, and therefore part of the foundation of government. A *trained militia*, Machiavelli believed (citing Britain as an example), could be more effective than a standing army. *Land allocation* was a fourth element identified by Machiavelli as vital to the Roman colonies. The settlement pattern, including the design of towns, that Oglethorpe synthesized from classical principles and embedded within agrarian equality is taken up in chapter 2.[43]

Promotional materials, Trustee records, and Percival's diary contain sufficient material to restate the "design" for the Georgia Colony in the form of a modern strategic plan. Several strategic planning models have been developed since the mid-twentieth century to facilitate organizational processes. The model applied here is often found in town and regional planning. It establishes a hierarchy, beginning with a vision statement, specific purposes (or goals), and guiding principles; a set of implementation strategies is provided in conjunction with each guiding principle.

Reducing the Trustees' design to this format highlights the essence of their intent.

Since the Trustees were of different minds about the purposes for establishing Georgia, the plan for the colony reflects Oglethorpe's intent, rather than common intent, as the core organizing influence. What emerges as the Oglethorpe Plan, therefore, subsumes the various purposes of the Trustees into a broad vision and a framework of guiding principles consistent with country party philosophy, Enlightenment humanism, and agrarian equality. The following list synthesizes these diverse components into a model that might plausibly be described as the strategic plan underlying the Oglethorpe Plan:

> *The Trustees' Vision and Goals:* To establish a place of opportunity for the
> industrious people of Britain and Europe who have suffered unemployment,
> poverty, financial misfortune, or religious persecution; to plant religious
> values in the New World whereby colonists are served by their church
> and Indians and slaves are educated, catechized, and converted to Christian-
> ity within a framework of tolerance and secular colonial administration; to
> populate, cultivate, and protect unsettled British territory south and west of
> the Savannah River, thereby (a) establishing a buffer between established
> British colonies and Spanish and French provinces in America, (b) prevent-
> ing the Spanish from inciting slave revolts through offers of freedom, and
> (c) reducing the threat of Indian uprisings in the region; to cultivate crops
> that must otherwise be imported from other countries and thereby to expand
> trade and commerce independent of and without strengthening foreign pow-
> ers; to establish a model frontier colony founded on humanistic principles
> and traditional agrarian values; and to create a new kind of society based on
> a system of agrarian equality with potential to renew traditional values in the
> homeland.

This is a long vision statement by modern standards, but necessarily so, since it represents multiple visions and wide-ranging goals. The following guiding principles and implementation strategies constituted the shared understanding of how the Georgia Colony would be developed.

- *Principle:* A more equitable society can only be established in un-
  settled territory where entrenched attitudes and practices do not exist.
  Strategy: Obtain a Charter to settle territory south of the Savannah
  River; adopt regulations under which the colony will be administered;

recruit settlers who agree to follow the regulations and make land grants subject to them; provide support during initial establishment.

- *Principle:* A more equitable society can be built on a system of agrarian equality that allocates land fairly and preserves the fair distribution of property. *Strategy:* Structure land grants to provide for home, garden, and farm lots; establish a maximum acreage for grants and accumulated land; set cultivation requirements as a condition of grants; set restrictions on giving credit; limit the size of towns to prevent over-commercialization.
- *Principle:* The viability (productivity, security, and sustainability) of a colony depends on the density and distribution of settlement. *Strategy:* Establish a hierarchy of towns, farms, and villages of specified regularity and density; provide roads and design elements for defense.
- *Principle:* A colonial frontier is a natural place of challenge, opportunity, and reward and as such builds individual character and national strength. *Strategy:* Require most citizens to be freeholders who work their land; provide for indentured servants who become landowners; prohibit slavery and minimize social stratification; require service in the militia.

The plan was a result of Oglethorpe's experience in Parliament with reform initiatives, from which he realized that mercantilism and urbanization were reshaping power and politics while increasing poverty and social disintegration. Oglethorpe saw the colonial frontier as a laboratory in which to cultivate reform without challenging established power, a place where the processes *ridurre ai principii* and *translatio virtutis* would precipitate change without the domestic upheaval. He quite plausibly may have understood, as would the historian Frederick Jackson Turner a century and a half later, that the juncture between civilization and wilderness is a place where a nation's strength and character are forged.[44]

The American frontier, where vast areas were still a blank slate, offered a place for the misfortunate to have a fresh start—in Burton's words, "to begin the world again." The intended self-sufficiency of the colonists would need to be sustainable, and to achieve that aim the system of agrarian equality would prevent accumulation of lands over time in the hands of a few. Land grants would provide each freeholder with a house lot in town, a garden lot nearby to feed the family, and a farm lot for income generation. Laws would be enacted to ensure the colony remained one of small, industrious farmers: the maximum acreage of an initial grant would be fifty acres for those supported by the Trust. Grants of up to five hundred acres would be made to those who paid their way to the colony and took servants to cultivate the land; servants would be entitled to their own grant of land upon completing service. The total amount of land any freeholder could accumulate through any means (purchase, inheritance, gift, or lease) would be limited to a maximum of five hundred acres. Percival wrote, "We considered that grants of larger quantities of land than men can cultivate is a weakening of the colony." Later he remarked that "large grants . . . would throw too great a part of our lands into few hands, the great bane of our other Colonies." Slavery would be prohibited, in part because it would discourage the colonists from working. Cultivation requirements would be placed as a condition of each land grant. Restrictions would be made on giving credit to prevent indebtedness (with the public stores providing free food and tools until the settlers were able to produce their own crops). The size of towns would be limited to prevent urbanization and overcommercialization (with all the attendant social ills) of the colony.[45]

Oglethorpe cited Machiavelli's analysis of Roman practices to emphasize the importance of density, distribution, and order in the settlement pattern of a colony. This design calculus for a successful colony resonated with Oglethorpe's worldview, a large part of which was influenced by Newton and Shaftesbury. Nature's God (in the parlance of the Enlightenment) had created beautiful laws that governed the universe, and man should honor that in his own creations. Careful attention would be paid to the geographic hierarchy of towns, farms, and villages in order to balance the colony's needs for farm production, commerce, defense, and accessibility. Absentee owners would not be permitted. When the question was raised, the Trustees' response was that they "do not propose to subsist any People in the Colony, Who do not intend to cultivate Land for their own Subsistance" and that grants of land would be vacated if a colonist left.[46]

Where Bolingbroke sought to restore the strength and character of Britain, which he believed resided principally in the gentry and the rural population working on their estates, Oglethorpe may have realized that there would be no return to the past and that Britain was changing permanently. Like Bolingbroke, he perceived moral decline in the migration of people from the rural estates to the cities. But unlike Bolingbroke, he did not believe that a return to "original principles" led by a new king would occur to reverse the course of events. The frontier would either provide a model for reform in the homeland, or it would become an external place of opportunity and renewal.

Oglethorpe believed the colonial frontier, a tabula rasa, provided that opportunity. A restoration of ancient rural values on the frontier would constitute an external renewal, perhaps with the potential to reinforce a more limited domestic return to founding principles. It would also constitute the natural and inevitable process of *translatio virtutis,* or the relocation of virtue from place to place. In such a frontier colony, most settlers would earn a living from the land through their own labor, not through the labor of servants or slaves. Indentured servants would be provided only for initial clearing and cultivation or for use by self-financed colonists on larger farms. Those servants, too, would become freeholders and work the land when they completed their service. Slavery would be absolutely prohibited, and other forms of social stratification would be minimized. Slavery was prohibited not only because as an institution it was an "abomination" and antithetical to the purpose of the colony, but also because it would create a threat to the colony's security by creating the potential for rebellion.

Oglethorpe did not conceive of the Georgia Colony as an evangelical mission, instead having merged his more secular mission with the religious purposes of the Bray Associates. Nevertheless, his religious convictions were sufficiently strong for Percival to count him among those who strongly supported the religious purposes of the colony. Oglethorpe's views on religion are reflected in the passages found in *Select Tracts* from Machiavelli suggesting its necessity as a moral foundation for society. He appears to have adopted Machiavelli's pragmatic view of religion rather than an evangelical one, seeing it generically as important to civilization. He also saw religion as fundamental to the alliance of interests that comprised the Trustees.[47]

From the founding of the colony, ministers and missionaries would be present to provide religious instruction and to educate, catechize, and convert non-Christians. Oglethorpe did not, however, view the colony as theocratic. It would be a secular province, tolerant of religious differences, administered by civil (and perhaps, when necessary, military) authority. William Stephens, the secretary to the Trustees in Savannah, mirrored Oglethorpe's pragmatic view of religion when he wrote that "sublime points of divinity" were "ill-suited with the present circumstances of this young colony, where the preacher's labor would most certainly be best bestowed, in plainly setting forth the sad consequences of a vicious life."[48]

The colony was an infant of the Enlightenment, and as such it made use of science and scientists in its establishment. Sir Hans Sloane assisted Oglethorpe in devising an agricultural plan for crops that could be grown on small acreages and selected a botanist to refine the plan and obtain new crops for the colony. The plan included land set aside for experimentation with crops, a ten-acre plot known as the Trustees' Garden. Experienced horticulturists were assigned to maintain the garden.

Crops such as vegetables and fruits were anticipated to be the basic staples of sustenance and local trade. Silk production, which could be managed by families as a cottage industry, held promise as an export commodity. Grape and olive production, thought to be suitable to the latitude and climate, also offered promise for wine and oil exports. Such exports would not require large plantations dependent on slave labor as was the case with rice production in South Carolina.

From the earliest stages of settlement, many colonists petitioned for changes to several of the laws and conditions placed on grants that were derived from the colony's guiding principles. Tail-male inheritance, limits on accumulation of land, and the prohibition of slavery were of particular concern to the colony's critics. Most of the petitions came from Savannah, where South Carolina traders and merchants convinced some of the colonists that they would never succeed with those restrictions. The Trustees initially responded with thoughtful but modest amendments, changes they believed would not alter their intent. Eventually, they altered the constraints on tenure and (after Oglethorpe stopped attending meetings) rescinded the prohibition on slavery.[49]

Many historians have concluded that the Oglethorpe Plan was an ill-conceived utopian scheme administered in an autocratic manner. It appears more likely, however, that the Trustees adopted a paramilitary organization for settlement of a hostile frontier (see chapter 3) but envisioned republican government based on country party philosophy once the colony was secure from external threats. While their vision failed to materialize, the humanistic colonial experiment put forth enduring ideas that would influence the course of British and American history.[50]

2

 The Plan for an Ideal City

The Trustees established five towns during their twenty-year administration of Georgia, three on the Savannah River and two on the colony's southern frontier. Only one of the towns, Savannah, would be laid out and substantially developed with a planned hinterland of farms, villages, and estates.

When Oglethorpe sailed for America, it is likely he carried with him a drawing of the regional settlement plan for Savannah, a prototype that would subsequently be applied throughout the colony. No copy has yet surfaced, and it remains the Holy Grail for many students of Trustee Georgia. However, the frontispiece for *Some Account* (Martyn's published version discussed in chapter 1), designed by John Pine, is an idealized regional development plan, engraved for printing at the time the actual plan was being prepared.

Pine's rendering, shown in figure 7, accurately reflects both the text in *Some Account* (both versions) and actual settlement that soon followed in the Savannah region. The plan depicted the town of Savannah as small and well fortified with a centrally located church; it is surrounded by a large common for surveillance and cattle grazing; a hierarchy of gardens, farms, villages, and yeoman estates beyond the town is shown laid out in a grid. Regularly spaced double lots reserved by the Georgia Trustees for community support purposes are shown amid what appear to be square-mile farm sections. The radial development patterns seen in the villages allowed for a defensible cluster of houses at the center. Wooded areas are preserved for firewood, lumber, and game. Peaks in the distance portrayed the colony extending from the coast to the Appalachian Mountains and beyond.

FIGURE 7   Idealized depiction of the Georgia Colony. This vision for the colony, the frontispiece of Martyn's *Some Account*, completed in 1732 by John Pine, was consistent with the Oglethorpe Plan as it was implemented the following year.

The plan was implemented on February 12, 1733, when Oglethorpe escorted more than one hundred colonists to the site that would become the town of Savannah, thus founding the Georgia Colony. A short history of settlement is provided in chapter 3, with special attention to implementation of the guiding principles and design details that make up the Oglethorpe Plan.

The layout of the town was initiated by setting a prime benchmark on a stretch of high bluff at a bend in the Savannah River. From that point, the entire town and the surrounding region—gardens, farms, and villages—would be laid out in accordance with the Oglethorpe Plan. The prime benchmark undoubtedly had special significance to Oglethorpe, a Freemason who would have seen it as a symbolic cornerstone.

Oglethorpe laid out the town with meticulous care and a sense of purpose, knowing that the town's unique design was tied to the success of the entire colony. Every action taken by Oglethorpe upon arrival in the colony was calculated to develop a new society based on the precisely formulated system of agrarian equality. Establishment of Savannah according to plan was as important as securing support from neighboring South Carolina and establishing good relations with indigenous (Indian) nations.

The precision, elegance, and simplicity of the plan for Savannah reflected the Masonic doctrine of perfect order in nature created by God, the Great Architect of the Universe. To Oglethorpe, Masonic doctrine encompassed the new science of Isaac Newton and the ancient knowledge of Greek and Roman civilizations at their peak, a synthesis holding great promise for humanity. The plan was thus an emulation of the beauty and perfection of design conferred by God to the natural world, celebrated by writers and poets of the period such as Oglethorpe's friend and fellow Freemason Alexander Pope, whose *Essay on Man,* written in 1732, reflected the sentiment with which Oglethorpe approached the colonial venture: "All nature is but art ... / ... / All discord, harmony, not understood."[1]

It was a precept of Oglethorpe's time that, underlying the appearance of randomness and discord in the world, there is a plan of perfect order and natural law that humans are capable of discovering and emulating. That fundamental precept guided Oglethorpe as he laid out the town of Savannah and the surrounding region.

After a year of labor, nearly one hundred acres had been cleared, the town laid out and built up, the colonists housed, and fortifications erected. A perspective map, or rendering, of the town as it stood in March 1734 was prepared by Peter Gordon, a colonist and bailiff in Savannah. Gordon's rendering, shown in figure 8, also depicts the town plan in outline form. Oglethorpe's tent is shown near the benchmark set for laying out the town. By remaining in a tent as houses were built for others, he demonstrated his willingness to sacrifice comfort and sublimate authority to earn the respect of the colonists and to establish a sense of fundamental equality among them.[2]

A year later Francis Moore, secretary to Oglethorpe and later storekeeper in Frederica, described the plan for Savannah as follows:

> The town is laid out for two hundred and forty freeholders; the quantity
> of land necessary for that number is twenty-four square miles; every forty
> houses in town make a ward, to which four square miles in the country belong; each ward has a constable, and under him four tything men. Where the
> town lands ends, the villages begin; four villages make a ward without, which
> depends upon one of the wards within the town.[3]

Moore went on to describe a settlement plan that provided villagers with a place of refuge in town where they could go in the event of attack, using the square in each ward as an encampment. He noted that beyond the villages were lots of five hundred acres granted with the stipulation

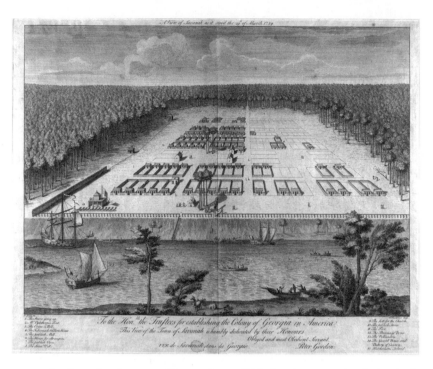

FIGURE 8   Peter Gordon map of Savannah, 1734. This famous perspective depicts both the town plan and the built environment one year after its founding. (Hargrett Rare Documents Library, University of Georgia)

that servants would be retained by the owners to clear and cultivate the land. His description of actual settlement resembled the theoretical model described in Oglethorpe's *Some Account* with only minor modifications.[4]

A map prepared several years after the founding of Georgia (figure 9) illustrates both actual settlement and idealized build-out under the Oglethorpe Plan. The map, published in Germany for prospective immigrants, was prepared from a sketch drafted in the colony, almost certainly under Oglethorpe's supervision. The map confirms the use of a square-mile grid for regional planning and the boundaries of the garden, farm, and village districts within the grid. The regional plan was designed to contain at a minimum four square miles of town and gardens, twenty-four square miles of farms, twenty-four square miles of villages, encompassing a fifty-two-square-mile area. Figure 9 shows a grid of nearly seventy square miles, an area that would include outlying estates and compensate for unusable land.[5]

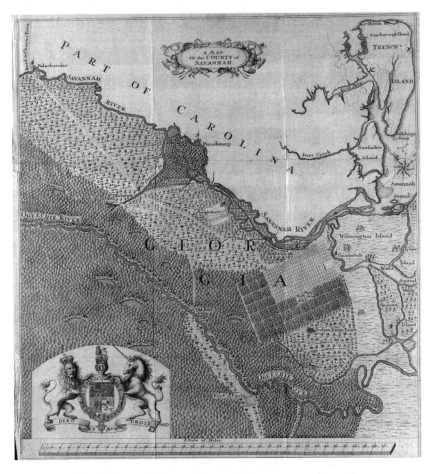

FIGURE 9 Map of Savannah County. Prepared between 1735 and 1740, this map illustrates the implementation of the Oglethorpe Plan in the Savannah region. The grid appears to have included the estates beyond designated villages, hence the number of grid sections exceeding the twenty-four that would be expected. (Hargrett Rare Documents Library, University of Georgia)

Terminology

Terminology surrounding Oglethorpe Plan has lacked clarity. Planning and design professionals often use the term "Oglethorpe Plan" to refer to the layout of historic downtown Savannah (see chapter 4), and, in popular usage, the term often encompasses the built environment added during the nineteenth century. Before proceeding with the deconstruction of the plan, the following definitions are provided.

Oglethorpe Plan. The plan to establish a new model society in the colony of Georgia comprising social, economic, and physical elements

Savannah plan. The integrated physical plan for the town of Savannah and its hinterland including a square-mile grid system and elements within the grid

Regional plan. The generic plan for towns and their hinterlands, including gardens, farms, villages, estates, expansion areas, and right-of-way surrounding a town

Town plan. The design of wards, riverfront development, right-of-way, and the common that made up the town of Savannah

Ward layout (or structure). The primary unit of physical development within the town, comprising four tything blocks, four trust blocks, a civic square, and right-of-way

The hierarchy of definitions seen here may not be intuitively obvious to those who have grown accustomed to using the term "Oglethorpe Plan" to describe the ward layout and the historic built environment it produced. However, Oglethorpe indisputably constructed a multilayered, integrated plan, one to which his name should properly be applied. Technical justification for these definitions is developed over the subsequent sections.

The Regional Plan

Oglethorpe's vision of a country party paradise can be seen in Pine's conceptual plan for the Savannah region (figure 7), discussed at the beginning of this chapter, where a small town is surrounded by farms beyond which lie villages and yeoman estates. Townspeople are shown working cooperatively on a construction project, a contrast with the anonymity and alienation of large cities. The town was limited in growth potential by the symmetry of its context, appearing to have only the common surrounding it in which to accommodate any expansion.

Pine's illustration was not merely an attractive frontispiece for Martyn's version of *Some Account* but, more importantly, a model for the colony's regional development plan ("land-use plan" in modern terminology), in which towns would be small central places in low-density regional settlements. Savannah was designed to be an agrarian town, not a city. Oglethorpe envisioned the metropolitan function of Savannah as a low-density capital city with a large hinterland of interconnected farms, estates, and villages.

The Oglethorpe Plan generally met the specifications of the Grand Modell for colonial settlement formulated by the 1st Earl of Shaftesbury. The model, which influenced town planning throughout the British Empire, had the following elements:

1. Planned urbanization, not dispersed settlement
2. Land rights to town, suburban, and country lots
3. Advanced layout of towns, before settlement
4. Wide streets framed within a square-mile grid
5. Civic squares
6. Standard lots, larger than in Britain
7. Plots reserved for public purposes
8. A town common

The plan for Georgia, however, was infused with details derived from Roman colonial practices and country party political philosophy.[6]

Figures 8 and 9 support the observation that the Savannah region was laid out for structured (and limited) development as depicted by Pine and generally as described by Oglethorpe in the original version of *Some Account*. Table 2 compares the hierarchy of regional planning units in *Some Account* with those in the final plan as implemented. Other detailed specifications for the regional plan are summarized in table 3.

Tables 2 and 3 reveal the complex interrelationships among physical, social, and economic facets of the plan. A limitation on land ownership of fifty acres per family, maintained by control of sale and inheritance, would ensure perpetuation of the agrarian design. Five-hundred-acre estates of self-supporting colonists would equate to fifty acres per future household, since indentured servants would be granted fifty acres of their own upon completing their term of service. The geometric distribution of population throughout the region would resemble Roman practices for claiming, settling, administering, and defending colonies.[7]

The Oglethorpe Plan anticipated that people would work their own land and that hard work would be amply rewarded. In Burton's words, "Industry and contentment will be attended by wealth and prosperity." Colonists were required to clear and plant according to a schedule, and they were provided with tools and provisions sufficient to establish themselves. Trust farms were set aside (at the center of each square-mile section of farm land) for communal use, and the profits from them would support charity when needed in future times. Slavery was prohibited because it was

TABLE 2   HIERARCHY OF REGIONAL PLAN ELEMENTS

Grid element	1731 concept	1732 plan
Region	Town and 20 villages 625 families	Town and 24 villages 480 families
Gentry	1 manor per square mile (1 lath)	1 to 5 manors per square mile
Yeomanry	4 estates per square mile (1 lath)	—
Village	1 lath on 1 square mile	1 tything on 1 square mile
Farm grid	32 farms per grid unit 20 acres per farm 2 for the constable 6 for public benefit	12 farms per grid unit 45 acres per farm 2 for public benefit
Gardens	Unspecified parcel in town	5-acre parcel near town
Common	1 square mile including town	1 square mile including town
Town	5 laths 125 families	6 wards housing 240 families
Lath	2 tythings and constable	—
Ward	—	4 tythings
Tything	2 comradships	10 families
Comradship	6 families	—

Sources: Oglethorpe, Some Account; F. Moore, Voyage.

inhumane and would corrupt the system of agrarian equality planned for the colony.[8]

The Oglethorpe Plan, as shown in chapter 1, was driven by distinct guiding principles and implementation strategies. Two of those principles, along with their implementing mechanisms, pertained to the physical plan for settlement in the colony. The principle of agrarian equality required equitable distribution of land in parcel sizes appropriate for family farming. The principle of viability required a density and distribution of settlement that would assure its acquisition and defense. Those two principles converged into a settlement plan of strategically located towns with well-defined hinterlands. Each town was to be ringed by four distinct districts: gardens, farms, villages, and estates.

The internal design of each town was correlated with the land-use plan for the surrounding region. Economically, the villages and estates formed

TABLE 3   STRUCTURE OF THE REGIONAL PLAN

Geographic hierarchy	
Town and commons	1 square mile
	240 house lots (Savannah)
Village	1 square mile
Estate	100 to 500 acres
Land allocation	
Charity colonists	50 acres, comprising
	0.12-acre town lot
	5-acre garden lot
	44.88-acre farm lot
Self-Financed colonists	500-acre maximum
	1 servant per 50 acres
Servants	20 (later 50) acres
Lot dimensions (charity colonists)	
Town (house) lot	60 feet × 90 feet
Garden lot	660 feet (sides)
Farm lot	1206 × 1601
Tenure	
Purchase and sale	Subject to trust approval
Accumulation	500-acre maximum
Inheritance	Tail-male
Cultivation requirement	
Area cleared, fenced and planted—50 acres	5 acres in 10 years
Area cleared, fenced and planted—500 acres	50 acres in 10 years
Mulberry trees planted—50 acres	50 white mulberry trees
Mulberry trees planted—500 acres	1,000 white mulberry trees

a hinterland for the town, and the town was designed to support them with a port, public stores, a public mill, and other essential facilities. Administratively, the town and its hinterland had one civil authority made up of bailiffs, constables, a storekeeper, a recorder, and a surveyor. Defensively, the town, villages, and estates were organized into militia units that together formed a battalion. Units of the battalion would train in civic squares placed at regular intervals in the town and would form in those squares to defend against attack.

The town plan harmonized with the regional plan, reinforcing and sustaining the principles of agrarian equality. The size of Savannah, the town prototype, was limited to 240 houses arranged within six wards. Wards were placed within a town common defined by a one-square-mile perimeter. A garden district lay immediately beyond the common, and a farm district lay immediately beyond the gardens. The small size of the town allowed residents easy access to their gardens and farms. Additional growth of the town would not be accommodated unless it occurred within the common, since it would disrupt the allocation formula linking town lots to surrounding garden and farm lots. New growth would be directed to the hinterlands and to other towns.

The conclusion drawn by many that Savannah was designed for indefinite growth by cellular (ward) replication runs counter to the agrarian design underlying the regional plan. Apart from an inference, drawn from country party philosophy, that Oglethorpe would not have wanted a large, growing city in the colony, there are statements to that effect by officers of the Trust in the colony. Peter Gordon wrote that the "town was intended to consist of six wards," and Francis Moore wrote that it was "laid out for two hundred and forty freeholds" and that "the quantity of [agricultural] lands necessary for that number [240 freeholds] is twenty-four square miles." Moore then added that there were twenty-four villages beyond the farms, requiring an additional twenty-four square miles within the regional grid. Both men worked closely with Oglethorpe in administering the colony and were privy to the details of the plan.[9]

While Savannah was not intended to become a densely developed city, it apparently was intended to be a new model city functioning as the "Metropolis of the Province." It would, however, be a *garden* metropolis, the center of a highly interconnected region of towns, villages, and estates. As such, the Savannah region would constitute an alternative to the dysfunctional rural-urban dualism afflicting Britain. It may be correct to conclude, as at least one author has, that the design of Savannah and its hinterland was a monument to Robert Castell, reflecting his work in *Villas of the Ancients*, which idealized the rural landscape. However, the primary reason for limiting the town's size was to preserve its virtue. As Percival said to Queen Caroline, "Populous towns have more roguery than little ones." There was a sense in British Enlightenment thinking that nature and nature's God were best harmonized over a rural landscape, not in the depravity of the city. Men were to be stewards of their lands, "paternal not plundering," as God was steward of the earth.[10]

The Oglethorpe Plan, viewed as a scheme to create a model agrarian society, may seem to have diminished modern relevance as a town or regional plan. However, an understanding of the intricacies of the plan reveals considerable relevance to contemporary planning, particularly in the debate over form versus function now taking place among contemporary planning paradigms. The Oglethorpe Plan is therefore more than a historic curiosity: parts of its tiered planning framework remain relevant to modern planning; its use of a scientific paradigm in modeling social behavior is still relevant as a cautionary example of overplanning; and most importantly, its function-based design led to elegance in form, very much a lesson for modern town planners to contemplate.

The Oglethorpe Plan, in its broadest sense, is an expression of traditional agrarian values and Enlightenment humanist philosophy. However, the narrowest interpretation of the plan, one that looks only at the ward layout, is what many think of as the Oglethorpe Plan. The latter view misses the crucial point, that Oglethorpe's plan was elaborate in its detail and in its interrelationships because it sought to create a harmonious new society. If the term "Oglethorpe Plan" is to do justice to its framer, it is best understood as a strategic plan in which physical design is subordinate to social and economic purposes. The elegant, remarkable plan for the town of Savannah nevertheless remains the most significant surviving component of the Oglethorpe Plan and deserves careful examination.

The Genesis of the Savannah Plan

Oglethorpe and his circle of planners were secretive about the utopian facet of their colonial plan, and unfortunately their detailed plan for Savannah is also shrouded in mystery. While the lack of information about central aspects of the colonial plan was intentional, the lack of information about town and regional plans is more likely due to a scattering or complete loss of documentation. Numerous theories on the genesis of the plan, particularly the layout of the town of Savannah, can be found in the literature on the early settlement of Georgia. Rather than repeat all such theories, the discussion that follows focuses only on those that have withstood strict scrutiny.[11]

The two-dimensional, spatial plan for Savannah and the surrounding region can be reverse engineered from surviving elements (primarily wards) and numerous maps produced in the eighteenth and early nineteenth centuries, beginning with the 1734 Gordon map (figure 8). The symmetry and regularity of the plan also offer hints about the original design, as does Moore's written description, cited earlier.

The plan for the Savannah region is particularly well illustrated in figure 9. The grid system framing the plan, based on square-mile units, had been standard in British colonies since the adoption of Shaftesbury's

Grand Modell. The Savannah regional plan, however, was innovative for the time, inspired in its detail by Roman town planning and unique in its precision as well as in its integration of sociospatial planning. The New World was a tabula rasa of opportunity for designing cities more perfectly, and grids were often a starting point in this pursuit.[12]

The Roman grid integral to the Oglethorpe Plan was in turn inspired by ancient Greek colonial planning. The grid system of city planning was first developed by Hippodamus (498–408 b.c.) for Greek colonial cities. His plan for the city of Piraeus was the basis for his study of city planning discussed in Aristotle's *Politics*. Oglethorpe, however, began his discussion of city planning in *Some Account* with Vitruvius (ca. 75–25 b.c.), the Roman architect and town planner whose principal work, *De Architectura*, was lifted from historical obscurity during the Renaissance. Leonardo da Vinci based his famous drawing the *Vitruvian Man* on the discussion of proportions in book 3 of *De Architectura*.[13]

Little is known about Vitruvius, and he appears to have been mysterious during his own time; nevertheless, he made a strong impression on Renaissance scholars, who eventually made his work accessible to English designers. The architect Inigo Jones introduced Vitruvian design principles to England during the seventeenth century; however, new interest in aesthetic philosophy during the early Enlightenment was prompted by Shaftesbury's *Characteristicks*. The architect Colen Campbell published *Vitruvius Britannicus* in successive volumes between 1715 and 1725, providing a catalog of designs by Jones and others influenced by Vitruvius. Robert Castell in *Villas of the Ancients* (1728) explored Italian architecture and landscape design influenced by Vitruvius. Oglethorpe's initial interest in classical design at Oxford must have led him Castell.[14]

The Oglethorpe Plan does not appear, however, to have been influenced by British interpretations of Vitruvius (with the notable exception of the Newcourt plan cited below). Oglethorpe seems to have gone directly to the Italian Renaissance for inspiration. Several Renaissance designers, including da Vinci, applied Vitruvian principles in a quest to design the ideal city. Others notable in that quest include Leon Battista Alberti (1404–1472), Georgio Vasari (1511–1574), Vincenzo Scamozzi (1548–1616), and Pietro di Giacomo Cataneo (ca. 1510–1574). Cataneo developed a concept of the "ideal city" remarkably similar to the Savannah ward structure and thought by some to be the basis for the layout of the city's wards. Cataneo, in turn, influenced post–Italian Renaissance town planners, including Richard Newcourt, who planned the rebuilding of London after the Great

Fire of 1666. The Newcourt plan was not adopted, but Oglethorpe may have seen it, and its unique repetition of wards may well have inspired the repetitive pattern in the Savannah plan.[15]

Another Renaissance designer, Bernardo Morando (1540–1600), synthesized earlier concepts of the ideal city. The principles he derived from his predecessors were applied to the plan of Zamosc, a historic city that exists today in Poland and retains a high level of similarity to Savannah, in terms of size and configuration, as seen in figure 10. The city has been designated a UNESCO World Heritage Site.

A recent theory proposed by John Reps, professor emeritus of city and regional planning at Cornell University, is consistent with this conclusion. Reps discovered a possible model for the Savannah ward plan in the historic design of Turin, Italy. The plan for the expansion of Turin, first published in *Theatrum Saubaudiae* in 1682, contained a design for the Piazza San Carlo (Piazza Carlina) that followed a Cataneo model. It is almost a perfect fit with Oglethorpe's Savannah wards. The plausibility of the Turin design as a model for the Savannah plan is enhanced by the fact that Oglethorpe served under Prince Eugene of Savoy, who made Turin his capital. Oglethorpe, his brother Theophilus, and George Berkeley, who was consulted on the plan for the Georgia Colony, were familiar with Turin.

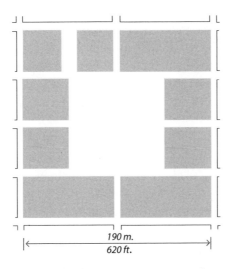

190 m.
620 ft.

FIGURE 10   Plan of Zamosc. The Zamosc central square and surrounding blocks resemble the Savannah ward layout, possibly sharing a common source in a Renaissance vision of an ideal city. (UNESCO World Heritage Site materials)

Another Renaissance influence may be traced to Andrea Palladio, discussed in the prologue, who had a pervasive influence on the rural aesthetic of eighteenth-century England. However, it is useful in the present discussion to call attention to the resulting formalization of English landscapes that occurred when the Oglethorpe Plan was being prepared. Palladian design, which Castell had helped popularize, may have influenced Oglethorpe to design Savannah as a utopian town-in-the-garden. The less formal approach to landscape design pioneered by Alexander Pope was insufficiently developed in the early 1730s to influence the Savannah prototype.

Other elements of the Savannah plan were also derived from Roman practices. Roman law provided for private, public, and common pasture land, which was reflected in town planning. The spatial arrangement of land uses and functions, including defense and public land, are evident in the Oglethorpe Plan. Oglethorpe's description of site selection in *Some Account* parallels Roman criteria. Roman surveyors, following the practice of Hippodamus, used rectangular gridding for the layout of towns and surrounding agricultural land.[16]

More important to Oglethorpe, Roman town planning in some instances supported principles of social justice through spatial equality, a point exemplified in the plan for the Roman city of Timgad (figure 11), founded in 100 a.d. Now a UNESCO World Heritage Site located in Algeria, Timgad bares a remarkable resemblance to the Savannah plan on all levels. It was built in a square grid system; it had wide, rectilinear streets that were both aesthetically pleasing and designed for maximum accessibility; its equally sized parcels and houses promoted a classless society. The town was built for retired soldiers, providing a reward for service that would have appealed to Oglethorpe, who was an advocate for British soldiers and sailors.

Roman town planning was strongly influenced by the gridiron design of *castra,* the formal encampments of the Roman army. A *castrum* was divided by two principal roads into four quadrants, the *cardomaximus* and *decumanus maximus.* A quadrant at the intersection of these roads defined the center of a *castrum.* Encampments became forts, and forts often evolved into towns, retaining the strict formality of the military design.[17]

While in the service of Prince Eugene of Savoy during the Austro-Turkish War of 1716–18, Oglethorpe may have been impressed with specific examples of the gridiron pattern of army encampments as well as towns built over Roman *castra.* The city of Timisoara, which he participated in

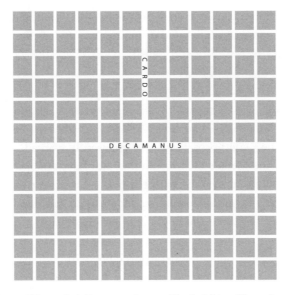

FIGURE 11   Plan of Timgad. A Roman colony in North Africa, Timgad used a
castrum grid to structure a socioeconomic system of spatial equity resembling that
adopted by Oglethorpe for Georgia. (UNESCO World Heritage Site materials;
satellite imagery courtesy of GeoEye)

taking, was built over a Roman fortress in the thirteenth century. He would
have noted the layout of axial streets defining a central square. However,
the city was rebuilt by the Austrians after the war, and it is not clear that
the town layout existing in 1716 was perpetuated in the present-day grid
and square that bear a resemblance to those of Savannah.[18]

Oglethorpe reconfigured the Roman town planning model where necessary to accommodate his goal of a just society based on principles of
agrarian equality. The spatial plan for the Savannah region would not only
provide for equal *initial* allocation of land; it would limit later acquisition
and consolidation to preserve the system of agrarian equality.

A critical stage of plan development occurred when agrarian equality was merged with the new paradigm of the Newtonian science. Several members of Oglethorpe's circle were scientists or lay members of the
Royal Society, and their influence is seen in two areas: (1) in maximizing
the efficiency, with mathematical precision, of the regional plan without
inducing urbanization and (2) in providing for continuous agricultural
experimentation.

The refinement of the land allocation system required maximizing
several variables. There had to be ample acreage per household to ensure

self-sufficiency, yet too large an allocation would have the detrimental effect of reducing accessibility and dropping density below a viable threshold. Regional accessibility and density had to be calibrated to maintain internal control and external defense.

For an intense period during 1732, Oglethorpe's inner circle of planners met with sufficient frequency to complete the task, although there is no record of such meetings. The design of the ward (the best-known surviving element of the Oglethorpe Plan) was apparently worked out during this period. The final details of the plan may not have emerged until shortly before Oglethorpe embarked with the first colonists for the New World. John Pine, the only professional designer affiliated with the Georgia Trustees, must have produced the final plan that Oglethorpe took with him to America.

Oglethorpe, the only member of his circle with military training, must have contributed the defensive elements. In *Some Account* he describes a physical and organizational plan for the defense of the colony. The country houses of the yeomanry would be clustered in groups of four and protected with perimeter ditches; villagers would retreat to the town, and the town would be fortified with walls and outer ditches: "Villagers and Townsmen being drawn together will form a Batallion of Infantry consisting of 625 Men." Additionally, the yeomanry would comprise 120 dragoons (soldiers transported by horses); gentry and servants would make up as many as 100 horsemen (cavalry). The same defensive structure emerged in the 1732 plan, with a smaller force of 480 men instead of 625 (plus yeomen and gentry) and tythings apparently replacing an earlier, larger unit call a lath (see table 2 for a comparison of 1731 and 1732 units).[19]

Oglethorpe's elaborate regional plan for equitable land allocation, efficient land use, and effective defense was, by design, spatially static, very much like the countryside of the English gentry and very much unlike the organic and chaotic development of cities. The plan ensured that each family would have a farm less than four miles from their house (it had been less than two miles under the 1731 concept plan put forward in Oglethorpe's *Some Account*). Growth would be accommodated by new towns rather than by infilling and disrupting the order and harmony of town, common, gardens, farms, and, villages: "If the first 125 Familys found a Town the Villagers and Yeomenry will be drawn together by the protection of it, and therefore each 125 Familys may be settled in a separate Town leaving the increase and the execution of the rest of the Design to time."[20]

The plan for the town of Savannah, the prototype for future towns in the colony, provided for six wards. Initially, as seen in the Peter Gordon drawing, four wards were laid out. The town was surrounded by the common, which was preserved by the Trustees for defensive surveillance and grazing land. Garden lots also occupied part of the common, but most were within a three-square-mile area to the east and west, straddling the town. Farm lots were laid out immediately beyond the common and gardens, creating a total area of twenty-four square miles occupied and cultivated by town residents. Beyond the farms, there were outlying villages for charity colonists and estates and manors for self-sufficient colonists. Some of the villages were immediately populated, but others were held in reserve for future growth. Those villages would absorb indentured servants upon completing their terms of service. Like the charity colonists, they would be granted fifty acres.

Each of these elements and their genesis are subsequently described in greater detail. First, however, a discussion of land grants explains the hierarchical structure of land allocation, and a discussion of surveying and measurement practices explains how each element was laid out.

Land Grants and Survey Methods

Colonists subsidized by the Trust, sometimes referred to as charity colonists, were granted exactly fifty acres. For those who would live in town, the grant consisted of three separate parcels: town, garden, and farm lots. Village residents were granted a single parcel within a radial cluster, as depicted conceptually in figure 7 and implemented in figure 12, an 1873 map in which the imprint of the Oglethorpe Plan can be seen 120 years after the Trustee period. The radial pattern appears to have been abandoned after the settlement of Hampstead village.

Land grants were tied to a contract with the Trust that required the grantee to remain in Georgia and cultivate a specified amount of land over a ten-year period. The colonists therefore did not own land on a fee-simple basis but through contract. Self-supporting colonists (those described by Oglethorpe in *Some Account* as yeomanry and gentry) who were granted up to five hundred acres by the Trustees, were also subject to a contract with residency and proportional cultivation requirements. However, they would be required to support one indentured servant per fifty acres, or ten servants for the maximum grant. Servants were rightful colonists, and larger estates were thus incubators for future landowners who would be granted lots upon completing a period of indenture. In this manner, the

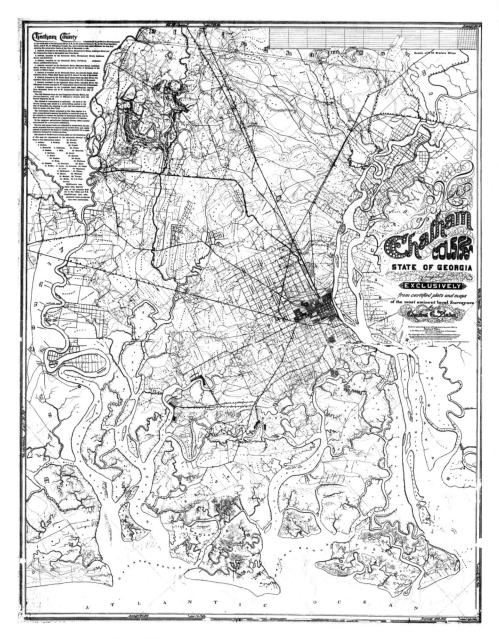

FIGURE 12   Map of Chatham County, 1873. The Oglethorpe Plan remained largely
intact after 140 years. Radial lots allocated in Hampstead Village are among the original
features than can be seen in this map. (Chatham County Engineering Department)

ratio of one colonist to fifty acres was preserved, and overall equity thereby maintained. The acreage allocated to each group is shown in table 3 (the fractional acreage of farm lots is explained later in this section).

Equitable land allocation required an accurate survey of the region. Oglethorpe established an initial point of reference, or "benchmark" in survey terminology, from which the grid system and all of its elements were laid out. This prime benchmark was set at the midpoint of the bluff on the Savannah River, three hundred feet from the riverbank (presently at the foot of Bull Street in front of city hall). The central location provided a half mile of high ground in either direction on which to build the town of Savannah.

The grid containing the town, delimited as seen in figure 13, the common, and the surrounding gardens, farms, and villages in theory would consist of a minimum of fifty-two square miles. In practice the grid would encompass a larger asymmetrical area of nearly seventy square miles to avoid unusable areas such as swamps. The town and common with adjacent gardens required a four-square-mile area, arrayed in a line along the river with the square-mile town and common at the center. Farms required twenty-four square miles, one for each tything, and villages also required twenty-four square miles, since there would be one affiliated with each tything. The remaining four square miles would have been available to offset unusable land. Yeoman or gentry estates would lie immediately outside the fifty-two square mile area.

The units of measurement applied to the grid, shown below, were those commonly in use by surveyors at the time.

Furlong	660 feet	8 per mile
Chain	66 feet	10 per furlong
Pole or rod	16.5 feet	4 per chain
Yard	3 feet	5.5 per pole
Cubit	1.5 feet	2 per yard
Ell	3.75 feet	0.8 per yard

Each unit is shown in terms of length in feet and divisibility into the next larger unit. Theories regarding the cubit and the ell as units in the plan are discussed later in this chapter. Detailed specifications underlying the Oglethorpe Plan, set forth in table 4, corresponding with figure 14, are provided in feet and acres. Figures represent components of the grid, the total area of which was at least sixty-six square miles.

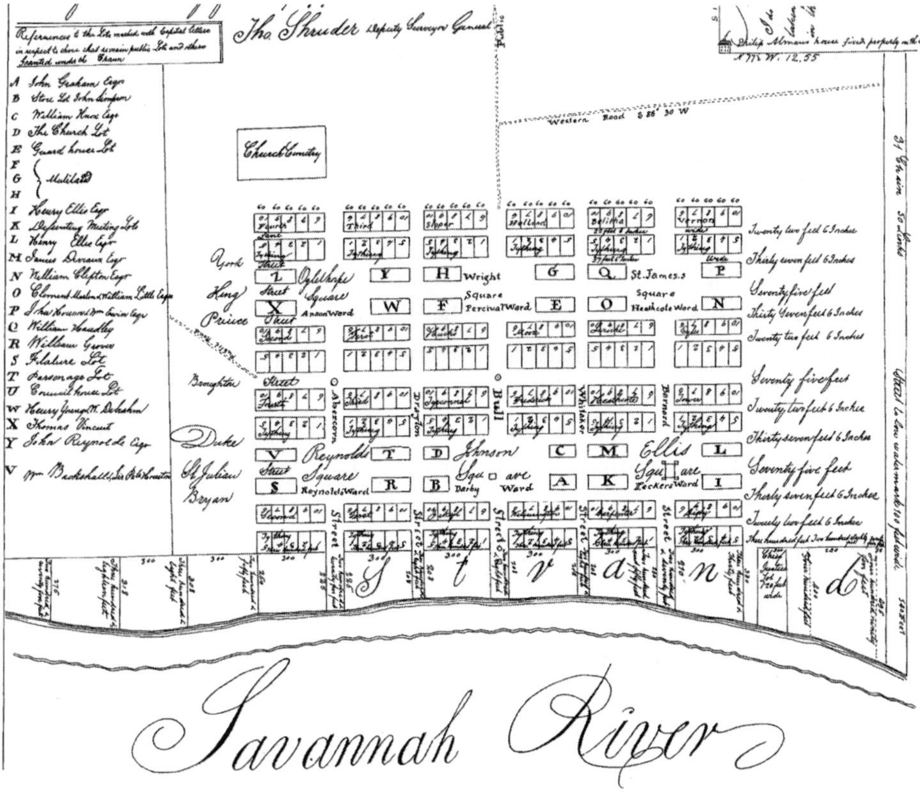

FIGURE 13 Completed six-ward plan for Savannah, 1770. (City of Savannah)

The fifty-acre grants yielded a fractional measurement of farm acreage, just under forty-five acres, as seen in table 3. Since decimal measurements were not used in planning and surveying the colony, the 44.88-acre figure is provided only as a convenience for the modern reader. Actual measurement of farm lots was formulated as 44 acres and 141 (square) poles. Archaic units of measurement used in the Oglethorpe Plan are discussed subsequently (see "Mechanics of the Plan").[21]

Garden lots were also measured in units that would facilitate surveying. Unlike the rectangular farm lots, they were laid out in pairs of equilateral triangles within a square furlong, and each square furlong filled one cell of a seven-by-seven grid within each square mile (figure 14). The area created by the eighth furlong making up the mile on each side of the larger grid section was allocated to right-of-way. The elegance of the regional plan coupled with the precision of its internal survey units permitted Savannah to be laid out and developed with no delay.

TABLE 4   SAVANNAH REGIONAL PLAN SPECIFICATIONS

	Area		Dimensions in feet	
	Square feet	*Acres*	*Width*	*Length*
Town and Common	27,878,400	640	5,280	5,280
Town	3,013,875	69.19	2,115	1,425
Ward	455,625	10.46	675	675
Ward + ROW[1]	540,000	12.40	720	750
Tything	60,750	1.95	300	202.5
Tything lot	5,400	0.12	60	90
Trust lot	10,800	0.25	60	180
Square + ROW	85,050	1.95	315	270
Square – ROW[2]	46,800	1.07	240	195
Broad streets	—	—	75	—
Through streets	—	—	37.5	—
Lanes (alleys)	—	—	22.5	—
Perimeter street (east–west)	—	—	75	—
Perimeter street (north–south)	—	—	45	—
Garden District				
Inner grid unit[3]	490,000	11.74	715	715
Garden lot	217,800	5	660	933[4]
Inner grid ROW[5]	—	—	55	—
Exterior ROW	—	—	165	—
Farm District				
Inner grid unit	2,376,000	54.55	1,225	1,633.3
Farm lot[6]	1,954,926	44.88	1,206	1,621
Inner grid ROW[7]	—	—	42.5	—
Exterior ROW	—	—	165	—
Village District				
Village	24,502,500	562.5	4,950	4,950
Interior ROW[8]	variable	variable	variable	variable
Exterior ROW	2,021,175	46.4	165	—
Estates or manors[9]	—	100–500	—	—

[1]ROW = right(s)-of-way.

[2]Assumes extension of 37.5-foot streets.

[3]A square area containing two triangular gardens

[4]Garden lots were triangular, with dimensions of 660 feet × 660 feet × 933 feet.

[5]Assumes plan had a diagonal right-of-way pattern.

[6]Deeded as 44 acres and 141 poles.

[7]Figures are plausible estimates.

[8]Intended to be a radial pattern.

[9]Tracts located both within and outside the gridded area.

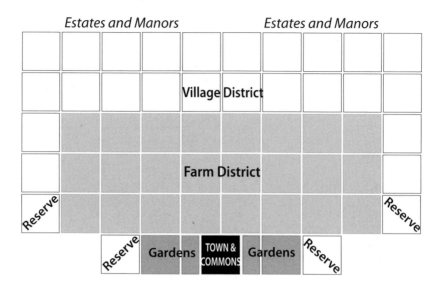

FIGURE 14   Conceptual regional plan of Savannah

Figures 7, 8, and 9 are conceptual in nature, although the Gordon map (figure 8) comes close to being a survey map by showing lot lines and right-of-way. The earliest actual survey map located thus far is one dated 1798 and signed by city surveyor John McKinnon (figure 15). McKinnon produced several maps, but this version is the only one that verifies the existence of internal right-of-way in the farm district, a critical piece of information for reverse engineering the Oglethorpe Plan. Although dated 1798, the map appears to be a palimpsest of a much older map, predating McKinnon's tenure as city surveyor. Recopying maps was a time-consuming process, and old maps were often revised and reused over a period of years before being replaced.

The McKinnon maps illustrate that the plan established substantial right-of-way between and within each square mile section of the grid. External right-of-way width appears to far exceed that required for roads but was likely needed for herding livestock. Since there is no extant plan or written record of how it was formulated, and since the later McKinnon maps are not drawn precisely to scale, determining the dimensions of the right-of-way and thus the configuration of garden and farm lots, in particular, requires considerable reverse engineering and still remains conjectural. The mathematics used to determine alignments of town, garden, and farm lots appears to have required complex calculations, perhaps even integral calculus, an invention of Newton in the late 1600s.

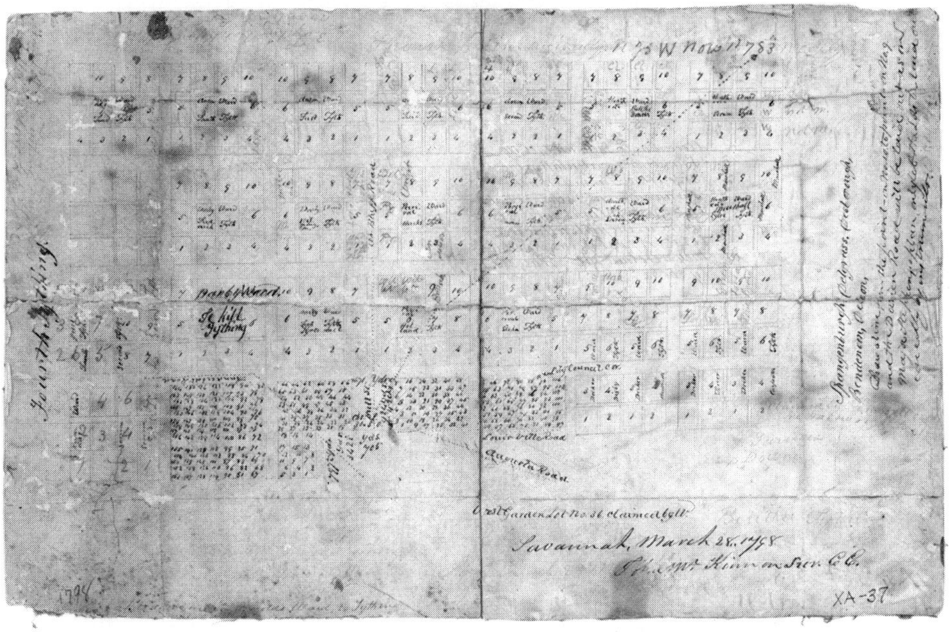

FIGURE 15   Savannah regional map, to 1798. This early map was probably used by city surveyor McKinnon as the basis for later maps. This map, however, unlike later maps, shows internal right-of-way in the farm district, aiding reverse engineering of the plan. (City of Savannah)

The Wards

Oglethorpe selected the mile-long bluff on the Savannah River because it was the closest site to the mouth of the river that would accommodate the town. It was also suitable as a point of departure for laying out the grid system, lying on a coastal ridge that extended ten miles southward. The town would require less than half the width of the bluff, with the common occupying a full square mile of high ground. Farther south, the ridge widened out, offering ample land for farms and villages.

Oglethorpe initially cleared sufficient land for four wards and surrounding fortifications, as shown in the 1734 Peter Gordon map (figure 8). The two additional wards called for by the plan would be laid out and developed two years later. The town would remain confined, as intended, to these six wards until the end of the eighteenth century. The term "ward" appears to have been uniquely applied by Oglethorpe in the colony, without any exact analog in England, where the word merely applied to a small administrative unit of a town.

The six wards making up the town were initially of identical design, thereby supporting Oglethorpe's principles of agrarian equality. There would be no wealthy section of town and no poor section. Each ward had the same number of house lots, all of equal size. The center of each ward was aligned and interconnected with the center of the other wards, creating a physical design that promoted spatial equality. A modification that Oglethorpe may have made while implementing the plan was a slight enlargement of the square in the ward nearest the prime benchmark, which would have accommodated town meetings or other large gatherings. The final layout of the original six wards is seen in figure 13, a colonial survey map dated 1770.

Each ward consisted of four elements, depicted in figure 16: four groups of house lots called *tything* blocks, four lots reserved for public uses called *trust* blocks, a central square for various activities, and access right-of-way. (Ward element dimensions are shown in table 5.) Each tything block contained ten house lots (or tything lots) in back-to-back rows of five. The term "tything" also referred to the unit of ten families in the block. Each trust block had sufficient area for one or two public uses such as transient housing or a public oven. Tything blocks and trust blocks were arrayed around a central square measuring 315 by 270 feet, or just over two acres, with the exception of the single larger square, which measured 435 feet by 270 feet (two lot widths wider).

The standard central square is reduced to one acre when perimeter street right-of-way is subtracted (i.e., the projection and perimeterization of the 37.5-foot streets). However, it is unlikely, given the absence of significant traffic in such a small town, that any separation of right-of-way was anticipated. The squares present today in Savannah (see chapter 4) were thus not delineated as such in Trustee Georgia.

The square served several purposes. In *Some Account* Oglethorpe said it would be "reserved for a Market place, and for exercising the Inhabitants." It would also provide a site for public gatherings, and in the event of an attack, each square was designated to accommodate a group of four villages as a place to retreat and encamp while defending the town. The square also established a "garden aesthetic" consistent with a region where agriculture would prevail and residents would remain rural at heart.[22]

Each of the six wards laid out by Oglethorpe was exactly 675 feet square, comprising an area of 10.46 acres, excluding perimeter right-of-way between wards. Ward dimensions increase to 720 feet by 750 feet, an area of 12.4 acres, when perimeter street right-of-way is included. Wards

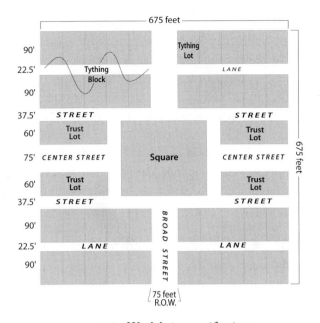

FIGURE 16   Ward design specifications

TABLE 5   WARD ELEMENT DIMENSIONS IN FEET, CUBITS, AND
ELLS (WHERE A CUBIT = 18 INCHES AND AN ELL =
45 INCHES)

Ward element	Feet	Cubits	Ells
Lanes (alleys)	22.5	15	6
Through streets	37.5	25	10
Perimeter streets (north–south)	45	30	12
Tything lot width	60	40	16
Trust lot width	60	40	16
Broad streets	75	50	20
Tything lot depth	90	60	24
Trust lot depth	120	120	32
Square depth	270	180	72
Square width	315	210	84
Ward width and length (internal)	675	450	180
Ward width (with right-of-way)	720	480	192
Ward length (with right-of-way)	750	500	200

contained four streets seventy-five feet in width approaching the central square. Two other streets 37.5 feet in width flanked the square on the north and south and separated tything blocks from trust lots. Streets separating wards on the east and west sides were forty-five feet in width, while streets separating wards on the north and south were ninety feet wide. The latter ninety-foot streets may have been designed as perimeter streets on the north and south edge of town, even though there were no other wards beyond that required separation.

As each of the six wards contained forty tything lots, the town was designed for 240 freeholders, the same number that would ultimately reside in the outlying villages. If one assumes an average family size of five, the population of the town and villages would be 2,400. Merchants, colonial officials, military personnel, and other travelers visiting Savannah would be housed in transient quarters. A "house for strangers" built on one of the trust lots is shown as site "6" on the Peter Gordon map (figure 8).

The physical plan for Savannah was meant to serve the principles of agrarian equality, not, as emphasized earlier, to facilitate urbanization and mercantilism. Each element of the plan related mathematically, in Newtonian fashion, to every other element. The town could not be increased in size without disrupting the hierarchical regional plan. To the extent that a larger city might have been envisioned by Oglethorpe, it would have been seen as part of a distant future when new, inland frontiers created a tableau for future agrarian colonies.

While Savannah would be the principal city in the colony, most growth would be accommodated by creating new towns, rather than by densifying the capital. Each new town would have its own region, or hinterland. Towns would be sufficiently far apart to allow for rural countryside in between. The countryside would be gradually settled by those who could afford servants to clear and cultivate large tracts of land (the yeomanry and gentry), who were eligible for land grants of up to five hundred acres.

During the twenty-year period of Trustee control of the Georgia Colony, two other towns were established using the Savannah ward design. New Ebenezer, settled by Salzburgers, was situated twenty miles upriver from Savannah. Its plan departs from the Savannah design principally in combining trust lots, thereby also eliminating two seventy-five-foot connecting streets. Darien, founded in 1736 on the Altamaha River, retained the basic configuration of the Savannah plan but increased the number of lots in a tything from ten to twelve. Two other towns established during the Trustee period did not precisely follow the Savannah model. Frederica, which became home base for Oglethorpe in 1736, was a garrison town laid out much like the Savannah model but with modifications for additional defense. Augusta, the only other sizable settlement established while Oglethorpe was in Georgia, was both a garrison town and a trading center in the Lower Creek nation; few elements of the Savannah model appear to have been implemented there.[23]

By the end of the Trustee period, Savannah was the only town in the colony that retained all of the original design elements and functionality of the Oglethorpe Plan. Darien, however, retained many of the basic elements. For another century, the ward element of the plan would be repeated in Savannah, while the regional elements (gardens, farms, and villages) would gradually fall out of use. Savannah would ultimately have twenty-four wards before city officials discontinued the ward layout for a conventional urban grid in 1851 (see chapter 4).

The origin of the ward element of the Oglethorpe Plan has been the subject of considerable research and speculation. John Reps has studied the range of theories and added some of his own. In 1960 he documented the similarity of the plans for Londonderry and Coleraine in Northern Ireland and offered plausible links to the Savannah ward layout. In 1984 he updated the theory and added a new one that demonstrated similarities between Hanover, Cavendish, and Grosvenor squares in London and Savannah wards. In 2006, Reps announced the entirely new theory, described earlier, of a plausible link to a plan for Turin that produced Savannah-scaled units, which can be seen today in the Piazza Carlina. The Turin connection is particularly compelling because Oglethorpe visited the city in 1716 and 1717.[24]

Ultimately, however, the question of origin takes one to the principles of agrarian equality and the historical context of the Enlightenment. Oglethorpe and those in his circle who worked out the details of the plan, designed the ward for spatial equality, geometric precision, and specific functionality. Other plans may have been instructive, but it is unlikely any served as an exact prototype. It appears more likely that the plan was unique and purposeful. In any case, none before or since has quite captured its elegance.

The Common

The common, within which the town's wards were situated, served several purposes. Martyn described it as follows: "Without the town, a mile square, which amounts to 640 acres, might be reserved as a common for the pasturing of the cattle and all within musket shot of the works should be cleared. This open space will contribute greatly to the health and security of the town as well as to the conviency of the inhabitants." Healthful open space was a particular concern after the Great Plague struck London in 1665–66. The common would also accommodate additional growth of the town, should it be warranted, although such a scenario was more likely neither envisioned nor welcomed.[25]

John Reps, an authority on the genesis of the Savannah ward, has also suggested various plausible sources for the layout of the Savannah common. Oglethorpe may have borrowed from the plan for Bath, from various plans for settlements in the Carolinas, or from the plan for Purrysburg in South Carolina on the Savannah River. Oglethorpe was familiar with Purrysburg's layout, which had a 260-acre common, having reviewed it in 1731. The plan was the first implemented under orders issued by Governor Robert Johnson. The governor's policies carried out a directive from the Crown to enhance settlement of South Carolina by creating twenty-thousand-acre townships laid out in a grid with the town situated on a river. The town would have a common not exceeding three hundred acres, and each inhabitant was to be granted a town lot and a fifty-acre farm lot beyond the common.[26]

The Savannah common included a ten-acre public garden, located on the east edge of town, the purpose of which was to test local viability of plants brought from throughout the world and train colonists in their cultivation. The garden was an initiative strongly supported by Trustee Stephen Hales and Trust advisor Sir Hans Sloane, both members of the Royal Society. The crop experimentation initiative, or "project" in the parlance of the time, reflected the tremendous interest in science and experimental methods characteristic of the British Enlightenment.

Botanists hired by the Trustees would supply numerous plants, many of which came from similar latitudes and thus were potentially adaptable. Crops were sought that would thrive in Georgia and supply England with products such as silk and wine that were imported from foreign countries. An expert in silk production would be hired to develop the garden into a nursery and educational facility (and one in fact was dispatched with the first colonists). The Trustees' Garden, as it later came to be called, was prolific during the first years of the colony. Later, it would be poorly managed and neglected.[27]

The Garden District

One of several works that influenced the Oglethorpe Plan was *Villas of the Ancients,* written by Oglethorpe's friend Robert Castell, whose death in prison led to Oglethorpe's leadership in prison reform. In part 3 of that work, garden lots are situated in suburban districts just far enough from town "as to be no annoyance" but sufficiently near to furnish it with produce for daily meals, a physical relationship that was clearly achieved in the plan for Savannah.[28]

The garden district was essential to the larger plan of agrarian equality. Gardens would swath the town in an agricultural setting and provide each family with a nearby source of food for daily meals, a desirable alternative to purchasing it from merchants. Children would acquire an ethic of hard work and learn farming techniques in the family garden before working the farm.

The five-acre, triangular garden plots, occupying half of a square furlong, were embedded in a seven-by-seven-square-mile grid section of ninety-eight gardens. Nearly two and a half square miles were thus required to accommodate 240 gardens required for the town's predetermined population. As shown in figure 14, the theoretical depiction of the Savannah plan, each side of the town and common was laid out first with a half square mile of garden lots and beyond that, aligned with the farm grid, a full square-mile garden section. The three-square-mile garden district straddling the town and common would have thus accommodated 294 garden plots, more than sufficient for the required number. The common, however, had additional capacity to provide reserve land to replace plots on unproductive soil.

Since the town was centered on either side of a line dividing the larger grid of square-mile sections, the gardens were laid out in a manner that restored the grid to the east and west of the town, as may be seen in figure 14, the early McKinnon map. The external right-of-way for the garden district thus aligned with that of the farms and villages. Although the McKinnon map does not show *internal* right-of-way for the garden lots, it is assumed an internal network existed for access and alignment with the town and farm grid sections.

Garden district specifications in table 4 are based on the following assumptions. A square-mile grid section in the garden district contained 490 acres (5 acres × 98 plots) of garden area. Right-of-way acreage is calculated by subtracting garden acreage from the acreage in a square mile (640 − 490 = 150 acres). The 150 acres of right-of-way would have to be accounted for by the combined area of internal and external right-of-way. It seems clear that internal right-of-way was provided in a grid that surrounded the square-furlong pairs of gardens, rather than separating the triangular garden along the hypotenuse, which would have elongated each square mile group of gardens. It appears that half, or 330 square feet, was allocated to external right-of-way and the balance allocated to internal right-of-way. The latter works out to a width of 55 feet. Thus seven rows and columns of garden lots and six interstitial segment of right-of-way yield an internal width of 4,950 feet.

The Farm District

Farm lots were allocated within an area immediately beyond the garden district. The farm district extended from there three miles south and spanned an area seven miles wide. The regional plan as conceived in London likely had a perfectly symmetrical arrangement, possibly spanning eight miles, east to west, centered on the right-of-way projecting southward from the prime benchmark (at the base of what is now Bull Street) and through the center of town. In practice, the plan was altered to conform to topography: land ended three miles to the east at the Wilmington River, whereas the upland extended four miles to the west.

Each square mile of farm area contained twelve lots, ten allocated to freeholders as part of their fifty-acre grant and two reserved by the Trustees for communal farming or lease. As envisioned by Oglethorpe, the Trust farms would generate crops or revenue "for supplying the Poor and Sick and the whole Town in case of War, Famine, or other accidents."[29]

Farm lots were allocated by tything, with each group of ten freeholders farming a square-mile grid section. All four tythings in a ward were allocated a cluster of contiguous square-mile sections of farm lots. The tythingman who led each tything for military training also presumably led his tything in clearing, fencing, and cultivating their farms.

The terms of land grants required each freeholder to clear, fence, and cultivate land within specified time limits (see table 3). Freeholders were specifically required to plant white mulberry trees to support the manufacture of silk, anticipated to be the colony's principal export. An expert in silk production was brought in from northern Italy to oversee establishment of the industry. Farms were expected to cultivate other crops as well, such as corn, wheat, and cotton. Grape vineyards and olive orchards were also thought to hold promise at the 30- to 32-degree latitude of the colony.

As discussed earlier, a botanist and gardener were retained to seek out promising crops for cultivation in the colony. Once a crop was determined to be suitable for cultivation as a result of experimentation in the Trustees' Garden, it was made available to farmers.

Early parcel maps were not drawn precisely to scale, and with the exception of the early McKinnon map, they did not show the presence of internal right-of-way. Nor is there any text from the period that describes exactly how the farm district was laid out. Consequently, a central problem in reverse engineering the exact parameters of the Oglethorpe Plan is to determine right-of-way specifications. The parameters supplied here represent a mathematically plausible scenario.

Farm district specifications in table 4 are based on the following assumptions. A square-mile grid section in the farm district contained 538.5 acres of farm area, comprising twelve lots of 44.88 acres each. Right-of-way acreage is calculated by subtracting farm acreage from the acreage in a square mile (640 − 538.5 = 101.5 acres). Farm lots were laid out in approximately a three-to-four side ratio, corresponding to the three-by-four array of lots within each grid section. Farm lot dimensions of 1,206 feet by 1,621 feet conform with this assumption and allow for external right-of-way alignment with the garden district and internal right-of-way of 42.5 feet in width throughout a grid section.

A later McKinnon map, seen in figure 17, was drawn roughly to scale, showing farm lots occupying an area measuring 1,320 feet by 1,760 feet, or 54 acres, rather than the 44.88 acres granted by the Trust, a difference of 9.12 acres of right-of-way per parcel. Apparently, over time, the intended delineation of right-of-way was lost or most of the acreage ceded to private property owners.

The Village District

The "out-villages," as the Trustees called them, were an integral part of the Oglethorpe Plan, creating the density and penetration in the hinterlands essential to establish the rule of law, to claim the colony for Britain, and to defend it if attacked. The villages would become defensive outposts for the town, and the town would be a place of refuge for the villages in the event of war. The village district also provided a reserve area that would be settled over a longer period of time than the town, absorbing the children

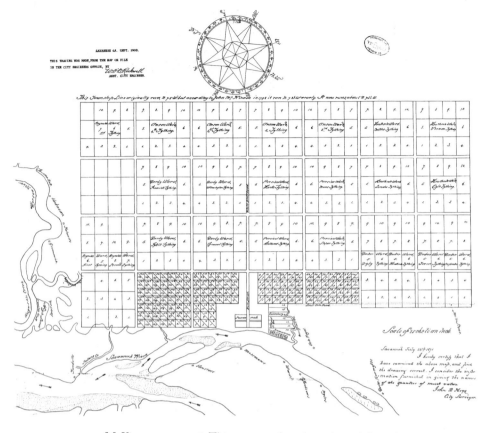

FIGURE 17   McKinnon map, 1798. This map may have been derived from the survey map shown as figure 15 and drawn with greater precision; however, internal right-of-way in the farm district has been left out. (Hargrett Rare Documents Library, University of Georgia)

of freeholders in town and indentured servants as they completed their terms of service.

In *Some Account,* Oglethorpe specified that every four villages, each with ten freeholders, would form a tything of forty families. Militia units would be formed from village tythings paralleling those in town and would be attached to counterpart tythings in one of the town's wards. Villagers would have use of the square in that ward if they required refuge during an attack.

Several strategically located villages were settled soon after the town was populated and fortified. Hampstead and Highgate were located to the south of town, immediately outside the farm district. In 1735, Francis

Moore described them as "pretty villages . . . where planters are very forward, having built neat huts, and cleared and planted a great deal of land." The two villages were named after ancient Saxon villages on the outskirts of London. Oglethorpe's villages, much like their namesakes, were situated at the gateway to Savannah on a central axis exactly four miles from the prime benchmark. Engravings of London squares in the early 1700s depicted Hampstead and Highgate villages on the horizon four miles distant. Other villages in the Savannah grid included Acton, located just south of Hampstead, and Thunderbolt, east of Savannah on the Wilmington River.[30]

Villages established outside the grid, and therefore not part of the planned area, usually commanded a strategic location. Abercorn was located on an upstream tributary of the Savannah River, Tybee was a barrier island near the Savannah River bar, Vernonburg was ten miles south of town on the Vernon River, and Skidaway Island was settled to take advantage of good land and timber. The settlement of villages is discussed further in chapter 3, where a complete list of villages can be found.

The village district was laid out in the same square-mile right-of-way grid as the gardens and farms. In *Some Account* Oglethorpe stated, "Each lath should compose a Village . . . and in it each family should have its Alotment [of] Farms thereunto adjoining in the same manner as the Towns People." When tythings of ten families replaced laths, a basic unit of organization of twenty-four families (see table 2), villages were reduced commensurately.

Hampstead, the first village to be settled, was platted in a radial pattern with a central cluster of houses, consistent with Pine's conceptual plan (figure 7). The ten freeholder grants per village were fifty acres each. It is unclear how the 62.5 acres inside the right-of-way were allocated. The radial pattern remaining on the 1873 map in figure 12 shows both twelve radial segments and a central common. The irregular lot pattern suggests that some of the original lots were subdivided. In that case, the central common with internal right-of-way accounted for the residual 62.5 acres.[31]

The radial pattern may have been applied to all three of the villages settled in the Savannah region during the Trustee period; however, the pattern probably did not show up on later maps because Hampstead was the only village fully settled to Oglethorpe's specifications. Portions of the perimeter right-of-way for the village district, preserved for public access, can be seen in the present-day Savannah road network (see chapter 4).

Estates and Manors

In *Some Account* Oglethorpe described two groups of people who would have larger grants of land beyond the villages. Yeomen were described as persons "who carry over their families at their own expense and agree with the Trustees on such terms as shall be for the advantage of the Colony." Gentry were described as "Men of Reputation and Character and such to whom the Trustees shall think fit for the increase of the Colony to grant Manors upon such terms as shall be agreed between them." Four yeomen would be granted the same amount of land as a village tything, or 125 acres. Gentry would be granted up to 500 acres.[32]

In practice, or perhaps as a result of later refinements to the plan, the distinction between yeomen and gentry seems to have disappeared. There were no further references to these two groups as distinct categories of settlers in later publications by Oglethorpe, in Martyn's short version of *Some Account,* in Egmont's diary, or in the minutes of the Trustees.

Over three hundred grants ranging from seventy acres to five hundred acres were issued to self-supporting colonists who agreed to the terms of the Trustees for settling the colony. Self-supporting colonists, like charity colonists, agreed to specific terms tied to their land grants. In addition to clearing and cultivation requirements, they were required to reside in the colony and support one indentured servant for each fifty acres (maintaining the household/land allocation ratio discussed earlier).[33]

Self-supporting colonists often had specific plans for the use of their land in addition to meeting the Trustees' basic cultivation requirement. These plans included timber harvesting, potash production, and vineyard cultivation. Late in the Trustee period the number of colonists supported by the Trust diminished, and the number of self-supporting colonists receiving larger grants increased following enactment of amendments to the system of agrarian equality. After the Trustee period many of the original estates and manors were enlarged into rice and cotton plantations that operated on the South Carolina slave-dependent plantation model.[34]

The Mechanics of the Plan

The new science and mathematics of Isaac Newton can be seen in the Savannah plan, just as it influenced nearly all aspects of the British cultural milieu. Newton's work was infused in art and literature, popularized in the press, and made accessible to laymen through the lectures of John Desaguliers, among others. It was carried into religious and philosophical realms through the influential writings and teachings of the 3rd Earl of Shaftesbury and other philosophers. It also became an integral part of Masonic symbolism. For Oglethorpe, who founded the first Masonic lodge in Savannah, a blend of new mathematics and ancient design principles was an ideal way in which "to begin the world again."

Oglethorpe's circle of associates who conceived the Savannah plan, as discussed earlier, included several Freemasons. As a group, they likely shared the Newtonian view of God as the Great Architect of the Universe, a view codified into freemasonry (see epilogue). It is also likely that they took a great deal of care in refining the geometric and mathematical structure of Savannah's prototype regional plan, so much so that it is reasonable to call it a Newtonian plan.

The mathematical regularity of the plan for Savannah, in fact, is one of its most remarkable features. The planning historian John Reps identified a base common denominator of 7.5 feet for street and lot dimensions, which the architectural historian Mark Reinberger found could be further reduced to 1.5 feet, or one cubit. The ancient cubit during Oglethorpe's time, according to Reinberger, was standardized at 18 inches (half a yard), although Newton famously researched the ancient measurement and determined that it was 25 inches. The English ell, a measurement of 45 inches, is another hypothetical common denominator. The ell, from "elbow," is approximately the length of a man's arm. English surveyors used a standardized rod called an ellwand for official measurements. Poles and chains were used to survey property lines, and the furlong measurement was used in the garden district grid.[35]

An arcane unit such as the cubit or ell may have been used by Pine and others in the initial plan for Savannah, imbuing it with ancient significance. All narratives and correspondence from the Trustee period, however, cite measurements in more conventional units of feet and yards, while deeds made reference to survey units including poles and furlongs. Table 5 illustrates how both the cubit and ell yield whole numbers for ward dimensions.

More interesting, perhaps, than the numerology of measurement in the plan is its geometry. It is rigidly hierarchical and symmetrical in structure. Every element of the plan exists in a square-mile metagrid, and every grid section contains another grid within which each functional element of the plan is arrayed. Thus the square mile of the town and common contains six wards, which in turn contain four tything blocks, which contain ten house lots. A square mile in the garden district contains a seven-by-seven grid of gardens, and each grid unit contains two triangular gardens. A square mile in the farm district contains farm lots in a three-by-four array surrounding a double-lot Trust farm. The metagrid and the subdivisions within it define a remarkable system of right-of-way that maximizes accessibility throughout the system, one that influences the urban morphology of the Savannah area to the present day (see chapter 4).

The geometry of the plan, more than its mathematics, reflects the influence of freemasonry, with its symbology of construction geometry (e.g., the sacred three-four-five triangle) coupled with the Enlightenment understanding of the world as a harmonious and perfectly designed system. Renaissance interpretations of ancient geometric proportions are also evident in the civic square, where the dimensions (315 by 270 feet) are in a desirable ratio of 1.667 prescribed by both Palladio and Alberti (interpreting Vitruvius).

Where Newton's mathematics is most evident in the plan is not in its physical design but in its third dimension of human ecology. As Oglethorpe made clear in *Some Account,* each physical element of the plan is numerically associated with an element of its human organization. Newton was not satisfied to understand the physical laws of the universe and their underlying mathematics but wanted to know what significance those laws had for humans, a concern that led him on a quest for ancient knowledge (see epilogue). Oglethorpe appears to have been on a similar quest, linking physical design to the deeper meaning of social organization.

The Brilliant Design of the Enduring Ward

The functionality, proportionality, and spatial equality offered by Oglethorpe's ward plan invites the conclusion that it is an ideal design for cellular urban growth. Eminent scholars who have studied Oglethorpe's ward design conclude that it "did not predict its ultimate borders"; that it allowed for "indefinite expansion"; that it was "a repetitive grid without implied boundaries"; that the "the modular nature of the original town . . . envisaged expansion by the addition of one or more units when the need arose"; and that the "cellular unit, the square and its twelve blocks, not only served as a fine module for growth by accretion, but also had within it the elements of growth by extension."[36]

The compelling notion that Oglethorpe's ward layout was intended to support replication reflects a modern bias. As argued in chapter 1, Oglethorpe and the Trustees did not envision the ward as a unit of indefinite growth. In the historic context in which they devised a model for colonial development, cities were seen as the source of social ills. The plan for agrarian equality prescribed small towns in permanent, harmonious balance rather than in a state of continuous growth. Town residents would own a house in town and a garden and farm within walking distance. Growth of the colony would occur by creating new towns, not by expanding existing ones.

Although it seems unlikely the plan for Savannah anticipated indefinite growth, the ward plan is brilliantly adaptable as a model of urban design. The symmetrical arrangement of residential and civic land uses around a square creates a sense of place and establishes a secure environment. Trust lots provide for the needs of residents of the immediate ward but also for those of other wards as well as visitors, thus avoiding excessive insularity. The square is perfectly sized to accommodate ward residents without seeming too large and to accommodate all residents of the town's freeholders without being too small. The right-of-way of each ward interconnects with other wards at up to twelve points. Broad streets align and interconnect each square with squares of adjacent wards. The design is functional in maximizing accessibility and defensibility. Its proportionality creates both comfortable spaces and aesthetic balance. And it establishes fundamental spatial equality by allocating land in equal parcels and creating neighborhoods of fundamentally equal composition.

The ward has sufficient complexity to support a vibrant, mixed-use environment. This characteristic makes it a particularly good model from the perspective of modern urbanism. The design historian Stanford Anderson studied the adaptive quality of the plan and concluded: "Because the underlying structure is comparatively rich in information, the appearance and use of the various elements cannot be wholly arbitrary. Consequently, highly distinctive environments, serving their own uses and complementing one another, can lie around the corner from one another. . . . The articulated ward plan contributed to environmental diversity and choice. In the long term, the underlying structure provides for possible evolutionary change." While this understanding of the ward layout is not what Oglethorpe envisioned, the underlying principles readily produce an ideal urban growth model, a rich potential explored in chapter 5.[37]

Conclusion

The driving purpose of the Oglethorpe Plan was to create an equitable society, which led to a layout for the town of Savannah that achieved fundamental spatial equity: equal lot sizes in symmetrical and interlocking wards of equal size, status, and accessibility. Spatial equity in the design briefly achieved Oglethorpe's vision of an equitable society, but the system soon collapsed under the pressure of outside influences. However, the richness of the design, which was substantially retained for more than a century, supported later desirable outcomes. In the nineteenth century, an outcome of underlying spatial equity took the form of neighborhood formation in approximately equal-sized units of equal accessibility. The spatial arrangement perhaps mitigated to some modest degree a pattern of microsegregation that became entrenched within and among wards.

In the early twentieth century, segregationist policies in combination with greater mobility (streetcars and automobiles) corrupted the design. However, in the late twentieth century preservation of the original ward plan with its latent spatial equity revived the sense of Oglethorpe's intent, modestly influencing architectural preservation, codified design principles, and enhanced landscape design standards. For the twenty-first century, the city has adopted specific guiding principles for development that emulate Oglethorpe's original intent. Outcomes are yet to be apparent, but there is new interest in social and economic equity—Oglethorpe's original principles. It would be a brilliant achievement and a great honor to Oglethorpe if such a *ridurre ai principii* were achieved.

3

Implementation of the Plan

Oglethorpe and 114 colonists embarked for America on November 17, 1732, departing on the frigate *Anne* from Gravesend, near the mouth of the Thames River. Their voyage took advantage of prevailing winds with a southward course to tropical waters off Africa, a westward course across the Atlantic to the Gulf Stream, and finally a shorter northward course to British America. After nearly two months at sea, they arrived at Charles Town (now Charleston) on January 13, 1733. More than six thousand colonists would cross the Atlantic to settle Georgia during the twenty-year period of Trustee administration.

The *Anne* remained briefly at Charles Town with colonists on board as Oglethorpe met with the governor and other South Carolina officials to discuss plans for settling the new colony. Anxious to have the wilderness to the south settled, envisioning it as a defensive bulwark, the Carolinians offered to assist Oglethorpe in locating and building the new, planned town of Savannah.

The *Anne* then proceeded to Port Royal, the southernmost settled area in British territory, where colonists were housed in new barracks at Fort Frederick, then under construction. Oglethorpe set out with local guides to find a suitable site for the new town. They found an ideal location on a high bluff along navigable waters sixteen miles upstream from the Savannah River bar. The river was sufficiently deep there for access by most vessels, and the mile-long bluff was over forty feet above mean high water, offering ample high ground on which to lay out the town according to plan. The Yamacraw people of the Lower Creek nation who inhabited the area were welcoming and saw the new town as an opportunity for increased trade. A trading post was also located nearby on the river, a short distance beyond the Yamacraw village.

Oglethorpe returned to the selected site with the colonists on February 1 (O.S.), or February 12 (N.S.), 1733, the date now celebrated as the day of the founding of Georgia. They were joined by Col. William Bull, a Carolina plantation owner and colonial official, who assisted in laying out the town. They were immediately heartened by the warm welcome they received from their Yamacraw Indian neighbors. About an hour after arrival, a delegation from the Yamacraw village, located about a quarter mile away, appeared from the woods to greet them. Following a ceremonial greeting of dancing and singing, Chief Tomochichi and his small delegation shook hands with Oglethorpe and discussed future relations.[1]

The Trustees were committed to a policy of "equity and beneficence" toward indigenous Americans, a policy articulated by John Burton in delivering the group's first anniversary sermon in 1733. Oglethorpe was personally committed to this policy and set out to establish good relations with the Indian nations from the beginning. Three nations with large populations were well established in Georgia, the Lower Creeks (including the Yamacraw on the Savannah River), the Upper Creeks, and the Uchees. The Cherokee nation occupied the southern Appalachians, and the Choctaw nation lay to the west near French Mississippi. Oglethorpe soon formed alliances with each.[2]

Mary Musgrove (1700–1765), or Coosaponakeesa, who owned the trading post near Savannah, forged a bond of trust with Oglethorpe and became a vital link between colonists and Indians. Half English and half Creek, like her husband and business partner, John Musgrove, she acted as translator, cultural interpreter, negotiator, and supplier.

Within the first five months, two blockhouses were outfitted for cannon, "musket shell proof and vary defensible," a substantial guardhouse was constructed, and a battery of six cannon was in place. Nine houses were built during this period, the first of which was framed and raised on March 1, a month after the colonists arrived on the site of the new town, with Oglethorpe driving in the first pin.[3]

It soon became apparent to Oglethorpe and the Trustees that the cost of supporting the colonists and defending the colony would be greater than anticipated, even with government funding and substantial private donations. Oglethorpe wrote on March 24 that he "was forced to buy a considerable quantity of provisions" including rice, arms, and tools, as well as gifts for the Indians. The variability of grants from Parliament (see table 6) would make colonial finances a chronic challenge.[4]

TABLE 6   CHRONOLOGY OF THE SETTLEMENT OF GEORGIA

Year	New charity colonists	New private colonists	New foreign colonists	Parliamentary grants (£)
1732–33	152	132	11	10,000
1734	341	168	104	2,561
1735	81	103	58	26,000
1736	470	229	129	10,000
1737	32	58	0	20,000
1738	298	86	163	8,000
1739	9	1	7	20,000
1740	138	24	134	4,000
1741	6	27	3	10,000
1742	320	96	230	0
1743	6	42	5	12,000
1744	27	17	0	0
1745	0	34	0	0
1746	77	61	75	4,000
1747	52	134	0	0
1748	0	200	0	3,000
1749	0	544	0	5,304
1750	65	481	63	3,304
1751	48	297	44	0
1752	0	748	0	4,000
TOTAL	2,122	3,482	1,026	142,169

It also became apparent to Oglethorpe and the Trustees during the first year that maintaining a pious attitude and strong work ethic in the colonists would be difficult, despite a careful selection and briefing process (see chapter 1). Oglethorpe wrote to the Trustees on August 12, 1733, that upon returning from a visit to Charles Town he found "the people were grown very mutinous and impatient of labour and discipline." He attributed the "petulancy" to drinking rum and found some of them willing to trade "wholesome food for a little rum punch."[5]

Demographics of Georgia Settlers

The Trustees proceeded as planned to populate the colony. Confident in their plan and in Oglethorpe's leadership, they were undeterred by the ripples of discontent. They authorized five embarkations of colonists and supplies and began arrangements to settle Salzburger Lutherans in the colony. The Board of Trade was petitioned to prevent mutinous colonists from obtaining land grants in South Carolina, a treaty with the Lower Creek nation was ratified, and it was agreed in concept to prohibit the importation and consumption of rum.

Jews who had come to England from Portugal, Germany, and Italy to escape the Inquisition were among the first settlers in Georgia. Ships arriving in July and November 1733 brought forty-two Jewish colonists, the largest group to arrive in colonial America. A Portuguese Jew, Dr. Samuel Nunes Ribeiro, treated rampant dysentery upon arrival and had a deep well dug to prevent further cases. The Trustees, however, were disinclined to approve settlement of the first Jews, particularly since they had not gone through the standard recruitment and briefing process when they arrived at Savannah. Oglethorpe resisted an order from the Trustees to send them elsewhere, and obtained a legal opinion that upheld the right of Jews to settle in Georgia based on the charter's provision that "there shall be a liberty of conscience allowed in the worship of God."[6]

By the end of the first year, Oglethorpe expressed optimism about the colony, or perhaps he felt the need to rally the Trustees with an encouraging report in his final letter of the year, writing, "Providence itself seems visible in all things to prosper your designs calculated for the protection of the persecuted, the relief of the poor and the benefit of mankind." In the same letter, he reported that three and a half wards (of the six planned for the town) had been assigned to colonists. Fifty houses had been built, and the remaining lots were being cleared or had houses already under construction.[7]

In January 1734 Oglethorpe provided the Trustees with more information on the settlement of the colony. The population of Savannah was 259, including 39 at Hampstead and 3 at Highgate (most likely depopulated as a result of poor soil conditions); additionally, there were 22 at Ogeechee, 33 at Abercorn, 18 at Skidaway Island, 5 on Hutchinson Island, 21 on Tybee Island, 5 at Cape Bluff, 4 at Westbrook, and 28 at Thunderbolt.[8]

In March 1734 the first group of persecuted European Protestants, Salzburgers, arrived in the colony. Oglethorpe settled the seventy-eight Salzburgers twenty-five miles northwest of Savannah, six miles from the river. The town would later be relocated to a more fertile site on the river nearly opposite the Swiss Protestant town of Purrysburg in South Carolina. The new colonists named their town Ebenezer.

Table 6 shows the number of colonists arriving in the colony by year. Over the span of twenty years, the Trustees created a diverse society in the colony, as seen in the following categorization.

Trust-supported colonists

Worthy poor. The Trustees recruited people who valued work but were unable to find sustaining employment and a meaningful life in England's cities, many of whom had migrated from declining rural areas in search of new opportunity. This category included people released from debtors' prisons, although there were few of these.

Soldiers. Soldiers were required in the colony to fortify the southern frontier. Most were granted land at Frederica and Darien, which they were expected to cultivate when not on duty.

Indentured servants. Single people were recruited to work for families for a fixed period of time, after which they were granted land for their own use.

Self-Supporting colonists

Yeomen. Working farmers and traders were encouraged to settle in the hinterlands on five-hundred-acre estates. They were expected to supply nine servants each to clear the additional land.

Gentry. More affluent farmers were also granted five-hundred-acre estates, subject to the same requirements and restrictions as the yeoman farmers.

Persecuted protestants

Salzburgers. Expelled from the province of Salzburg (now part of Austria) by the Catholic Church in 1731, the Salzburgers were among the first to settle in Georgia. The first group of thirty-seven families landed at Savannah in March 1734 and were greeted by Oglethorpe. From there they were led to Ebenezer (meaning "stone of help"). By 1741, the town had grown to a population of twelve hundred.

Moravians. Descendants of ancient Hussites, the Moravian *Unitas Fratrum* were led by Count Nikolaus Ludwig von Zinzendorf. As conscientious objectors they would not take up arms, which created a dilemma for the Trustees, who required all settlers to be trained for defense of the colony. Oglethorpe was an advocate for their rights and a friend of Zinzendorf; however, they had nevertheless relocated from Georgia to Pennsylvania by June 1740.

Bohemians. Bohemia lost freedom of religion at the same time as Moravia. A number of Bohemians joined the Moravians in settling in Georgia during the Trustee period. Bohemia and Moravia make up the present-day Czech Republic.

Palatinates. Count Palatine governed a region of southwest Germany in the Holy Roman Empire. Palatinates, as his subjects were called, were among those recruited by Lutheran ministers to settle in Georgia. Most who went to Georgia joined the Salzburgers in Ebenezer. Many elected not to emigrate to Georgia because of the inheritance restrictions.

Swabians. Three vessels carrying Swabians to Georgia arrived in the colony between 1750 and 1752. Swabia is a region in the southwest of Bavaria in present-day Germany.

Vaudois. Protestants from the western canton of Vaud in Switzerland adjacent to the former Duchy of Savoy, absorbed into the Kingdom of Sardinia following the Treaty of Utrecht, were surrounded by Catholic states, leaving them with no refuge in the region. They petitioned to settle in Georgia in May 1734. Some settled in Purrysburg.

European Jews.
Sephardic and Ashkenazi Jews from Portugal, Germany, and Italy were among the earliest colonists. They established Mikve Israel, now recognized as the third-oldest synagogue in America.

After settling the European colonists, Oglethorpe returned to England, departing Savannah for Charles Town on March 23, 1734, sailing from there to England on May 7, and finally reaching London on June 20. While there, he successfully assuaged Trustee concerns about communication, funding, and political support. Accompanying him for part of the period were Tomochichi and his wife, a substantial entourage, and trader John Musgrove, who served as interpreter. Their reception by the Trustees was depicted in a painting by William Verelst (figure 18). The Native Americans were well received, which enhanced the prevailing goodwill toward the Georgia venture.[9]

In Georgia, however, Oglethorpe's long absence allowed disagreements to arise among administrators, and dissent reached a toxic level among colonists. In particular, a dangerous bond began to develop between discontented colonists and merchants thriving on the slave-dependent South Carolina plantation economy. The discontented colonists would become known as the Malcontents.

FIGURE 18   The Georgia Trustees, painted by William Verelst. The Trustees are depicted receiving Tomochichi and entourage in July 1734; Oglethorpe is front center, standing. (Winterthur Museum)

Relations with neighboring South Carolina, particularly Charles Town merchants, began to decline soon after the settlement of Savannah. Georgia's new laws and regulations were hindering South Carolina's rum-infused trade with the Indian nations through an extension of the slave trade south of the Savannah River. Charles Town merchants envisioned a wealthier neighbor with a lucrative slave-based plantation system like their own. Another source of distress to the Carolina merchants was the threat of a total prohibition of importation and consumption of rum, a major trade commodity. Consumption of distilled spirits had a corrupting effect on the poor in London, and the Trustees saw it as a threat to public health and productivity in the new colony (Trustee Stephens Hales published influential books on the subject in 1734 and 1736).

The souring attitude in Charles Town was described in several letters written to Oglethorpe by Georgia colonists while he was in England. In September 1734 William Bateman wrote:

There could be no description of any place (without the malice of hell itself) be made so dismal as the people of [Charles Town] endeavour to make of Georgia. Though in short a person may soon see through their artifice and that it is fear only of the great progress that has already been made in Georgia in so short a space of time will greatly damage their trade and force them to be more industrious and more diligent than what they really are at present. For of all the places I have ever yet been at I never see the inhabitants so indolent, so proud nor so malicious as themselves.[10]

The Trustees envisioned a colony of small farms, not one of large plantations, and they intended to defend that vision and carefully foster its implementation. Toward that end, early in 1735 the Trustees approved three laws: prohibition of slavery (by law rather than merely policy), prohibition of importation and consumption of rum, and regulatory provisions for maintaining peace with Indians in the province. The laws were subsequently approval by the Board of Trade and the king and Privy Council.[11]

Oglethorpe remained in England most of the year, working to get the new laws enacted and to secure funding from Parliament. News from the colony was generally positive during the early years, except for the protestations of the Malcontents. Many colonists wrote encouraging accounts and remained committed to the Trustees' regulation of tenure and inheritance and their prohibition of slavery and hard liquor.

Believing matters in hand at Savannah, Oglethorpe gradually shifted his attention from civil matters to security on the colonial frontier. Increasingly, he saw both the Spanish and the French as threats to the existence of the colony. As part of an initiative to bolster security, Oglethorpe arranged to settle a contingent of Scots Highlanders on the Altamaha River, the southern boundary of the colony. They would establish the towns of Darien and Frederica. The latter, named after Frederick, Prince of Wales, was the site of a new fort that became Oglethorpe's headquarters.

Over six hundred colonists embarked from England and Europe for Georgia in 1735, making it one of the most active years during the twenty-year Trustee period. The number included Moravian Protestants, who were settled between Savannah and Ebenezer. The Trustees also supported the settlement of additional Swiss Protestants at Purrysburg, a town established before the settlement of Georgia.

Oglethorpe departed for Georgia in November 1735 with brothers John and Charles Wesley, both Anglican ministers. They arrived in Georgia in mid-February 1736 with 257 Scots colonists, depositing them at Frederica and then traveling overland to Savannah. John Wesley was appointed minister in Savannah by the Trustees and also had responsibility for instructing Indians in Christianity. Charles Wesley was appointed secretary of Indian affairs, but Oglethorpe made greater use of him as personal secretary. Scandals caused both men to leave the colony earlier than planned, Charles after only five months and John after two years. However, the impression that this early experience was a failure is inaccurate on two levels. Certainly, both men were jolted into greater maturity as a result of their difficult physical and emotional challenges. However, both men also substantially completed their missions and left their mark.[12]

Oglethorpe remained in the colony from February until October 1736 before returning again to England. His first action upon returning to Savannah was to hold court and give all the people an opportunity to state their grievances. He required their petitions to be made in writing and received over three hundred responses, reporting to the Trustees that "settling the domestic affairs of this colony and regulating what has been amiss, encouraging the good and industrious and reducing the mutinous and disorderly and punishing the wicked, will be a difficult part but not so hard as the others."[13]

He was apparently able to restore confidence among the people in Savannah. Carolina merchant Samuel Eveleigh, an obsequious friend of the Trustees and subtle advocate for slavery, wrote favorably about progress toward spring planting: "There's a vast alteration at Savannah for the better. The generality of the people are grown there very industrious, the most of them have cleared their five-acre lots and the major part of their five-and-forty."[14]

Soon after returning for a second stint in the colony, Oglethorpe quickly resolved a number of matters in Savannah and then focused attention on Frederica and the southern frontier, much as he had done earlier in establishing settlements along the Savannah River. Several Trustees were uncomfortable with Oglethorpe's expansion of the colony, believing he should concentrate his efforts in Savannah and its hinterlands before settling the Altamaha frontier. Also concerned about the cost of expansion, they directed Oglethorpe by letter in March to confine settlement efforts to the area between the Savannah and Ogeechee Rivers (a band less than twenty miles wide, as seen in figure 19). However, there was little they could do to influence Oglethorpe, who was convinced that colonial security depended on establishing settlements and forts on the southern frontier. Defending his actions, Oglethorpe countered with a letter containing the "very disagreeable news" that the Spanish were building up their forces at St. Augustine in preparation for war.[15]

Trustee concern about lack of attention to Savannah proved valid

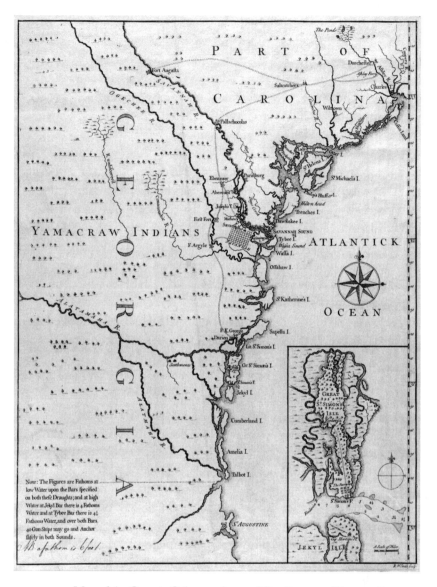

FIGURE 19 Map of the Georgia Colony and part of Carolina, 1741. (Hargrett Rare Documents Library, University of Georgia)

later in the year as reports of deteriorating conditions came in. Thomas Causton, the storekeeper in Savannah, who was well versed in the Trustees' principles of agrarian equality and often appalled at violations by the townspeople, wrote a prescient account to the Trustees, observing, "This your town of Savannah daily improves. . . . But it is too plain to be seen that many in this place don't think of planting. . . . Tis too plain to be seen that the same vices or frailties which probably drew on the people's misfortunes elsewhere attends them here."[16]

Oglethorpe, however, saw the need for advocacy in England as greater than the need for his guiding hand in the colony. He departed Savannah in November 1736, arriving in England in January 1737 and remaining there until July 1738. The focus this time was on the threat posed by Spanish forces in Florida and French forces to the west. British dominance in the region was in jeopardy, and the colony would need continued financial support and a strong military presence to survive. It is quite likely Oglethorpe believed not only that national defense would assure support for the colony but that military discipline was required to restore the principles on which the colony was established.

Percival found Oglethorpe's account of the colony "very satisfactory" in clearing up various matters "whereof the Trustees were in doubt." However, Oglethorpe confided in him that two-thirds of the people in Savannah had gone into debt, and he believed the only way for many to pay it off would be to sell their town and garden lots to tradesmen and live on their forty-five-acre farms, an admission that agrarian equality would require modification. Such an alteration in the original plan would also enhance the defensive network built into the plan by increasing the outlying population.[17]

Although Oglethorpe's account of the colony mostly satisfied the Trustees, concern about communication persisted, leading them to retain William Stephens in April 1737 for the new position of secretary of the province (also described as secretary of the affairs of the Trust). Stephens was a former MP who had recently been retained by a businessman to report on his investments in South Carolina and was thus familiar with the region. He would be assisted by his son, Thomas (later to become a leader of the Malcontents). Stephens was granted five hundred acres under the same terms as other self-sufficient colonists. The Trustees were hopeful that he would "constantly" correspond with them, "a thing we have wanted much." Stephens arrived in Savannah in November 1737, while Oglethorpe was still in England.[18]

The Trustees received the first report from Stephens in January 1738, with a finding of "much ill blood and bandying of faction," as Percival paraphrased it. John Wesley left Savannah not long after Stephens's arrival, reaching England in early February. He reported to the Trustees that about a hundred idle persons had left the colony, the corn crop at Savannah was sufficient to feed only about half the population, and the Trustees' Garden was unattended and about half the trees were dead. The Trustees were confounded by conflicting reports of conditions in the colony but remained hopeful that Stephens would sort out the inconsistencies.[19]

Stephens's arrival in the colony had little effect on colonists' behavior, even though his role in reporting conditions to the Trustees was known to all. The Malcontents intensified their efforts and did little to improve their land, while others kept faith in the Trustees' design and worked diligently to carry it out. The contrast was recorded by Stephens from his arrival in 1737 until at least 1745, the last year for which his journal entries were published. He was convinced that the Malcontents' "malicious and base designs" were "their pastime and delight."[20]

Some of the more diligent colonists wrote directly to the Trustees to refute the Malcontents. One suggested that plows would increase productivity and put an end to the argument that slaves were needed to develop the colony: "It might be of great service to the colony if Your Honours would please to assist them with a few English plows, for I am sure that one man and a boy with but a couple of oxen or horses shall do more than ten men with their hoes and much better done and, I think, would be better also than that inhumane and abominable using of Negroes."[21]

A number of Trustees doubted Oglethorpe's ability to administer both civil and military functions in the colony and pressed for a division whereby Stephens would assume greater administrative authority in the north. Oglethorpe may not have been far from opposing such a separation of powers. Perhaps he also reflected on Roman colonies, such as Timgad, that were successfully populated with army veterans. If so, he may well have envisioned a military presence in the colony that would populate it with dedicated and governable citizens, with civilians following once the founding principles of the colony were well established.

Oglethorpe returned to Georgia in September 1738 and remained in the colony until July 1743. He had little time to waste on the Malcontents, however, spending only two weeks in Savannah in October. William Stephens was grateful for the visit, however short, since Oglethorpe was able to clear up several administrative matters and deal with persistent mismanagement of the store by Causton. Afterward, Oglethorpe would need to focus his attention on the southern and western frontiers; encourage the system of agrarian equality where it was succeeding, notably in Ebenezer, Darien, and Frederica; and let those successes serve as a counterexample to the agenda of the Malcontents in Savannah.[22]

George Whitefield, a new minister who arrived in the colony in mid-1738, had a favorable first impression. However, he later became more critical of the Trustees' design for the colony, in particular the prohibition of slavery. It is an irony of history that Georgia enhanced the careers of both Whitefield and John Wesley, founders of evangelicalism and Methodism, while also contributing to the stream of secularist political philosophy in the British colonies (see epilogue).

In December 1738, the Malcontents sent a petition signed by 121 "settlers, freeholders, and inhabitants" to the Trustees. They listed as "the two following causes of these our present misfortunes and this deplorable state of the colony" the lack of fee-simple title to their land and the want of slaves "with proper limitations," which they maintained were necessary to subsist on their land.[23]

The Trustees remained committed to a policy of prohibiting slavery in the colony and sent a strongly worded rejection to those who had recently petitioned for it. They were backed up by a counterpetition from Darien rejecting the contention that slaves were needed to make the colony productive. Hugh Mackay, a lieutenant in Oglethorpe's regiment, testified "that white men can work in Georgia in the heat of summer without injury or complaint." The Salzburgers at Ebenezer also wrote a letter discrediting the claims of some that slaves were necessary in the hot Georgia climate.[24]

In mid-1739, the Malcontents sent Thomas Stephens, the errant son of William Stephens, to England to agitate on their behalf. Stephens's efforts would become a major distraction for the Trustees at a time when they needed to objectively reexamine the law on tenure. Young Stephens believed he could deliver a fatal blow to the Trustees with a statement to the House of Commons. Toward that end, he prepared a tract entitled "Observations on the State of the Colony." At the same time, several Malcontents who had moved to Charles Town, led by Patrick Tailfer, wrote a similarly damning tract entitled "A True and Historical Narrative of the Colony of Georgia in America."[25]

Sensing that young Stephens, whom Percival described as a "rash, vindictive fool," might actually succeed in overturning their design for Georgia, the Trustees acted to get an objective assessment of conditions and recommendations of reasonable reforms that might be enacted within the framework envisioned for the colony. Testimony was obtained from sea captains servicing the colony and military officers who had recently returned. Their assessments were more encouraging. While it was clear that reforms were needed, they could be accomplished within a broadened framework of agrarian equality.[26]

Thomas Stephens continued his campaign for three years, but counter-efforts by the Trustees gained traction in Parliament. Percival, whose entries were few by this time, wrote in June, "The House of Commons came to a resolution in their Committee that the petition of Thomas Stephens contains false, scandalous and malicious charges."[27]

William Stephens remained loyal to Oglethorpe and the Trustees throughout the ordeal. Suffering great "pain of mind" in learning of his son's disloyalty, he eventually disinherited him. The long battle with the Malcontents had, however, led to several amendments to their policies, and the Trustees appeared likely to consider more, although cautioned by Oglethorpe to hold the line.[28]

According to William Stephens, as well as Thomas Jones, bailiff for Savannah, the motives of the Malcontents had more to do with idleness and self-interest than with real adversity. The Malcontents increased their efforts to obtain slaves when their leaders formed an alliance with Charles Town slave merchants, who envisioned importation of slaves into the colony. A relentless effort to revoke the law prohibiting slavery ensued, during which the Malcontents stirred discontent, petitioned the Trustees repeatedly, and eventually petitioned Parliament. Jones countered their arguments of hardship, reporting in 1738 that he had "not seen any part of the world where persons that would labour and used any industry might live more comfortably."[29]

Meanwhile, tension with Spain increased over the southern extent of British territorial influence. Spain began to reassert its historic claim to territory as far north as 34 degrees latitude, the position in the Gulf Stream where their ships left the American coast on the voyage home. Spain's historic claim took in the entire South Carolina coast. Oglethorpe prepared for war and planned to take the Spanish fort at St. Augustine.

Before doing so, it was necessary to stabilize the western frontier. French strength was increasing in the lower Mississippi region, and Indian dissatisfaction with the English (principally South Carolina traders) was increasing. Oglethorpe was an advocate for the Indians, and he felt an unusually strong kinship with them. He would take it upon himself to travel through the region to affirm treaties and alliances. He set out in July 1739 from Savannah to visit the nations and reaffirm past treaties, returning to Savannah on September 23. It was an arduous trek for Oglethorpe, ailing with severe fever, but he achieved his objectives.[30]

In July 1740, with alliances affirmed and the military at ready, Oglethorpe led his forces to Florida and began a siege of the Spanish citadel at St. Augustine. The siege ultimately failed, but it left the Spanish acutely aware of their vulnerability and the potential to lose any claim to the disputed territory north of St. Augustine. For the British, the defeat provided justification for a buildup of forces on the southern frontier.

In 1741, in order to help Oglethorpe meet the Spanish threat and to further their ongoing effort to improve local administration, the Trustees implemented the plan to divide Georgia into two counties, the County of Savannah and the County of Frederica, separated by the Ogeechee River; the southern boundary was to be formalized when a proper map of the province was received. William Stephens was appointed president for the County of Savannah. Oglethorpe was recommended for appointment as president for the County of Frederica, a title he never actually employed, as he never assented to the diminished authority it entailed.[31]

On July 5, 1742, Spanish forces greatly outnumbering those of Oglethorpe landed on St. Simon's Island, the southern extent of the colony. Oglethorpe and his men retreated, and the Spanish took the nearby fort. The following day, as Spanish forces advanced toward Frederica on a narrow road, Oglethorpe marshaled his forces. Still outnumbered, they ambushed the Spanish in rainy conditions from hidden positions, throwing the larger army into confusion. The skirmish became known as the Battle of Bloody Marsh. The Spanish left the island and never returned.

An ironic collision of utopian plans occurred during Oglethorpe's final months in the colony when Christian Gottlieb Priber was arrested by South Carolina authorities in early 1743. He was turned over to Oglethorpe, the designated military commander in the region. Priber had planned a utopian commonwealth in America, which he began implementing with the Cherokee. After he learned the language, adopted their customs, and gained their confidence, he set about establishing an ideal society that he called "The Kingdom of Paradise." The new nation would counter the advance of European domination, while accepting people of all races and circumstances and placing them on an equal footing in a communal society. One may speculate about conversations between the two idealists, both of whom welcomed intense philosophical discussion; however, no record of any such exchange has been discovered.[32]

Efforts to subvert the colonial plan by the Malcontents, abetted by special interests in South Carolina and Spanish agents and accelerated to take advantage of the crisis, had taken a toll on the Trustees. At the time of

Oglethorpe's final departure for England on July 22, 1743, it was apparent to most of the Trustees that the utopian vision was failing, and there was little prospect of restoring the precision of the original design. The goal of creating a system of agrarian equality, closely tied to an intricate physical development plan for towns and regions, succumbed to inconsistent leadership and the allure of Carolina prosperity founded on slavery.[33]

Oglethorpe arrived permanently back in England in September 1743, ten years and ten months after his first departure for the New World. For the first time, Georgia would be administered without his presence or specter of authority. William Stephens's pragmatic civil authority would afterward prevail in the colony without the benefit of Oglethorpe's intellectual, moral, and military authority. Oglethorpe, nevertheless, would remain a forceful advocate for the principles on which Georgia was founded for over five more years.

The Trustees saw in William Stephens the practical, civil leadership they needed to maintain stability in the colony. However, they were soon forced to remind Stephens about their commitment to the prohibition of slavery in the colony, writing that they were "surprised to find that any expectations are still kept up among the People of their being allow'd the use of Negroes." Stephens was ordered to "take all opportunities to discourage the same, and to convince the people that their own industry will prove much more usefull to them" and admonished that by using slaves "they would soon become such themselves, by being debtors to the Negro merchants."[34]

The meeting of the Common Council on January 19, 1749, appears to be the last Oglethorpe attended. Afterward, the Trustees responded to increasing pressure for change in the laws and policies of agrarian equality with more amendments to restrictions on tenure and inheritance. In May 1749 the Trustees received a response from William Stephens to the reaffirmation of the prohibition of slavery stating that a large number of slaves had been introduced despite their efforts and that enforcement of the prohibition was infeasible. This time, without Oglethorpe, the Trustees relented and petitioned the king to repeal the act of prohibition.[35]

In 1750, with agrarian equality disintegrating and funds running low, the Trustees began a process of disengagement from administration of the colony. The following year they sent a report to the king on progress in the colony and the inability of the Trust to continue to support civil government and a military detachment. To allow for local governance, they approved a constitution of an Annual Assembly of the People in Georgia.

On January 11, 1752, the Trustees sent a petition to the House of Commons stating that the king had accepted the Trust's offer of surrender of the colony and that Georgia would "soon prove a beneficial Colony to Great Britain" because of its ports, location, and trade, especially silk production. The final meeting of the Trustees was held on June 28, 1752.[36]

During the twenty-year Trustee administration, more than 6,296 colonists were settled in Georgia, approximately a third of whom received charitable support. Five towns and numerous smaller settlements listed below were established during this period.

Savannah County (situated between the Savannah and Ogeechee Rivers)

Towns
    Savannah
    Savannah Town (small settlement near Augusta)
    New Ebenezer
    Joseph's Town (five miles upriver from Savannah)
    Augusta

Villages
    Abercorn
    Acton
    Bethany (upriver from New Ebenezer, settled by Swabians in 1751)
    Highgate
    Hampstead
    Irene (near Savannah on Pipemaker's Creek, settled by Moravians in 1735)
    Londonderry (northeast of Augusta, settled by Palatinates)
    Newington
    New Windsor (near Augusta in South Carolina, previously known as Old Savannah)
    Ogetie (Ogeechee)
    Thorpe
    Thunderbolt
    Vernonburg (near Savannah, settled by Swiss Germans, laid out as a potential town)

Other places
    Cape Bluff
    Fort Argyle
    Ockstead (estate settlement of Thomas Causton)

Purrysburg (opposite New Ebenezer on the Savannah River, in
South Carolina)
Skidaway (island settlement southeast of Savannah)
Tybee (island settlement at the mouth of the Savannah River)
Westbrook

Frederica County (situated between the Ogeechee and Altamaha Rivers)
Towns
Frederica (garrison town on St. Simon's Island; Oglethorpe's base,
1737–43)
Darien (settled by Scots in 1736)
Villages
Unnamed settlements on the Altamaha River, thirty miles from
Darien
Other places
Fort King George
Jekyl Island

Many of the settlements can be located in figure 19, a map of the region
published in 1741.

Assessment of the Oglethorpe Plan

The preceding account demonstrates that the purposes for establishing
the colony of Georgia as stated in its charter were accomplished to varying
degrees, a conclusion admittedly at variance with that of many historians.
The colony was indisputably successful in becoming sufficiently strong to
secure it from Spanish and French designs on the region, an achievement
attributable entirely to Oglethorpe's military leadership and his ability to
forge alliances with the Indian nations. The colony also arguably bore out
its promise to become a productive province in Britain's mercantile empire,
demonstrating significant agricultural potential (though not yet generat-
ing much wealth), before the Trustees surrendered their charter. Finally,
the colony created new opportunity for thousands of those it sought to
assist, namely, struggling families in Britain and persecuted Protestants
in Europe, in spite of the relentless efforts of the Malcontents and their
Carolina allies.

Oglethorpe's *unstated* purposes for establishing the colony, by contrast, were not achieved during the twenty-year Trustee administration. The system of agrarian equality was reluctantly dismantled by the Trustees themselves, at first through a series of changes to tenure and inheritance requirements, then by revoking the prohibition on slavery in May 1749 (four months after the last meeting attended by Oglethorpe). Swept aside along with agrarian equality was the envisioned working model of country party political philosophy that was to shine a light on the original principles of British nationhood. Nevertheless, the debate stirred by Oglethorpe's effort to create a model society set the stage for later social reforms and advancements in human rights, thereby making a notable contribution to the Enlightenment (see epilogue).[37]

The prospects for success of Oglethorpe's vision of a model society depended on controlling countless variables from the beginning of settlement. Oglethorpe seems to have understood the magnitude of the challenge, as he worked thoughtfully and diligently on the intricacies of the plan, enlisting help from the best minds available to him. Oglethorpe's circle of planners was undoubtedly energized by the optimistic notion prevalent during the middle Enlightenment that reason and the tools of science would prevail over any obstacles.

Nevertheless, Oglethorpe must have known that the prospects for success were dicey. It is unlikely, therefore, that he went to Georgia with an all-or-nothing attitude. He quite likely saw the colony's geopolitical purpose as vital to the nation on a historic scale and valuable as well to his career. Such a hypothesis explains his transition over a ten-year period from founder to administrator to frontier diplomat to regional military commander. While he never gave up on agrarian equality, he readily took up other causes that would positively define his role in settling British America.

Many factors converged to close the Trustee chapter of Georgia history. They can be reduced to two broad categories: internal flaws in the plan and external threats to its implementation. Internal flaws can be identified in the design of agrarian equality and in the plan for colonial administration. External threats to the plan include harsh environmental conditions, potential enemies in the region, and the poisonous influence of South Carolina's plantation economy.

Flaws in the Design of Agrarian Equality

Many of those who have studied the central initiative of the Oglethorpe Plan, agrarian equality, either dismiss it as an unworkable economic system or do not bother to dignify it with serious analysis. Such a stance reflects a modern assumption that viable economies range between those that are minimally regulated (neoliberal economies) and those that are moderately regulated (Keynesian economies).

The position taken here is that *definitive* judgment on the efficacy of agrarian equality should be withheld. It is sufficient to acknowledge, in hindsight, that a utopian plan was not going to produce a model society, while reserving judgment about the efficacy of specific concepts. Planners, after all, are presently reaching into the past for more sustainable, mixed-use development models that were until recently thought quaint but archaic (see chapter 5).

One can readily imagine combinations of events and trends that could lead to more heavily regulated forms of capitalism with features not unlike that of agrarian equality (e.g., land ownership by contract). Similarly, it is easy to imagine population decentralization scenarios that challenge the modern assumption that cities are the economic drivers of advanced nations and the proper habitat for most of their citizens. The dangers of a minimally regulated and densely developed world have become evident: nonstate warfare, loss of personal freedom for greater security, infectious disease pandemics, and dependence on monoculture food production—trends that may prove unsustainable and lead to less dense, more agrarian (albeit technologically advanced) forms of future development.

The principal flaw of agrarian equality was not small-scale land economics but the assumption that social organization could be reduced to precise mathematical and geometric relationships. The basis for this assumption, explored further in the epilogue, was the adoption of the Newtonian scientific paradigm and concomitant empiricism of Locke and Berkeley. The power of science and reason, it was believed, could be harnessed to control and improve all facets of human activity.

The order and harmony in Oglethorpe's model of agrarian equality glossed over variability in human nature and complexity in the natural environment. It expected that most members of society would be content with equal grants of land, and they would maximize productive use of their land. The model wrongly assumed that social conformity would prevail over pursuit of individual objectives. When colonists became frustrated by having to wait for their parcels to be surveyed, or in finding the soil unsuitable for their crops, they began to look for alternative ways of sustaining themselves, such as hiring out for labor or selling contraband rum, thereby fraying the fabric of agrarian equality.

Oglethorpe appears to have built flexibility into the physical plan for land allocation by establishing a somewhat larger grid for development than would be necessary if all land was productive. However, the rigidity of grouping land grants by tything made it difficult to reallocate land. Slowness in surveying and recording grants, coupled with insufficient labor for initial clearing and fencing, further restricted the ability to alter land grants. As the colonist and register John Brownfield reported to the Trustees in February 1737, his colleague, the surveyor Noble Jones, was unresponsive to the urgent need to allocate land, or to reallocate lots that were unusable.[38]

As a consequence, some colonists wrote of doing well, while others were left at a standstill. Colonist Elisha Dobree reported a good crop on his land in 1735, with "fine salad, peas and cabbage plants . . . almost ready to eat." Colonist Arthur Johnson, by contrast, reported during the same year that he was making no progress because his garden lot was "one entire swamp."[39]

Martin Bolzius, the Salzburger leader, revealed another flaw in the plan, underestimation of the importance of experience in farming. He wrote that his people, who were experienced at farming, "like and appreciate the land here, and have no wish to go back." The difficulties experienced by the English at Savannah, according to Bolzius, were a result not only of the rigid land allocation process ("If they had liberty to pick their land, the colony would have prospered much sooner") but also of the English colonists' limited knowledge of farming and their having "never worked in the field in their life." By using family labor and cooperative farming methods, the Salzburgers prospered.[40]

The lack of experience with farming cited by Bolzius was accompanied by another serious flaw in the plan, inadequate provision for wage labor. The Trustees believed that indentured servants would adequately supplement family efforts during initial stages of clearing and planting. The challenge of farming virgin land, however, was grossly underestimated by the Trustees. Letters from colonists frequently requested more servants. Lacking adequate manpower to efficiently clear their land, many colonists put themselves up for hire, preferring a steady wage over the uncertainty of planting crops.[41]

A last flaw in the design of agrarian equality was its framework for land ownership and inheritance. By limiting land holdings to fifty acres for charity colonists and five hundred acres for self-sufficient colonists, the plan sought to prevent huge disparities in wealth from occurring over time.

While the limitation per se may have been a reasonable and workable feature of the design, two of the methods of achieving it proved unworkable.

The first was the framework of contractual land ownership in place of fee-simple ownership. By allocating land through a contract, the Trustees could take it back if a grantee did not meet basic clearing and production standards. The owner, however, had a reduced incentive to work the land because of the threat of losing it. The problem might have been resolved at an early stage by linking the contract to other perquisites such as access to supplies, but the Trustees were slow to address the issue because they viewed themselves as benevolent administrators and did not readily perceive that a colonist could be less than trusting of them.

The second unworkable regulation for land ownership was the system of tail-male inheritance. It was implemented to ensure that a family would not amass land holdings beyond the acreage limitations. The restriction clearly had nothing to do with any intent on the part of the Trustees to promote patriarchy, as Percival on several occasions asserted in his diary. The restriction was objectionable to many colonists, however, because it was seen as having the potential to *reduce* family land holdings. Most were less concerned about how the restriction would prevent them from amassing additional land than they were about seeing legitimate heirs deprived of property.[42]

The Trustees debated the merits of well-intentioned colonists, as well as the arguments of the Malcontents, and for several years they responded thoughtfully but firmly, asserting that no changes would be made. Eventually, but only after careful study, they began amending regulations on both tenure and inheritance. After Percival's death in 1748 and with Oglethorpe's disengagement, the Trustees gave up on efforts to modify agrarian equality and removed most restrictions on inheritance, amassing of property, fee-simple ownership, and eventually slavery.

Administrative Deficiencies

The Trustees carefully planned a system of colonial administration, but they failed to institute procedures that worked with consistent effectiveness. In part, this was due to an overreliance on Oglethorpe, who ultimately could do only so much on his own. The Trustees may have been overly confident that inexperienced men, led by Oglethorpe, would rise to the occasion. Had Oglethorpe remained in Savannah, perhaps they would have. Ultimately, a lack of strong, consistent leadership proved to be the single greatest deficiency in implementing agrarian equality.

John Brownfield wrote to the Trustees that Charles Town merchants took advantage of Oglethorpe's absence by taking debtors' mortgages, thereby discouraging improvement of land. Local officials, he went on to report, were also creating difficulties. Since Oglethorpe left the colony (on his first trip back to England), Brownfield wrote, "the Surveyor's and Register's duty have been much neglected. For want of having their lands the people stayed in town, run into debt, grew effeminate and that active spirit, which might have been turned to the public benefit by being rightly employed, busied itself in little parties and thereby disturbed the whole body."[43]

Once back in Georgia, Oglethorpe wrote to the Trustees in June 1736, "Having settled the frontiers with foreigners a more difficult task is arose. The people of Carolina (instigated by some merchants of Charles Town who have a profit in sending rum up the river) have set the Assembly against this province." Even though he strictly administered the prohibition on rum, he was never able to stem the tide of increasing rum sales in the colony. He complained that rum sellers were acquitted despite evidence against them and that the Savannah magistrates were not cooperating in the enforcement process.[44]

The colonist Samuel Marcer, who had been licensed by Oglethorpe to sell liquor, estimated that there were twenty houses illegally selling rum and other liquors, including those of Thomas Christie, the recorder, and other officials. People were purchasing it on credit and going into debt. Rum sellers were getting wealthy, because "so long as the people can get rum they never will buy any other liquor." Rum was a valuable commodity because it would keep through the summer, whereas beer and wine would not.[45]

Peter Gordon described other forms of administrative chaos in correspondence to the Trustees in 1735. The "frequent holding of Courts," he said, reduced available labor by up to one-third with jury duty requirements, witnesses, and spectators. Additionally, Gordon claimed that Mr. Causton, while holding court, "insulted and abused many of the best freeholders," and when he disagreed with juries, he called them "fools and blockheads."[46]

Oglethorpe corrected many of these problems when he returned to Savannah in May 1736, but by 1737 the Trustees, at Vernon's urging, concluded that Oglethorpe alone could not administer the colony, especially in view of his insistence on dispersing settlement to the southern boundary. It was then that the Trustees appointed Williams Stephens secretary of the colony to administer civil matters and encouraged Oglethorpe to attend to defense. By separating civil and military administration in 1737 and dividing the colony into northern and southern counties in 1741, the Trustees believed they were improving administration. Oglethorpe often ignored the division, but it gave him cover to assume the role of military commander, a role for which he was well prepared by temperament and experience. In reality, however, Oglethorpe never ceded any power, and Stephens never fully assumed authority. Stephens's journal documents repeated cycles during which problems would worsen in Savannah until Oglethorpe came up from Frederica to resolve them.[47]

Stephens was a loyal servant of the Trust, a fact made perfectly clear in his journal, but he was a pragmatist and a better diplomat than leader. He understood the mechanics of agrarian equality, and he appreciated its philosophy, but he lacked the persuasiveness and zeal to enforce it.

Environmental Conditions

The Georgia Colony faced numerous environmental threats, many of which were unanticipated or underestimated. Individually, those threats posed serious challenges; collectively they had the potential to swiftly destroy the colony. The harshness of physical conditions in the lower Atlantic Coastal Plain from the Outer Banks of Carolina to Florida constrained the size of settlements until compensating technological advances of the twentieth century made denser human habitation more feasible.

The challenging physical conditions in the southern lowlands were poorly documented by explorers, early settlers, and scientists. Lacking substantial empirical data, the Trustees relied on generalized principles of geography such as latitude in assessing the potential for productive settlement. Governor Robert Johnson of South Carolina, an early supporter of the Georgia Colony, realized that he should warn the Trustees about the difficulty of frontier life in the region. However, his letter detailing those conditions arrived after Oglethorpe and the first colonists had sailed.[48]

Although the Georgia charter provided for limitless westward expansion, the treaty forged by Oglethorpe with the Indian nations effectively limited British settlement to the coast and along the Savannah River. The terrain of this area consists of barrier and back barrier islands, sandy coastal ridges, and richer alluvial but flood-prone lowlands. None of these areas was ideal for the geometric grid of small farms envisioned by the Oglethorpe Plan. While Savannah was brilliantly situated for trade, defense, and flood protection, it was located on a ridge with poor soils.

As shown in figure 8, the town was surrounded with pines, common on sandy ridges.

Water for human consumption and for irrigation of crops was available from springs, creeks, rivers, and sometimes rainfall. However, long-term storage of water left it subject to contamination, especially during the long summer season, and therefore a potential source of dysentery. Water quality of streams varied seasonally with rainfall and tidal influence. With high tides ranging from seven to ten feet above mean low tide, coastal rivers and water bodies were brackish to about twenty-five miles upstream. Areas with the best alluvial soils were low and marshy or subject to tidal inundation.

Climate posed another threat to the survival of the colony. William Stephens repeatedly expressed dismay over unexpected weather conditions. Variability and extremes in temperature and rainfall, far greater than anticipated (as reported by Stephens), made agriculture a dicey venture. Meteorological records reveal a pattern of greater-than-average variability in both temperature and rainfall in coastal Georgia. Damaging storms reported by Stephens may have been hurricanes, although the Georgia coast is somewhat less vulnerable to them than Florida and the Carolinas.[49]

Pests abounded during the growing season, and mold ruined many crops after they were harvested. Adding to other challenges of farming was the difficulty of penetrating virgin forests filled with poisonous snakes, panthers, alligators near water bodies, and other dangerous wildlife. Stephens reported a child in Darien was eaten by an alligator.[50]

Environmental health threats faced by the colonists are not known with any certitude. William Stephens recorded frequent "fevers and agues" that occurred during hot, wet weather. Half of his indentured servants were ill at any given time; his son, Thomas, nearly died of a fever; and on a visit to Frederica he found Oglethorpe in ill health with "a lurking fever that hanged on him for a long time past." Dysentery is a broad category of intestinal infections caused by bacteria, protozoa, and parasitic worms that undoubtedly encompassed many of the fevers Georgia colonists suffered.[51]

Malaria, yellow fever, and dengue fever may also have been present at the time Georgia was settled, introduced through the Carolina slave trade. Malaria is a protozoan infection of the genus *Plasmodium* transmitted by the *Anopheles* genus of mosquito; yellow fever and dengue fever are viral infections transmitted by the *Aedes* genus of mosquito. These diseases require a concentration of mosquitoes and people to become established, and it is uncertain to what extent they were present in the colony during the Trustee period. Native mosquito vectors were present, and it is plausible the diseases spread rapidly among the first settlers. Malaria had become endemic throughout the colonies prior to the founding of Georgia and constituted a significant public health threat.[52]

Oglethorpe and the Trustees have been justifiably criticized by historians for applying a rigid land allocation system and overly specific farming requirements on terra incognita. They have been criticized for creating a "political landscape" with a crippling "disparity between the[ir] projected ideals" and the actual "experiences of the settlers." However, scientists of the mid-eighteenth century lacked empirical knowledge of geographic variability and ecological complexity. The Trustees relied on the best science of the time, drawing on Royal Society luminaries for guidance. Their failure to respond to conditions might more accurately be attributed to the prevailing scientific paradigm rather than their own lack of responsiveness. As discussed in chapter 1, they believed their plan was built on sound science and the best available empirical data.[53]

Furthermore, Oglethorpe and the Trustees have been criticized for failing to incorporate environmental opportunities such as fishing, hunting, and timbering in the plan for the colonial economy. They are portrayed as having been fixated on sedentary agriculture with crops typically found in a Mediterranean climate. However, Oglethorpe and the Trustees believed that sedentary agriculture was the best means of claiming and defending territory, and family farms were an ideal form of permanent settlement. The hunting and gathering orientation in French colonies, it might be pointed out, contributed to loss of territory. The Trustees believed that their experimental garden would refine the range of crops cultivated in the colony and maximize productivity.[54]

Potential Enemies in the Region

The Trustees believed that they faced at least four threats from potential adversaries. The first was indigenous Americans, whose reception of the colonists upon their arrival could not be predicted. Several Indian nations already well known to South Carolina traders were potential adversaries. Good relations with these nations was a high priority for the Trustees, as discussed at the beginning of the chapter. Oglethorpe was personally engaged in treaty negotiations and always had a competent liaison available to address issues as they arose. Oglethorpe saw in the Indians an admirable people who held a reverence for the land consistent with his own values. He respected Indian culture and territorial rights and negotiated mutually beneficial agreements. His close friendship with Tomochichi, the Yamacraw chief who accompanied him to England, was legendary. Oglethorpe's productive alliance with the Indians was among his greatest achievements.[55]

Where South Carolina traders pursued a lucrative rum trade with little regard for the concerns of Indian leaders, Oglethorpe emphasized personal relationships and mutual benefits. The resulting rapport with Indian leaders created allies out of potential adversaries. Tomochichi and other Indians served with British forces in the 1740s during campaigns against the Spanish. The Lower Creeks were strategic allies against both the Spanish and the French, while the Choctaw on Georgia's de facto western frontier were an important buffer against the French.

A second major threat was posed by the Spanish in Florida, who had historical claims to not only Georgia but South Carolina. Oglethorpe attempted to establish harmonious relations with the governor in St. Augustine, reaching an accord in 1736. The governor, however, was soon replaced, after which time the Spanish reasserted their historical claim to territory that included Georgia. Defending Georgia's southern flank required Oglethorpe to vacate Savannah and relocate to Frederica. It also required him to spend more time in England to convince the government that a threat of attack was growing imminent and that he would require command of a regiment to defend the colony.

A third threat was posed by Britain's European archrival, France, which had colonized the Mississippi River basin and was probing eastward. Hostilities never broke out between the British and French over Georgia, but beginning in 1739 French aggression against Choctaw Indians and rumors of invasion plans required constant vigilance by Oglethorpe. From 1736 until he left the colony in 1743, Oglethorpe was preoccupied with defense on multiple potential fronts.[56]

The fourth potential threat was the large slave population in South Carolina, which could potentially rebel and overrun the fledgling Georgia Colony en route to promised freedom in Spanish Florida. The number of slaves in South Carolina in the 1730s far exceeded the white population; as one observer noted in 1737, "Carolina looks more like a negro country than like a country settled by white people." Slave owners were aware of the potential for rebellion and vigilant to prevent it. The offer of refuge by the Spanish in Florida intensified the potential for rebellion and added to the importance of Georgia as a buffer colony. That role, however, represented a threat to the young colony and increased the need for a sedentary population with a well-trained militia.[57]

While the distraction of maintaining good relations with the Indians and strong defenses against other potential adversaries diminished Oglethorpe's ability to enforce agrarian equality, the single greatest challenge came from South Carolina. Avaricious Indian traders and rum merchants were a serious problem, but the slave-dependent plantation system, the very antithesis of agrarian equality, constituted a challenge to the existence of the colony.

The Threat from South Carolina

South Carolina, initially presumed to be a nurturing ally, quickly proved to be Georgia's most serious external threat. The affluence of landowners in South Carolina had a seductive appeal for some colonists, and Charles Town merchants reinforced that appeal to further their own agenda.

Oglethorpe described the tension between the two colonies in a letter to the Trustees dated July 1, 1736: "The people of Carolina desire to have [the Georgia Colony] entirely destroyed, and united to theirs, that they may have the benefit of the improvements here, and the liberty of oppressing both the Indians and the English poor, as they do their own."[58]

The Charles Town merchants encouraged the Malcontents by convincing them that prosperity awaited them if only they adopted the South Carolina economic model. South Carolina's large plantations produced economies of scale made possible by slaves, who were readily available to clear and work the land at virtually no cost. Africans could feed and clothe themselves, whereas indentured servants had to be fed and clothed at great expense.[59]

The Malcontents were not merely vocal victims of an ill-conceived plan rigidly administered by an authoritarian Trust, as suggested by some writers. They were conspirators who were in league with South Carolina merchants to undermine agrarian equality and replace it with a slave-based plantation economy. William Stephens, whose aversion to the Malcontents was noted earlier in this chapter, described a conversation with one who admitted to the "inveterate ill-will" toward Georgia he found in Carolina.[60]

Thomas Jones, who served as bailiff and storekeeper, summarized the character of the Malcontent instigators in a letter of September 1740, in which he described them as "a company of proud, idle and turbulent-spirited Scotch" who had put their "unhappy servants" out for hire rather than using them to improve their land and used the revenue to support "idleness and extravagance for some years." When their servants' indentures expired, "poverty began to stare them in the face," but rather than "stoop to anything they imagined unbecoming gentlemen" they raised a group of followers from among drunks and idlers and "contrived also several falsehoods, which have been industriously spread in England."[61]

According to Jones, the Malcontents increased their efforts to obtain slaves when Patrick Tailfer, one of the group's leaders (who barely escaped jail for murdering a servant), formed an alliance with Robert Williams, whose brother was a Carolina slave merchant. The two envisioned having a monopoly on importation of slaves into the colony, which began an incessant effort to revoke the law prohibiting slavery.

Tailfer was one of those behind an appeal sent to the Trustees in August 1735 that asserted, "We, all having land in your colony of Georgia and having come here chiefly with a design to settle upon and improve our land, find that it is next to an impossibility to do it without the use of Negroes." He argued that (1) white servants "can't bear the scorching rays of the sun in the summer"; (2) Negroes were less expensive and more self-sufficient; (3) white servants were good for only three to five years, and upon termination of service their masters would need to go to Britain to recruit replacements or hire villains who were removed from Britain for their crimes; and (4) slaves were more likely to be sent back when they ran away. Tailfer proposed to use slaves for hard labor only, not trades, and to limit the number in the Georgia Colony to suit the Trustees.[62]

Repeated letters, petitions, and tracts, as well as vicious personal attacks on Oglethorpe and the Trustees by Thomas Stephens and others stirred debate in Parliament and raised the issue of slavery in public consciousness, thereby contributing to the course of events leading to abolition.

Thomas Causton, the overzealous storekeeper, remained an advocate for the Trustees' design. Lamenting the attacks by the Malcontents, he wrote, "Experience teaches that few designs are so well formed as to admit of no disappointments. So in the case of this settlement, it is too plainly verified that persuasions and fond imaginations riveted an early opinion that the gain of hire was preferable as being more certain than that of planting. Happy also had it been if those who are bold enough to disquiet the minds of the people by ensnaring schemes and cram their dissuasions to planting on everyone who attempted it had never come into the colony." Those "prone to contention, idleness and luxury" should be distinguished from those who quietly labor to improve their land.[63]

The Salzburgers in Ebenezer wrote to Oglethorpe in opposition to slavery, contradicting the claim that colonists would be unable to work through the hot summer: "We are told by several people after our arrival that it proves quite impossible and dangerous for white people to plant and manufacture any rice, being a work only for Negroes, not for European people. But having experience of the congregation we laughed at such a tale, seeing that several people of us have had in the last harvest a greater crop of rice than they wanted for their own consumption." Their leader, Martin Bolzius, remained adamantly opposed to slavery in the face of increasing pressure from the Malcontents in Savannah, describing it "as a most abominable thing not consistent with reason and Scripture which presages nothing else but God's Punishment."[64]

Colonists at Frederica and Darien, where Oglethorpe had greater administrative authority, also expressed their opposition to slavery. The message was delivered personally to the Trustees by Lt. William Horton, sent to London by Oglethorpe to brief them. Horton remained in London for some time and actively advised the Trustees on the prohibition of slavery and other policy issues.[65]

Oglethorpe may have been tolerant of slavery in Carolina when he arrived in America, but his firsthand exposure to the practice converted him into a lifelong abolitionist. Writing to the Trustees in January 1739, he condemned slavery in the strongest terms:

> If we allow slaves we act against the very principles by which we associated together, which was to relieve the distressed. Whereas, now we should occasion the misery of thousands in Africa, by setting men upon using arts to buy and bring into perpetual slavery the poor people who now live free there.
>
> Instead of strengthening we should weaken the frontiers of America, give away to the owners of slaves that land which was designed as a refuge to persecuted Protestants, prevent all improvements of silk and wine and glut the markets with more of the present American commodities which do already but too much interfere with the English produce. I am persuaded therefore you will speedily reject the petition. And as soon as your resolution is known, the idle will leave the province and the industrious will fall to work, many of whom wait 'till they see the event of this application.[66]

The Trustees resisted constant appeals to remove the prohibition on slavery by instructing William Stephens in no uncertain terms that it would never be allowed. With a hope of putting an end permanently to the letters and petitions, they adopted a strongly worded resolution on

March 17, 1748, with an instruction to Stephens and his assistants to make it clear that anyone continuing to advocate slavery should vacate Georgia and relocate to another colony where it would be permitted. In their reply to Stephens and his assistants, Martyn conveyed a stern warning: "The Trustees order me to say, that you had sufficient Power . . . [to stop slavery]. They observe at the same time in the Journal, that Negroes have been creeping into the Colony at Augusta, and other Places. And they cannot but wonder that you have not before this put a Stop to such Practices, nor propos'd to them the Means of doing it; but have contented your Selves with seeing it, and complaining of it now."[67]

The Malcontents, however, had already begun circumventing the prohibition, bringing slaves across the Savannah River so frequently that a dependency had set in. Stephens and the assistants determined the colony was past the tipping point. In May 1749 they wrote to the Trustees that the prohibition was no longer viable. Large numbers of slaves were working in the colony despite their best efforts. They maintained that to enforce the prohibition after such a dependency had developed would depopulate the colony.[68]

Stephens's appeal to the Trustees followed the death of Percival in May 1748 and Oglethorpe's withdrawal from active participation as a Trustee by February 1749. Without the resolve of the two visionaries, the Trustees relented and referred the matter to committee to draft language lifting the prohibition on slavery with certain restrictions and regulations. The law prohibiting slavery had been approved by king and council because it lay outside the powers given to the Trustees in the charter. Thus its repeal would also require their approval. A petition for the repeal was forwarded to the king in August. While it was never acted upon, the Trustees ceased all efforts to enforce the prohibition on slavery.

Vernon and Shaftesbury emerged as replacements for Percival and Oglethorpe with new priorities. Vernon was principally concerned with the colony's religious institutions and religious instruction for enslaved people. Shaftesbury, whose early solidarity with both Egmont and Oglethorpe upheld the principles of agrarian equality, was now older and more pragmatic and concerned principally with colonial administration.

Rebirth of Oglethorpe's Reform Agenda

The Georgia Colony under the Trustees is often portrayed by historians and Oglethorpe's biographers as a failed effort. The Trustees have been described as impractical idealists whose "persistence in their vision for Georgia ultimately led to their downfall." They are said to have "refused to abandon their dreams even when it became obvious that they were only fantasies."[69]

Some historians have essentially endorsed slavery and deleterious Indian trade as the proper and inevitable road to prosperity for European settlers. Trustee policies were "cramping the poor, small farmers of Georgia in their competition with rich, large landowners in South Carolina" with a "policy coloured too much by moral and military considerations and too little by the economic and human factors." The "human factors" apparently referred to European humans only. Another historian concluded that the South Carolina model offered a "better template" for prosperity. And yet another criticized the Trustees' "smothering property constraints" that "stunted" Georgia's economy, preventing development of a slave-based plantation system, as if holding slaves was not "smothering."[70]

In a detailed study of Trustee Georgia's economy, the labor economist Paul Taylor concluded, "No clear judgment of the progress and prosperity of Georgia was possible then, nor is it now, without an understanding that men's views differ as to what properly constitutes progress and prosperity." Slave-dependent, large-scale plantation agriculture that displaced the Trustees' owner-worked farms created quicker wealth, but only by disregarding the human rights of enslaved people. However, plantation agriculture and agrarian equality are noncommensurable systems. The former was contrived to concentrate wealth in the hands of a few at the expense of many, and the latter was designed to improve the lives of the worthy poor.[71]

Much criticism of Trustee Georgia overlooks the transitional role of the colony in stimulating debate on emerging issues of slavery, humanism, secularism, and colonial policy. The "dreams" and "policies" they "refused to abandon" were in fact egalitarian principles that ultimately achieved "success in symbolic terms," in the words of the historian Sylvia Fries, and later prevailed in Britain through political evolution and in America through revolution.[72]

The institution of slavery was effectively challenged and debated in England and America for the first time. Years of lobbying by the Malcontents to permit slavery in Georgia met with rejection when Parliament defeated a motion on their behalf by a vote of 35 to 18. When slavery was eventually permitted in the colony, the worst cruelties of the practice as seen in South Carolina were prohibited. Trade with Indian nations, based on a humanistic policy of mutual advancement, stood in sharp contrast to the rum-driven trade promoted by South Carolina merchants. When importation of rum was reluctantly approved by the Trustees, it was to be strictly regulated. Secular civil authority was emphasized, but Christian education for both freeholders and slaves was pursued with such determination that it became an accepted institution. Thus even though the system of agrarian equality, with its prohibition of slavery, eventually collapsed during the Trustee period, all of the stated goals of the colony, and even modest elements of its unstated goals, were achieved.[73]

While Trustee Georgia failed as a utopian experiment, it succeeded in advancing Enlightenment ideals and in planting an enduring physical design embodying those ideals. Thus, to proclaim that the utopian plan failed is to judge it narrowly. The debate over agrarian equality became a national debate about class, slavery, and equality, while the physical plan for the town of Savannah, so closely associated with humanistic ideals, later emerged as a model for modern urban design.

4

The Plan Today

Oglethorpe's elegant six-ward design was multiplied four times by successive generations of Savannahians, creating an area now preserved as a National Historic Landmark District. Savannah's acclaimed Landmark District, however, is not merely a relic of another age but, more important, a vibrant downtown and a regional hub of business, government, higher education, culture, and entertainment. Oglethorpe's ward design has proven remarkably adaptable and well suited to the demands of modern urban society. The design has consequently drawn praise from urban designers and town planners in academic as well as applied fields.

The complex and multifaceted nature of the Oglethorpe Plan is, however, often overlooked by those who study it. Notably, the little-understood *regional* structure of the plan continues to influence development throughout the Savannah metropolitan area, yet it receives little attention. Of broader importance, the plan's less understood guiding principles, which influenced the progression of humanistic ideas leading up to the birth of democracy, offer prescient insights for modern town and regional planning, a prospect taken up in chapter 5.

The more obvious physical design features of the plan that draw the most praise are found in its ideally proportioned and interconnected civic realm, which provides a seemingly contradictory geometric yet natural aesthetic that places functionality within a context of beauty. The genesis of such a remarkable heritage rests with the fact that Savannah was designed to be a new kind of town, a garden metropolis that united town and country and preserved agriculture and open space in perpetuity. Growth would occur through formation of outlying villages and estates rather than through densification or consumption of farmland and green space (see chapter 2).

The legacy of the original physical design—once intended to support a complex, humanistic plan—can readily be seen today in the form of a blended environment that accommodates nature and formal structure equally well. It is a city interpreted from its civic squares, city parks, promenades, tree-canopied streets, and a dense urban forest, elements that contribute to a rare urban aesthetic evolving from the exceptional composition originally conceived by Oglethorpe.

Oglethorpe's eighteenth-century plan, coupled with an extensive overlay of well-preserved nineteenth-century architecture, constitutes a resource that facilitated twentieth-century redevelopment and now holds promise for twenty-first-century revitalization that in some respects goes full circle back to Oglethorpe's holistic approach to planning (see chapter 5). With a vibrancy not seen since bygone eras preceding suburbanization, downtown Savannah now has sufficient private capital to drive sustainable public policy objectives. Figures 20 and 21 depict thriving mixed-use residential and commercial wards. Furthermore, the critical mass of downtown revitalization has inspired reinvestment in areas contiguous to the historic district, as discussed later in this chapter.

Revitalization coupled with preservation would not have been possible, however, without several catalysts. Most notably, city and county governments reinvested in the Landmark District when private capital was moving to the suburbs. Local government also invested meager available funds into tourism infrastructure on the theory that it would be followed by private investment. The nonprofit sector worked with even less funding but intense dedication to halt and reverse the flight of businesses and residents to the suburbs, a trend that if left unchecked would result in the destruction of historic resources. Most notably, the Historic Savannah Foundation, chartered in 1955, stepped in at a critical period to halt the loss of architectural resources. Those efforts paid off when Savannah College of Art and Design was founded in the Landmark District in 1978. Since then, the college has drawn thousands of students to downtown Savannah and renovated more than fifty buildings in and near downtown Savannah.

The National Historic Landmark District

Savannah is home to over eight thousand historic and cultural resources, many of which are preserved in the Landmark District and eight other historic districts designated as representative of successive eras of

FIGURE 20 Urban residential character. Housing densities in the historic district average approximately thirty units per acre, with densities of more than one hundred units per acre in some blocks. Even at high densities, the urban forest softly textures the cityscape.

FIGURE 21 Urban commercial character. Preservation of the town plan and historic architecture facilitated revitalization in the wake of suburbanization; many downtown buildings are mixed use, with residential units above retail and office uses.

development. Each district preserves land-use patterns and architecture unique to an era, but all were influenced in various ways by the Oglethorpe Plan.[1]

The prestigious Landmark District designation was received from the Department of the Interior in November 1966 for an area that encompasses most of Oglethorpe's town and common. The designation was based on the significance of the original town plan and the architecture of subsequent eras. Architecture in the Landmark District was originally surveyed in 1962 by historic preservationists from the University of Virginia and the Historic Savannah Foundation. This original survey was amended in 1977, 1985, 1992, and 2005. As a result of these surveys, the Landmark District is recognized as containing significant buildings in colonial, Federal, Gothic Revival, Greek Revival, Italianate, Second Empire, neoclassical, Beaux-Arts, International, Moderne, Art Deco, Queen Anne, and folk Victorian styles.[2]

The attractiveness of Savannah, which draws over six million tourists annually, is, however, attributable as much to the Oglethorpe Plan as to the city's rich architectural legacy. The interconnected public rights-of-way integral to the Oglethorpe Plan enables visitors to view the city's historic architecture from attractive civic spaces that soften impacts typically associated with urban congestion. With a major convention center and more than four thousand hotel rooms concentrated in and around the Landmark District, Savannah is one of the nation's major destinations for cultural tourism, maintaining high occupancy rates year-round and virtually full occupancy in the temperate spring and fall seasons.[3]

Figure 22 shows the boundary of the Landmark District (upper middle), which encompasses the original six-ward town and the later wards that followed the Oglethorpe model. Areas within the district not following the original ward pattern include the historic riverfront and gridded areas laid out after 1851. The entire district is 570 acres (0.9 square miles), nearly half of which is laid out in the historic ward pattern.[4]

Figure 23 is a conceptual map of the original six wards laid out by Oglethorpe (numbered 2, 3, 4, 8, 9, 10) and the eighteen wards that followed the original pattern in later periods. While Oglethorpe's pattern was followed for over a century, various dimensional adjustments were made to fit new wards into an expanding urban grid. Wards to the east and west of the original six were narrowed by two lots, while those in the lower tiers were increased in depth, first to 100 feet, and then to 120 feet. In the late nineteenth and twentieth centuries, new forms of development resulted in numerous anomalies and discontinuities depicted in the shaded areas. Specific alterations to the original plan are discussed in the next section.

Of the original wards, three were named for Trustees: John Percival, George Heathcote, and the Earl of Derby. A fourth was named for Sir Matthew Decker, a member of Parliament, director of the East India Company, and benefactor of the colony. These first four wards were depicted on

FIGURE 22 National Historic Landmark District and other historic districts.
(Chatham County–Savannah Metropolitan Planning Commission)

1. Franklin Ward / Franklin Square
2. Decker Ward / Ellis Square
3. Derby Ward / Johnson Square
4. Reynolds Ward / Reynolds Square
5. Warren Ward / Warren Square
6. Washington Ward / Washington Sq.
7. Liberty Ward / Liberty Square
8. Heathcote Ward / Telfair Square
9. Percival Ward / Wright Square
10. Anson Ward / Oglethorpe Square
11. Columbia Ward / Columbia Square
12. Green Ward / Green Square

13. Elbert Ward / Elbert Square
14. Jackson Ward / Orleans Square
15. Brown Ward / Chippawa Square
16. Crawford Ward / Crawford Square
17. Pulaski Ward / Pulaski Square
18. Jasper Ward / Madison Square
19. Lafayette Ward / Lafayette Square
20. Troup Ward / Troup Square
21. Chatham Ward / Chatham Square
22. Monterey Ward / Monterey Square
23. Calhoun Ward / Calhoun Square
24. Wesley Ward / Whitfield Square

☐ Tything block   ▨ Trust block   ■ Square

▨ Tything block - modified   ◪ Trust block - modified   ▨ Anomalous blocks

FIGURE 23   Historic wards and squares of Savannah. This schematic map illustrates the evolution of the Oglethorpe Plan after the Trustee era and identifies anomalies in the urban fabric.

the 1734 Gordon map (see chapter 2, figure 8). The remaining two wards laid out by Oglethorpe were simply named the "lower new ward" and the "upper new ward," later becoming Reynolds Ward and Anson Ward.

The four tything blocks in each ward and several streets were also named for Trustees and benefactors of the colony. Oglethorpe included several South Carolinians among those names. Bull Street, the central axis through town, was named for Col. William Bull, who assisted Oglethorpe in laying out the town of Savannah. Broughton Street, which formed a perpendicular axis with Bull Street at the center of town, was named for Thomas Broughton, lieutenant governor of South Carolina at the founding of Georgia, and later governor. In an exception to the practice of naming elements of the plan after people, Oglethorpe named York Street, below the three lower squares, to honor his Yorkshire heritage.[5]

The Savannah Plan after the Trustee Period

The foresightedness of leadership in the public and nonprofit sectors in the 1960s and 1970s prevented what for a time seemed inevitable: obliteration of the last functioning elements of the Oglethorpe Plan. However, the story of preservation in Savannah goes much further back. For more than a century after the Trustee period, successive generations reapplied Oglethorpe's ward layout, with only minor modifications, increasing the number of wards from six to twenty-four by 1851. After that, the city adopted a conventional urban grid as a template for new growth.

The design of the original six wards was extended with practical modifications into the town common. A design that preserved the established road network was extended to the east in two additional tiers and to the west in one additional tier. In both cases one lot in each tything was eliminated, thereby reducing ward width by 120 feet. Southward extension produced three additional tiers, completing a five-by-six grid of thirty wards, only six of which diverged from Oglethorpe's basic pattern.

Further extension of the model was prevented by existing city streets and other infrastructure, leading to use of the more conventional grid pattern. By the end of the nineteenth century, the remainder of the town common and most of the original farm grants directly south of the common were developed in a conventional grid layout.

The city of Savannah grew inward more than outward over the first 150 years of its history. Inward growth (densification) occurred by subdivision of lots from the original sixty-foot width specified in the Oglethorpe Plan to narrower lots of twenty or thirty feet and by increasing the typical height of buildings to three and four stories. The resulting population densification transformed Savannah from Oglethorpe's agrarian town built on a fabric of spatial equality to a modern city with a design fabric that accommodated segregation by race and class.

Two southern tiers of wards were laid out between 1847 and 1851, with eight of the twelve new wards following Oglethorpe's specifications. Two anomalous wards to the east were among the first areas developed in a conventional rectilinear grid. The new wards were laid out in the 1840s to accommodate African American railroad worker housing. The act of developing those areas differently not only violated the physical design of the Oglethorpe Plan but also violated the plan's prescription for spatial equality as a foundation for social and economic equality, matters taken up later.

During the mid-1800s, the city also expanded outside the original boundaries and began laying out new wards in a rectilinear grid. With the development of Forsyth Park in 1851, the alignment of lots to the east and west was altered to face the park rather than being associated with a civic square. Street widths were slightly altered during this period. Jones Street, famous for its stately townhouses, was designed with a seventy-five-foot width. Gwinnett Street, at the southern end of the end-of-town common, was designed with a ninety-five-foot width. The Oglethorpe ward pattern was discontinued until recent times, although its success inspired new design features that maintained a vibrant public realm.

After 1851, when the original ward pattern reached its farthest extent, various disruptions to the pattern were justified in the name of progress, as seen in figure 24, an 1856 map that shows the city developed to the southern edge of the common. This is particularly evident to the west, where Montgomery Street was pushed through four wards in the 1930s to accommodate a linear alignment for U.S. Route 17, the principal East Coast highway serving Savannah. Large civic uses such as the county courthouse complex and the civic center, both oriented to the U.S. 17 corridor, further altered the ward plan. The highway has since been realigned with the Savannah River bridge outside the historic district, but the spatial layout of wards remains an aberration to the original plan.

Many wards that were not disrupted by infrastructure and other major projects saw internal modifications, often to accommodate larger building footprints. Such departures from the original design include the DeSoto Hilton Hotel site, the Holiday Inn site, the new federal building, and Chatham County School System offices. All of these involved combining two tything blocks into a single block in order to accommodate larger-scale development.

Trust blocks (set aside for civic and business uses) that have been combined include site of the historic federal courthouse in Percival Ward and a church in Jasper Ward that were permitted to unite the lots and incorporate the principal street between them into their property. Most other

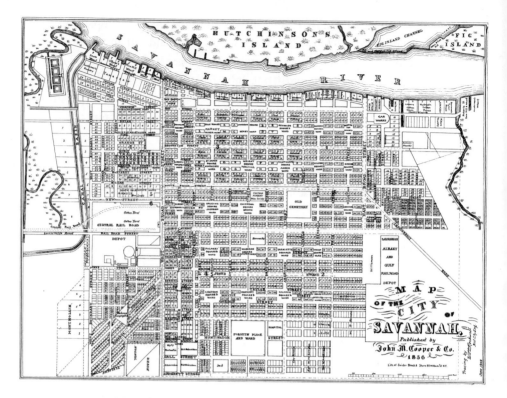

FIGURE 24   Map of the city of Savannah, 1856. The entire area of the original town
common was nearly filled with new wards, adapted from the Oglethorpe layout;
a conventional grid was applied south of the common after 1851. (Hargrett Rare
Documents Library, University of Georgia)

irregularities are associated with the disruption created with the former
U.S. 17/Montgomery Street alignment.

Twenty-one of the twenty-four traditional wards are substantially
(more than 70 percent) consistent with Oglethorpe's specifications. Consistency by this assessment is measured at the scale of tything and trust
blocks and the central square but not in terms of lot size. By the same
measure, four of the six original wards are 100 percent consistent (including newly restored Decker Ward). The other two are 92 and 73 percent
consistent, respectively. Four other wards laid out after the Trustee period
are also 100 percent consistent. The pattern of consistency can be seen in
figure 23, where anomalies are shaded in gray.

While block configurations within wards remained generally consistent
with Oglethorpe's specifications, the finer-grained pattern of lots *within*
tything and trust blocks was substantially altered by the mid-1800s. Inward

growth, as described earlier, split Oglethorpe's standard sixty-foot lot into smaller lots. Twenty-foot residential lots became the new standard, while lots of thirty feet, or multiples thereof, became the standard for commercial land uses. The new lot specifications gave rise to the prevailing nineteenth-century pattern of town houses and "main street" businesses now preserved by the city's historic district design standards.

Inward growth gave way to outward growth when greater mobility offered by streetcars led to the popularity of garden suburbs. By the end of the nineteenth century, growth was being absorbed in the farm district south of the town common, an area now referred to as the city's "streetcar suburbs." The next element of the Oglethorpe Plan to fall to urban expansion was the village district, which began four miles south of the river (or, more precisely, the prime benchmark). That area began developing in response to the additional mobility offered by automobiles in the 1920s. By the 1950s, suburbanization had consumed Oglethorpe's village district and was growing into the estate district, by then comprising farmland and woods.[6]

Most Savannahians were delighted with the new suburban era. Shopping centers, malls, and fast food arrived; backyards became big enough for family activities and garden parties. Meanwhile, Savannah's historic downtown fell into economic decline, and its older structures fell into disrepair. As residents and businesses moved to the suburbs, Savannah, like other cities during the emerging era of automobile dependence, responded by widening streets and building parking facilities to accommodate increased vehicular traffic.

Savannah briefly embraced urban renewal, the federal program created in 1954 to revitalize neglected urban areas, which had become a particularly acute problem after World War II when suburbanization attracted most public and private investment. The city envisioned a revitalization initiative that would transform downtown Savannah and its urban neighborhoods into a model of modernism. In 1956, amid excitement over the emergence of suburbia and prospects of modernizing the downtown area, the *Savannah Morning News* editorialized that "bold new concepts" should be implemented, including a freeway to be built through downtown (over Bull Street) in order to speed the commutes of workers from their suburban homes to their downtown workplaces.[7]

The Golden Heritage Plan, prepared in 1958, offered a new template for growth that would retain but substantially alter Oglethorpe's ward layout. The new model sought to encourage large modern commercial buildings while retaining open space and preserving significant historic structures.

New zoning adopted in 1960 codified into law the concepts underlying the plan, enabling urban renewal projects to move forward.[8]

The plan to modernize Savannah, to be funded largely through urban renewal grants, would have eviscerated the Oglethorpe ward layout. The impact of the 1960 zoning ordinance, which would have forced large lot development over the fine-grained Oglethorpe pattern, was mitigated by the rise of an effective preservation movement, which heightened awareness of the threat; by the designation of the National Historic Landmark District in 1966; and by adoption of historic district zoning overlay standards and development guidelines in the early 1970s. The 1960 zoning ordinance remained in place but was essentially held in check by the newer standards and guidelines, which were administered by an appointed preservation board.

The City of Savannah now has a policy of restoring Oglethorpe's original design as wards are substantially redeveloped. The first example of a major restoration can be seen in Decker Ward, where Ellis Square has been restored to civic space (with parking below grade provided as an accommodation of the automobile). Ellis Square was the site of the historic City Market complex until it was demolished in 1954 and replaced with a parking lot, the city's first urban renewal initiative. A redevelopment plan for Decker Ward was initiated in 2007 and completed in 2010. The plan for reintegrating the ward into the historic fabric of the city was based on historical analysis depicted, in part, in figure 25, which illustrates an evolution from a mode of growth and compaction through 1900 to a disintegration of historic urban fabric between 1950 and 2000. The before-and-after appearance of Ellis Square is seen in figures 26 and 27.

Elbert Ward will follow the model of Decker Ward when the city builds a new civic center convention facility immediately west of the Landmark District, restoring Oglethorpe's layout of tything and trust blocks arranged around a central square. The restoration could be accomplished either by total demolition and redevelopment or through a long-range plan of phased-in improvements. Liberty Ward is the only altered ward that cannot soon be restored to the original pattern, although the City of Savannah urban design consultant Christian Sottile believes that it too will eventually be redeveloped according to plan. Chatham County, which is redesigning the courthouse complex that occupies much of the ward, has developed a new plan that makes minor concessions to the Oglethorpe Plan without restoring its basic functionality.[9]

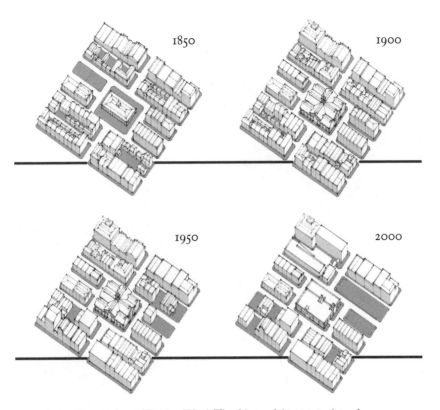

1850 1900

1950 2000

FIGURE 25 Restoration of Decker Ward. The fabric of this original ward was severely altered over successive generations in an effort to accommodate new forms of development. In 2010, the city implemented a restoration plan, reopening Ellis Square and reconnecting Decker Ward visually and functionally into the fabric of the town. (Sottile & Sottile)

Other disruptions in the historic fabric of the city will also be corrected. In 2009, the urban design firm of Sottile & Sottile identified all current street closures and private right-of-way within the Oglethorpe Plan for the city's Historic District Ordinance in a move toward reconnecting the original network of public streets.[10]

Thus, restoration and preservation of twenty-three of the twenty-four wards designed to Oglethorpe's specifications is anticipated. Moreover, a planned extension of the ward design into redevelopment areas adjacent to the Landmark District, discussed in the next section, demonstrates the contemporary relevance of Oglethorpe's town plan, a thesis explored at a more technical level in chapter 5.

FIGURE 26 Ellis Square parking garage. The garage was built in response to strong competition from suburban retail and entertainment venues in the 1950s, when parking was a higher priority than the civic realm.

FIGURE 27 Ellis Square restored. Renewed interest in the Oglethorpe Plan and the vital function of civic space led to restoration of Ellis Square. A parking facility was built under the square.

Present and Future Use of the Ward Design in Savannah

In 2006, Savannah adopted a new comprehensive plan (the *Chatham County–Savannah Tricentennial Plan*) that designated former industrial areas outside the Landmark District for redevelopment in a manner consistent with the Oglethorpe Plan. The downtown expansion areas, areas to the east and west of the historic district (see figure 22), would facilitate growth of the city's central business district, without the full range of zoning and design review requirements in the National Historic Landmark District, but in a manner that would be complementary to the historic town plan and architecture. New wards would be laid out with tything and trust blocks and center squares, thereby resuming the historic growth pattern where it left off in 1851.[11]

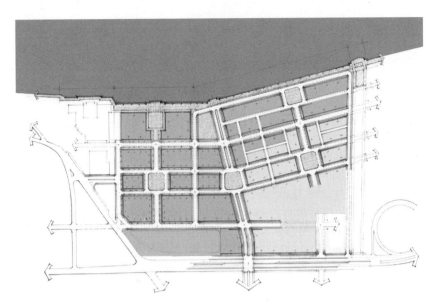

FIGURE 28. Civic Master Plan, East Riverfront. The plan ensures redevelopment consistent with basic elements of the Savannah plan. (After an original illustration by Sottile & Sottile)

A Civic Master Plan adopted in 2006 ensures the compatibility of future development with the historic ward plan. The Civic Master Plan provides an overlay of design standards for redevelopment in one of the adjacent downtown expansion areas. Figure 28 shows an application of the new standards immediately east of the National Historic Landmark District in an area known as the East Riverfront. Resubdivision of land in this area in accordance with the plan has been accompanied with a $60 million investment in infrastructure, in the form of streets and public squares, thereby assuring that future development will assume the ward pattern.[12]

The city's Historic District Ordinance was amended in 2009 to update development review standards, thereby increasing the compatibility of new development with historic patterns. A more comprehensive Downtown Master Plan will be adopted subsequently to ensure that growth in the Landmark District and the downtown expansion areas conforms with "guiding principles" and detailed standards derived in part from the Oglethorpe Plan. Additionally, the city's zoning ordinance will be updated to address recommendations in the comprehensive plan. When all of these pieces are in place, the city will have successfully melded an ingenious town plan from the eighteenth century and architecture largely from the nineteenth century with contemporary urban design practices. The resulting integrated plan will almost certainly secure a place for Savannah among the world's best-planned cities.[13]

Savannah's emerging planning policy framework recognizes that it may not always be possible to fit modern development needs onto eighteenth-century land parcels or into nineteenth-century building envelopes. Lot specifications under the Oglethorpe Plan, for example, were larger than desirable for development in the nineteenth century and smaller than required after that. Larger lots will be permitted, provided they do not alter the plan at the tything- or trust-block level, with few exceptions. A design solution recently applied to large-footprint developments is to segment more massive structures to look like a series of smaller buildings. Such an approach, however, has its limitations. While it may satisfy visual compatibility standards (i.e., form), it may violate other principles, such as maintaining a fine-grained mix of uses (i.e., function). The 2009 historic district amendments addressed this issue with stricter limitations on building footprints within the Savannah plan.

Savannah's first test in balancing form and function will likely occur in the East Riverfront area, where the Civic Master Plan was first applied. New development on former industrial land along the Savannah River will occur within an extended ward design with interior squares that approximate traditional ward dimensions. It is possible that much of the new development in this area will take the form of typically large-footprint land uses such as offices, retail outlets, condominiums, and hotels. Early designs showed less massive units that would be arranged around the central squares. Civic space is being preserved, and pedestrian connectivity (virtually nonexistent previously) will be established between the Landmark District and the newly developed expansion area, as seen in figure 28. Although it is too early to observe results, the longer-term planning challenge in this area may be to sustain visual interest and promote natural human interaction along three-hundred-foot city blocks if they are not divided sufficiently into smaller buildings and ownership patterns.

In the expansion area to the west of the Landmark District, the Housing Authority of Savannah, in coordination with city planners, has embraced a concept of redesigning a large public housing complex to create smaller blocks that match the city's historic ward and grid patterns. Following this prototype, the Housing Authority envisions redevelopment of all public housing in the downtown area in a manner that will physically integrate it into the historic and functional fabric of the city.

Other sites in the downtown area that are being planned for larger building footprints and contemporary land uses may be allowed zoning variances or exemptions from design policies, provided they apply creative, context-sensitive design. The civic center (a convention center that now occupies ten city blocks within two wards), for example, may be redeveloped with parking structures over a tything-block footprint, arrayed around a square or other civic space. A new stadium being planned for the city might take a similar approach in order to accommodate event-related parking.

On the Hutchinson Island riverfront facing downtown Savannah, designated as a downtown expansion area, development is also being encouraged to follow the principles of the Oglethorpe model. Both the comprehensive plan and the draft Downtown Master Plan specify that it should apply the historic ward pattern or at a minimum provide pedestrian connectivity and open space consistent with that in the Landmark District. There has been resistance to city policy, however, on parts of Hutchinson Island and elsewhere in the downtown area, in the form of proposals for "gated" development, which is perceived to add value to private residential development.[14]

Much of the difficulty the city will face in implementing the policies of the Downtown Master Plan, with its emphasis on the Oglethorpe Plan and pedestrian connectivity, will be in educating developers. Most of them specialize in conventional products and have little appreciation of the reciprocal benefits of developing in historic or environmentally exceptional areas. To their credit, city officials have recognized that they will need to partner with developers to design and build compellingly attractive and convincingly safe public spaces with sufficient cachet to offset the marketability of walled and gated private development.

Toward that end, the city adopted a policy of "reciprocity" in the 2006 comprehensive plan, whereby new development in areas adjacent to the Landmark District contribute to the historic public realm from which they receive substantial added value. The new policy invokes the mutual benefits of an expanding urban environment with concomitant application of Oglethorpe's design principles. If the city is successful in implementing this policy, it will avoid repeating the mistakes of the past when it allowed its historic center to become ringed with automobile-oriented, large-footprint developments. For decades such development precluded expansion of Oglethorpe's remarkable town plan.[15]

Savannah has a tradition of reverence for the Oglethorpe Plan, protecting it from threats such as urban renewal and expanding it into new areas.

The city's contemporary interpretation of historic design principles has engendered a richly textured, thriving urban environment often cited as an exceptional model by planning professionals. Yet the basic principles of the Oglethorpe Plan, elaborated in chapters 1 and 2, which make the city's success possible, are little understood and seldom applied.

While Savannah has risen to the challenge of reapplying Oglethorpe's design principles, the greater challenge the city faces is to apply Oglethorpe's principles of social and economic equality to the redevelopment of the downtown area. Mayor Otis Johnson articulated the latter challenge in 2004 in a position paper that addressed the interdependence of affluent and disadvantaged communities. Mayor Johnson called for a leveling of opportunity much like that prescribed by Oglethorpe. Policies were subsequently adopted in the 2006 comprehensive plan and other documents that emphasized local entrepreneurship, livable wages, and affordable housing—policies that Oglethorpe, with strong humanitarian instincts, would have deeply appreciated.[16]

Oglethorpe's Imprint on the Savannah Region

Oglethorpe's plan for Savannah and its hinterlands was embedded in a grid system of square-mile sections spanning an area 8 miles long and 6 miles wide. As discussed in chapter 2, the grid included a network of perimeter right-of-way estimated at 330 feet in width. The ample width allowed for eventual development of an intricate network of roads, while also allowing for other activities such as movement of livestock. As seen in figure 7, the network was envisioned to be tree-lined, thereby defining public and private space, creating visual interest, and providing shaded places to rest.[17]

After the Trustee period, gardens, farms, and villages often expanded into unused rights-of-way. The rights-of-way clearly seen in the early McKinnon maps entirely disappeared in later maps (see chapter 2). However, sufficient rights-of-way were preserved to enable successive generations to expand the road network in a manner largely consistent with the original plan. Where an original right-of-way was privatized, it was often reacquired to extend or widen roads. As recently as 2009, planners were considering a purchase of land within the original network, where it defined the division between the farm district and the village district.[18]

Many of the principal roadways in Savannah and Chatham County follow the original square-mile grid. Within square-mile grid sections, rights-of-way that defined wards, gardens, and farms allowed for development of secondary roads. Two major diagonal roads in Savannah appear to follow the triangular pattern of garden lots illustrated in chapter 2. The original grid established by Oglethorpe is shown in relation to the 1873 grid that formed the modern road network in figure 29. The town, gardens, and farms occupied the upper four square-mile tiers of the grid, while villages were designated for the lower two tiers. The rectilinear grid in the former area promoted compact growth through the streetcar and early suburban eras. The absence of such a grid invited curvilinear growth patterns and separation of land uses characteristic of post–World War II suburbanization.

The town developed within the boundaries of the common, while other land uses, initially agriculture and later industry and transportation facilities, were located in lower, flood-prone areas to the east and west. Farms located to the south, where the coastal ridge widened, were logical areas into which the city could expand its residential area.

East–west oriented streets in or near the original rights-of-way include Gwinnett Street, Victory Drive, Columbus Drive, DeRenne Avenue (offset slightly from Hampstead Avenue), Eisenhower Drive, and Montgomery Cross Road; north–south roads following the original rights-of-way are Bull Street/White Bluff Road and Waters Avenue. Each would be readily recognized by anyone familiar with Savannah as a major road corridor. Hampstead Avenue is an example of a historic right-of-way preserved to the present time, now serving as the northern boundary of Hunter Army Airfield.

The farm district in the Oglethorpe Plan occupied higher ground on the coastal ridge, whereas the garden district largely fell in the lower, flood-prone areas to the east and west of the town (explaining the reallocation of some garden lots to the common). As a consequence of this pattern, Savannah's residential expansion took place in the former farm district, whereas later rice plantations and industrial land uses occupied the former garden district.

As downtown Savannah approaches the limits of its growth potential, the former garden district has been targeted in the city's comprehensive plan for redevelopment, primarily in the downtown expansion areas. These generally lower, flood-prone areas were formerly too expensive to develop because of the high cost of fill and drainage structures. However, the demand for real estate adjacent to the historic district has risen dramatically, increasing the feasibility of more expensive site preparation. Growth in these areas is likely to provide business and residential real estate opportunities that are increasingly difficult to find in the Landmark District.

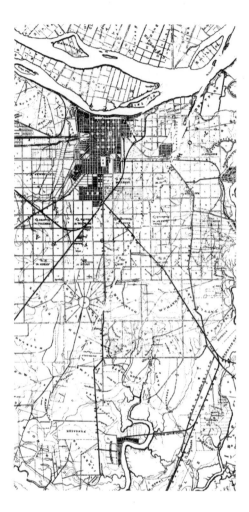

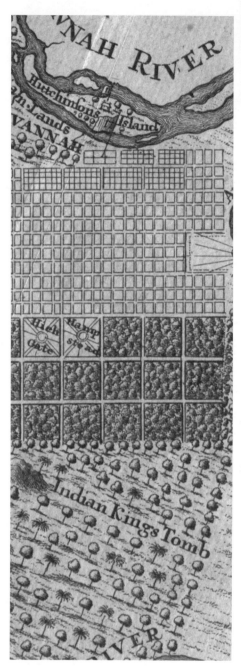

FIGURE 29. Savannah in 1873 (*above*) and the original grid (*right*). Ogle-thorpe's regional plan can be seen as having shaped the city's later growth. (Hargrett Rare Documents Library, University of Georgia; Chatham County Engineering Department)

Present-Day Status of Other Planned Towns

The settlement plan for Georgia anticipated that towns, villages, and estates would be distributed regularly throughout the colony. A number of those places exist today by name, while some retain characteristics of the original plan. The regional plan for Savannah remained a structuring influence to the present day, and many place-names from the Trustee era have been retained. Figure 19, the map of 1741, shows the location of several towns, villages, and other places that are recognizable today.

Outlying villages in Savannah's immediate hinterland, as well as small towns beyond, were, like Savannah, generally laid out according to predetermined specifications. Villages were generally settled within the grid of square-mile sections described in chapter 2 (see figure 9). Those within the grid were laid out to accommodate ten families within a one-square-mile grid section. Villages outside the grid were sited in strategic locations, usually with water access, rather than in a geometrically systematic manner. While the villages no longer exist as distinct settlements, the place-names of many survive to the present day.[19]

The town of New Ebenezer, located twenty miles upriver from Savannah, was laid out by Oglethorpe to closely follow the plan for Savannah, as seen in figure 30. Ebenezer survives to this day as a center of Salzburger culture, with a museum and meeting facilities, although the original town no longer exists. The town of Augusta, 250 miles upstream from Savannah (100 miles by straight line), was a garrison town and trading post far outside the preplanned Savannah hinterland. It was laid out in a gridiron pattern rather than with Oglethorpe's more intricate wards. Today, it is the second-largest city in Georgia.[20]

Oglethorpe established two other towns, Frederica and Darien, on the southern frontier of the Georgia Colony. Today, Fort Frederica (including the town) is a National Monument, and Darien is the county seat of McIntosh County. The plan for Frederica accommodated a regiment commanded by Oglethorpe and was a modified form of the Savannah plan. The fort occupied a central position on the river, and the town was laid out in a grid; however, garden and farm lots were laid out around the town as done elsewhere.

The plan for Darien, however, was nearly identical to that of Savannah. The town was laid out with four wards, two of which remain substantially intact. Traffic circulation has been altered in one case to convert the square to a roundabout. Figure 31a shows the Darien plan with four original wards

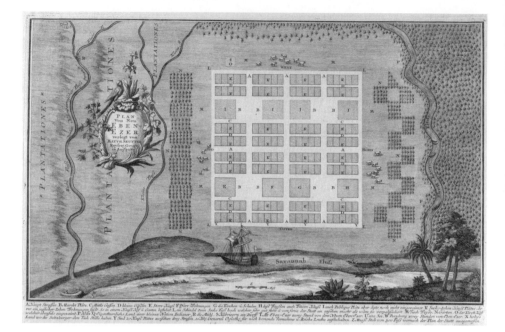

FIGURE 30.   Plan of New Ebenezer. The town settled by Salzburgers was planned with a layout nearly identical to that of Savannah; a departure can be seen in the single trust lots to each side of the public square. (Hargrett Rare Documents Library, University of Georgia)

and a later addition; Figure 31b shows the ward dimensions, which were larger than those of Savannah. Darien is a small town, with a population of 1,719 in 2008, the county seat of one of the poorest counties in Georgia. Despite its handicaps, the town has made strides in recent years in attracting investment and redeveloping its historic waterfront. In its 2008 comprehensive plan, the town envisioned restoring the original wards and redeveloping in a manner consistent with Oglethorpe's design.

Oglethorpe's Wider Influence in Georgia

One of Oglethorpe's highest priorities after establishing the town of Savannah was to create a transportation network linking settlements, forts, and trading posts. Referring to both road construction and charting of navigable waters, Oglethorpe wrote to John Percival, president of the Georgia Trustees, in 1736 that "there is no true way of civilizing a country without communications." It was at this point, two years after establishing the colony, that Oglethorpe's primary concern began to shift from the

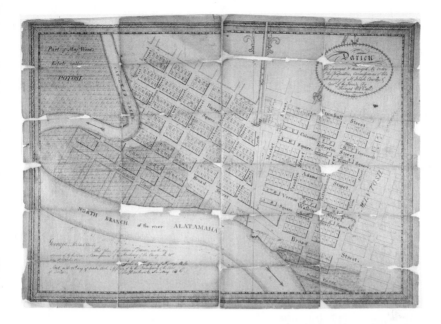

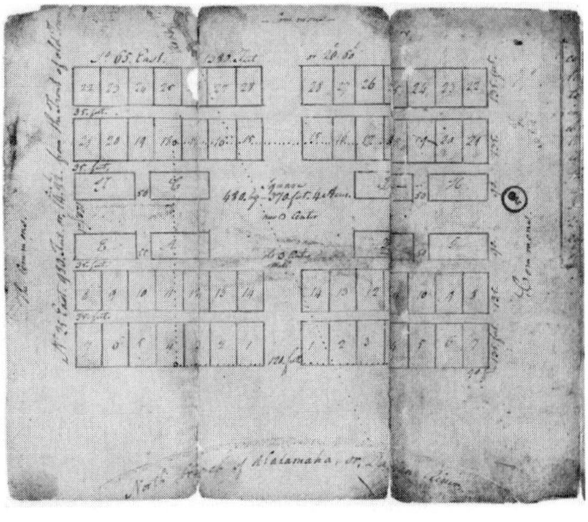

FIGURE 31A   Plan of Darien, 1806. The town was laid out with four wards, larger than but nearly identical in form to those in Savannah. Two wards have been preserved, and the others are designated for restoration. (Georgia Archives)

FIGURE 31B   Plan of Darien, ward design, 1788. This exact copy of an expansion plan drawn in 1767 contains ward design specifications. (Georgia Archives)

settlement of Savannah and the surrounding region to strengthening defenses on the colony's frontier. He became intent upon settling the southern and western frontiers of the province, and a road network would spur development and strengthen defense.[21]

The first roads in Georgia were constructed to increase connectivity within the Savannah region. A twenty-mile road to the south connected Savannah with Fort Argyle, located southwest of Savannah on the Ogeechee River. Another road paralleling the Savannah River connected

Savannah with Mary Musgrove's trading post and Ebenezer, the Salzburger settlement sixteen miles upriver.

After 1736, Oglethorpe was intent on deterring attack by the Spanish
in Florida, which required settling the southern border region along the
Altamaha River. He set about linking the southern border region by road
and charted waterway to Savannah. Letters written at the time reported
that workers were engaged in building a ninety-mile road connecting the
two areas. It was Oglethorpe's plan to have a village every six miles along
the road and a ferry at every river crossing.[22]

In order to facilitate Indian trade, which became increasingly important
to the colony, and to regulate competing (often illegal) trade by South Carolina merchants, a road to Pallachocolas, eventually to extend to Augusta,
was constructed. The road tied into an existing inland road to Charles
Town (now Charleston), creating an overland route from Savannah that
provided an alternative to difficult travel by small boat along the coast, a
journey that could take three weeks.[23]

Figure 19 in chapter 3 shows the road network completed by Oglethorpe in 1741, near the end of his residency in the colony. Georgia Route
21, the principle highway from Savannah to several towns to the northwest,
traces the colonial route from Savannah to Ebenezer. It intersects with
U.S. 301, which crosses the Savannah River at the point of the old Pallachocolas (now called Parachucla) settlement. U.S. 17 is a historic route
stitched from local roads that served colonies from northern Virginia to
Florida. It incorporates much of Oglethorpe's original right-of-way that
linked Savannah to settlements on the Altamaha River. Eventually, Inter-
state 95 would parallel the same route. In the Savannah metropolitan area,
Abercorn Street (which, west of Savannah, becomes Georgia Route 204)
follows the original road from Savannah to Fort Argyle.

The Oglethorpe name now appears throughout Georgia, where it is
applied to more than thirty roads. The name has been applied more frequently to places Oglethorpe opened to settlement but also to places and
institutions elsewhere in the state, in honor of the man considered to be the
founder of the state. Oglethorpe County, located between Augusta and Atlanta, was created a half century after Oglethorpe left Georgia. Oglethorpe
University in Atlanta was named after the colony's founder and honors
him annually but has no geographic connection to settlement during the
Trustee period. Many shopping centers, hotels, and subdivisions bearing
the Oglethorpe name are found in all parts of the state. No other name
from the colonial era has been applied so frequently throughout Georgia.

Numerous modern place-names originated with the colony, far too many to fully cite here. They include Jekyll Island, named after Sir Joseph Jekyll, an early supporter of the colony and in some respects an intellectual mentor of Oglethorpe's; McIntosh County, named after one of the original Scots settlers, Lachlan McIntosh, brought to Georgia by Oglethorpe; and Fort Frederica National Monument, which preserves Frederica, the southern garrison town where Oglethorpe spent much of his time after 1735, named in honor of Frederick, Prince of Wales.

Later Development Inspired by the Oglethorpe Plan

Oglethorpe's town plan was discontinued in Savannah in 1851, but its virtues continued to impress those who guided later development (the post–World War II era of suburbanization and urban renewal being one of the few exceptions). Successive eras of development borrowed elements of the plan, blending them with contemporary development styles. During the Victorian era of the later nineteenth century, the city grew around Forsyth Park, a sixty-acre central park, reflecting an appreciation of the public realm engendered by the Oglethorpe Plan. During the streetcar era that followed, a new central park, Thomas Square, was created as a focal point for the new part of town. After World War I, during the early automobile era, when development moved still farther away from the historic downtown Savannah, small parks, similar to ward squares, were reintroduced to the community's design palette. In recent decades, new subdivisions have frequently provided arrangements of houses around a square that invoke Oglethorpe's ward design, one of which highlighted that feature in its name, Legacy Square.

Elsewhere in Georgia, during the later colonial period, several towns adopted elements of the Savannah model. Brunswick laid out six squares in 1763 that were nearly identical to those in Savannah. Surrounding blocks, however, were laid out in a conventional urban grid. Also in 1763, the towns of Hardwick and Wrightsborough adopted plans that appear to have been inspired by the Savannah plan.[24]

Outside of the United States there have been few applications of Oglethorpe's ward design. Oglethorpe's close friend, the abolitionist Granville Sharp, borrowed elements of the plan for his design of Freetown, Sierra Leone, as discussed in the epilogue, an area that for some time was known as Granville Town. Sharp was also involved in the design of Adelaide, Australia, and elements of the plan remain present in that city's downtown area. More recently, the author has participated in an application of the design to initial redevelopment plans for Galeshewe, South Africa, one of six model redevelopment programs funded by the national government.[25]

In the next chapter potential new applications of the Oglethorpe Plan are explored, particularly as they might complement or build upon design elements adopted by New Urbanism. The potential broader relevance of the Oglethorpe Plan to modern planning is also examined.

5

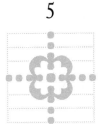

The Future of the Plan

The Oglethorpe Plan was a revolutionary, comprehensive, and highly detailed plan "to begin the world again." The thoroughness of the plan's preparation, however, was undermined by the suddenness of its implementation. While swift action was necessary to seize an opportune moment in history, a more cautious approach to settling the Georgia Colony might have protected it from internal subversion and external threats. A more effective leadership plan could have prevented the colony's Malcontents from sowing discord, and a formal agreement with South Carolina may have prevented its slave-based plantation economy from infecting Georgia's system of agrarian equality, which prohibited slavery. If not for those deficiencies, Georgia might well have become a colony of family farmers that would have matured over time eventually to reinforce Thomas Jefferson's vision of agrarian democracy.[1]

Although the social and economic system envisioned by Oglethorpe was compromised early in the colonial experiment, his plan remains highly relevant today on two levels. First, as a planning paradigm it suggests alternative approaches to current practice, including structural integration of complex information; increased emphasis on human-scale planning; and furtherance of basic egalitarian principles, often termed "social equity." Second, as a contemporary urban design model, with Savannah as an urban laboratory, it offers new perspectives on current urban design practices. The fact that Oglethorpe's vision and the Savannah design are revered by so many, including prominent urban theorists, such as those quoted below, attests to its enduring value.

> The famous Oglethorpe plan for Savannah . . . made a unique use of the
> square in the design, nothing like it having appeared in a town plan before

or since. Here, in Savannah, the square by frequent repetition becomes an integral part of the street pattern and creates a series of rhythmically placed openings which give a wonderful sense of space in a solidly built townscape.—Paul Zucker

[It is] a plan so exalted that it remains as one of the finest diagrams for city organization and growth in existence.—Edmund N. Bacon

The grid pattern of Savannah ... is like no other we know in its fineness and its distinguishable squares. . . . Once seen it is unforgettable, and it carries over into real life experience.—Allan Jacobs

Savannah occupies a unique position in the history of city planning. No complete precedents exist for its pattern of multiple open spaces.—John W. Reps[2]

Yet the fact that planning practitioners have not applied the design to new development suggests that there is a fundamental lack of understanding and appreciation of its mechanics.

Planning Paradigms

The Oglethorpe Plan, given its comprehensiveness, might usefully be compared with three modern planning models, or paradigms: comprehensive planning, sustainable development, and urban design. These dominant paradigms were established with three distinct forms of leadership: the first from government, the second from academia, and the third from practitioners. A comparison of the three reveals fundamental deficiencies, and the Oglethorpe Plan sheds light on the most glaring of those shortcomings—the lack of a humanistic foundation of social equity.[3]

Comprehensive planning was widely adopted by local governments after passage of the Housing Act of 1954, which created Section 701 planning grants and the now infamous urban renewal program. These new programs supplied more than a billion dollars for planning that enabled cities to raze entire urban neighborhoods and accelerate suburbanization, a process already speeding along after World War II, fueled byroad building and Federal Housing Administration mortgage insurance. Section 701 grants were intended to coordinate postwar growth with comprehensive plans for housing, urban redevelopment, new employment centers, and infrastructure. The resulting plans, however, consisted largely of land-use plans that depicted enlarged cities with vast suburbs and downtown redevelopment plans that justified urban renewal funding. Physical form was presumed to create the necessary preconditions for economic opportunity and social equity.[4]

The antiurban bias embedded in the legislation reflected the long-held belief, dating back to Oglethorpe's time, that cities were a cause of social pathology. This strand of thought was carried forward in Jeffersonian agrarianism, nineteenth-century anti-industrial movements (ranging from Luddites to socialists), the early twentieth-century Garden Cities movement, and mid-twentieth-century modernism that created the "tower in the park." Organic urban neighborhoods, viewed as blighted and overcrowded, were replaced with downtown high-rises and low-density suburbs.[5]

In Savannah, a city-county Metropolitan Planning Commission was created in 1955 to draft Section 701 plans for razing "overcrowded" downtown neighborhoods and "blighted" business districts. The historic intricate, mixed pattern of uses would be replaced with the larger footprint of gleaming modern buildings. Streetcar suburbs lying between the city and new automobile-oriented suburbs were rezoned with suburban lot standards to ensure their transformation over time to the new aesthetic of greener low-density development. Savannah's historic structures and the underlying Oglethorpe Plan would have been destroyed but for the efforts of preservationists.[6]

By the 1970s, many cities had begun to question the wisdom of wholesale transformation from historic development patterns to modernist prescriptions for larger buildings and more open space. At the same time, the Section 701 program ended, and states in high-growth regions began exerting more influence over local government planning. Most of those states shifted emphasis from land-use planning to strategic planning, a change that required local governments to obtain broad public participation in setting goals and objectives for future development. With modernism falling into disfavor, new concerns came to the forefront, including historic preservation and environmental quality.[7]

Comprehensive planning evolved into a process paradigm under which local governments had to satisfy the requirements of state enabling legislation, in many cases through a regional intermediary such as a council of governments. Local plans had to address specified substantive areas ("elements") and reflect the aspirations of constituent groups ("stakehold-ers"). A few states enacted planning legislation that required local govern-ments to adopt specific practices in various areas, notably environmental protection. Florida was among the first, amending its process-oriented planning act of 1975 with environmentally oriented growth management requirements in 1985. The Florida Planning Act established a new template for state-mandated comprehensive planning that would influence other states as they migrated from process plans and to substantive plans.[8]

The environmental focus of planning in the 1980s led to increasing concern that rapid suburbanization ("urban sprawl") had adverse conse-quences, a concern that dovetailed with that of historic preservationists, community organizers, and investors seeking new opportunities in older urban districts. Modernism gave way to "postmodern" architecture charac-terized by new designs with enhanced "visual interest" inspired by historic structures.

The comprehensive planning paradigm acquired the ability to rapidly evolve once it replaced centralized land-use planning with strategic plan-ning. Yet despite an emphasis placed on formulation of a guiding vision for planning, social equity is seldom addressed. Moreover, there is a chasm that separates the vision statement, goals, and objectives of a plan from its implementation. This disconnect arises from a vertical structure ("silo") of funding and regulation that inhibits local interagency coordination. As such, the complex problem of social equity—arguably the prime direc-tive of comprehensive planning—becomes lost in myopic government bureaucracy.

The second paradigm, sustainable development, emerged in the 1970s in part as an academic response to many of the same issues confronted through comprehensive planning, but with greater emphasis on systemic environmental stewardship. Sustainable development as a concept became widely recognized after appearing in the report of the United Nations Brundtland Commission in 1983, which defined it as development that "meets the needs of the present without compromising the ability of future generations to meet their own needs." It was subsequently formalized into a paradigm by the United Nations Agenda 21 initiative, which described it as an integrated program of environmental and economic planning, social advancement, and democratization. The Earth Charter Initiative, a coali-tion of organizations based in Costa Rica, has further advanced a holistic framework for sustainable development with a strong emphasis on peace, democracy, and human rights.[9]

The principles of sustainability were initially applied to developing countries through aid agencies. Early projects emphasized culturally and environmentally responsive "appropriate technology," an approach influenced by Mahatma Gandhi through British economist E. F. Schumacher (*Small Is Beautiful,* 1973), over massive projects such as hydroelectric dams. Since then, sustainable development has encompassed projects of larger scale by placing emphasis on outcomes with long-term viability.

The principles of sustainable development as defined by the United Nations and other groups are implemented through a wide range of strategies. For example, the principle that sustainable infrastructure should be decentralized produces very specific implementation strategies for storm-water management and flood protection. Such strategies include use of wetlands for natural detention, limitations on impervious surface coverage, and deployment of multiple rainwater collection systems within a community.

A relative of this paradigm is found in "resilience theory," formulated by the ecologist C. S. Holling in 1973, which maintains that humans and nature are coevolving and must be considered as a social-ecological system. Social equity, including access to resources, is a central component of this theory.[10]

Sustainable development in the United States is typically seen through an environmental paradigm, although it increasingly includes social and economic components. The Coastal Georgia Comprehensive Plan (2005), for example, established local, coordinated action to ensure long-term compatibility of shore and marsh development, critical marine habitat, viable fisheries, and the emerging industries of ecological and heritage tourism. Such applications of sustainable development generally occur on an ad hoc basis because its academic practitioners lack the legislative and financial process components available to public- and private-sector planners. Although sustainable development implementation strategies are gradually entering the practice of planning, the paradigm remains comparable to a wholesaler with few retail outlets or marketing strategies.

Although aspects of sustainable development have entered the mainstream, its prescription for integrated environmental, economic, and social planning remains elusive for most practicing planners. The Oglethorpe Plan created an integrated framework much like that envisioned under sustainable development, but planners today remain focused on environmental and design issues, while abdicating direct responsibility for strengthening democracy and building social equity.

Urban design constitutes a third planning paradigm because it provides a framework through which most development is conceived and built. As such, the design paradigm to a great extent both reflects and shapes market forces. Although various schools of thought exist within the design professions, urban design may be considered a single paradigm, since it is primarily driven by the private sector and because it presumes to shape social and economic facets of society through urban form.

The urban design paradigm presently consists of two prominent schools of thought, New Urbanism (a movement formalized as a chartered organization) and landscape urbanism. New Urbanism began a rapid rise to prominence in the 1980s by advocating a return to "traditional neighborhood design" characteristic of the late 1800s and early 1900s, an era that preceded automobile-oriented suburbs. It offers an alternative path to that of the modernism that drove postwar suburbanization, one of compact, walkable neighborhoods and strong civic institutions. Subsequent refinements and initiatives expanded New Urbanism beyond neighborhood and town planning into a theoretical model of regional development, thus completing its evolution as a school within the urban design paradigm.[11]

There are now noticeable areas of overlap in the environmental principles of New Urbanism and those of sustainable development. Where they fundamentally differ is in their assumptions about society. New Urbanism postulates that a well-conceived design formula will produce desirable social outcomes. Its argument with earlier schools of urban design, particularly modernism, is that their design formulas were flawed, not that they failed to address social complexities. Just as modernism sought to design a humanistic alternative to the industrial city, New Urbanism seeks to design a humanistic alternative to suburbanization. The question as to whether urban design is a model for, or merely a component of, a better society, will be taken up later.

Landscape urbanism is a school of urban design that advocates placing the design of habitable structures within the context of regional systems such as infrastructure and natural habitat. Proponents of landscape urbanism have recently broadened their perspective into "ecological urbanism" in order to create a more socially and environmentally integrated approach to planning and design. Landscape urbanism has embraced sustainable development and resilience theory to a greater extent than New Urbanism.

In contrast to both comprehensive planning and sustainable development, the urban design paradigm is led by professional urban designers trained as architects and landscape architects. While many leading proponents of both schools hold university faculty positions, they are also practitioners (notably deans Elizabeth Plater-Zyberk at the University of Miami and Moshen Mostafavi at Harvard).

A consolidation of best practices from each of the three planning paradigms occurred in 1996 when a coalition of organizations created the Smart Growth initiative. Smart Growth is unlikely to emerge as a new paradigm, since it does not engage directly with development or regulatory activity. However, its influence on planning practitioners will continue to promote a synthesis of concepts and practices among the three dominant paradigms. The rapid pace of synthesis, as illustrated by an increasing number of shared concepts (such as the use of natural and passive systems for storm-water management), suggests that planning has entered a highly creative but unstable period before the emergence of a new, dominant paradigm. Thomas Kuhn, in his influential work on scientific paradigms, referred to such instability as "the essential tension" preceding a revolution.[12]

The central tenet of the Oglethorpe Plan, social equity, offers an organizing principle for a revolution in planning that would synthesize the precepts of the three dominant paradigms. Planners should investigate not only that organizing tenet of the plan but also the rich context of the Enlightenment and the principles of social equity embodied in the democracies it produced. Just as the motto "life, liberty, and the pursuit of happiness" is at the heart of American democracy, a fundamental sense of social equity must reside at the heart of planning for it to produce meaningful and enduring results.

The code of ethics adopted by the American Institute of Certified Planners emphasizes social equity in stating that planners have a "primary obligation to serve the public interest," to recognize the "long range consequences" and "interrelatedness of decisions," and to "seek social justice." However, it is often difficult to prioritize social equity, even in public meetings and charrettes (intensive planning and design workshops) that promote democratic participation. Very often the complexity of process and multiplicity of objectives serves unintentionally as a smokescreen for special interests and aesthetic biases. Xavier Briggs, in a study of democracy and problem solving, has pointed to weaknesses in ostensibly democratic processes that can magnify social inequities, including overreliance on the technical competence of planners and urban designers. Where the Oglethorpe Plan lacked democracy and suspended representative governance, it established a code of contractual rights and responsibilities designed for the colony's survival in a hostile frontier environment. Within that context, it formed an equitable system of tythings and wards (neighborhood units) that expedited communication and created a foundation for republican government at a future time. The lesson for planners is that representation is only as good as its underling organization.[13]

Planning for three Sea Islands, located between Savannah and Charleston in Beaufort County, South Carolina, illustrates the difficulty of achieving social equity. Hilton Head, St. Helena, and Daufuskie Islands were settled by the Gullah people, descendants of slaves who made a living through agriculture and fishing after the Civil War. In recent decades the pristine islands have been attractive to resort developers.[14]

Hilton Head Island was the first of the three to be developed. Private land acquisition and planning with little public oversight ultimately produced eleven gated "plantation" resorts marketed to affluent residents and visitors. The plantations occupy more than two-thirds of the island's area, and employees must pass through security (Apartheid-like, as some have characterized it) checkpoints to enter. Since incorporating in 1983, island planners have improved public access to community facilities and amenities; however, an emphasis on environmental sustainability and aesthetics primarily benefits higher-income residents. There is a general sense of disenfranchisement on the part of the remaining Gullah people and lower-income residents.

St. Helena Island is recognized as a center of Gullah culture. Beaufort County gave special attention to the island's culture when it adopted its first comprehensive plan in 1997, developed from a process that required a rich matrix of public participation methods. The plan created a "cultural preservation area," identified unique settlement patterns, and recommended maintaining public access by prohibiting gated communities; zoning was subsequently adopted that enforced the provisions of the plan.

Duafuskie Island was home to a sizable Gullah population and a thriving oyster industry until recent times. Pat Conroy published *The Water Is Wide* (adapted in the film *Conrack*) about his experience as a young teacher on the island in the 1960s. Resort plantation development following the Hilton Head model has dominated the island economy in recent years. Following a lengthy public participation process, Beaufort County recently adopted a plan for the unincorporated island and has prepared a form-based code to regulate development. The code will use a "transfer of development rights" technique to preserve the character of unique island communities while allowing intensive resort development in other areas.[15]

Planning in each case followed the principles of the paradigms discussed earlier. Hilton Head's landscape design philosophy of "nature blending" draws heavily from the environmental principles of sustainable development. The plan for St. Helena was derived from the comprehensive planning paradigm, but with considerable effort to examine the human ecology of the island. The plan for Daufuskie drew from the design and transect theories of New Urbanism. Without evaluating the three approaches in detail, it is readily apparent that social equity was absent as a factor in at least the early stages of planning Hilton Head Island. Planning for St. Helena, which emphasized social equity, has resulted in maintaining the character of the island in the face of intensive growth pressures. Planning for Daufuskie has also emphasized social equity, but it remains to be seen whether the added emphasis on design will do more to preserve the island's character or gentrify it. Clearly, however, social equity as a philosophical force behind planning can achieve desirable results regardless of the techniques that implement its principles.

Before we examine the modern relevance of technical details in the Oglethorpe Plan, it is worth noting that the utopian system of agrarian equality may have an emergent modern counterpart. Modest trends toward a "new ruralism" in recent years may conceivably accelerate, thereby renewing interest in agrarian economic theory. At present, the trend is driven primarily by social sorting and flight from urban schools and secondarily by growing interest in local food production and access to natural environments. It may gain momentum as a result of many potential threats, including weapons of mass destruction, consequences of climate change, infectious disease, or a collapse of the food supply monoculture. It would be myopic to assume the tide of urbanization will forevermore flow in one direction. In fact, leaders in the planning and design professions are acknowledging the trend and theorizing that decentralization (though not necessarily de-densification) may be essential to sustainability, as first maintained by resilience theory.[16]

Several new planned towns illustrate the prospect of a shift toward "new ruralism." Serenbe Farms near Atlanta was designed as a constellation of interconnected hamlets and offers organic farming and abundant green space. Bundoran Farm near Charlottesville, Virginia, is planned with an "economic and social model" based on three elements: agriculture and land management, environmental stewardship, and "homeownership and residency on a working farm." The St. Joe Company has marketed its land holdings in north Florida for communities that foster "an intimate connection with the land."[17]

A technical comparison of the Oglethorpe Plan, an Enlightenment paradigm, with the three modern paradigms is also useful. The Oglethorpe Plan was developed at a scale and with a level of complexity that presaged the need for an ecological or systems-based approach to planning. Where modern planning paradigms are vertically organized, dependent on a hierarchy of regulatory agencies for implementation, the Oglethorpe paradigm, by contrast, was more horizontally integrated. In a vertically integrated plan, functions are organized into an administrative hierarchy (the "silos" mentioned earlier). In the area of transportation, for example, the process today is organized into a federal-state-local funding and regulatory silo that is often disconnected from other local planning processes. The Oglethorpe Plan, in sharp contrast, first established a long-range land-use plan for regional build-out, which included a system of integrated right-of-way, and then a road network was planned and developed within that framework.

The Oglethorpe Plan was developed to manage a complex social and economic system through, in modern terms, protocols, guiding principles, and an integrated system of land planning. Protocols are similar to the "sound science principles" and "best practices" now common in planning, except they have a more global level of recognition and application. A protocol may be applied to a plan as a universal concept, whereas guiding principles are specific to a place, representing locally recognized standards for growth and development. Integration is achieved by ensuring that protocols and guiding principles reinforce one another.[18]

Protocols embedded in the Oglethorpe Plan may be summarized as follows:

- Colonization, settlement, and defense based on well-documented Roman practices
- An economy based on the Roman practice of equal land allocation overlaid on traditional British rural social organization
- Agriculture, the primary industry, based in and refined through application of the scientific method
- Separation of civil and religious authority based on practices introduced to England by the Dutch after the Glorious Revolution

The guiding principles for development of the Georgia Colony described in chapter 1 collectively created a framework much like that of ecological urbanism and another new perspective known as landscape scale conservation that advocates a horizontal, interdisciplinary planning process spanning political, regulatory, and academic boundaries.[19]

Consistent with the aims of these new approaches to planning, the Oglethorpe Plan accomplished the following:

- *Integrated geographic structure.* The Oglethorpe Plan treated towns and their hinterlands as systems within the unified system of the colony.
- *Integrated public-land allocation.* The plan set aside acreage for public use within each square mile of farmland and within each ward for civic purposes.
- *Integrated right-of-way network.* The grid system in the plan was used to set aside ample and equal access to all areas. Accessibility was a high priority at the landscape scale.
- *Integrated economic system.* The agrarian economic system devised by Oglethorpe was integrated with the spatial (land-use) plan. Integration ensured equitable land distribution, maximum accessibility, sufficient intensity of land use to ensure productivity, and adequate population density to create a viable settlement pattern.
- *Integrated system of social equity.* Social equity was at the heart of the plan: land was allocated equally and without preferential location.
- *Natural-resource integration.* Natural areas between town-hinterland systems were preserved through growth boundaries and minimum separation distances between towns.
- *System feedback.* The most notable feature of the plan from a modern perspective is its scientific orientation. The plan promoted agricultural best practices through experimentation and feedback loops between scientists and practitioners.
- *System long-term viability.* The plan limited the size and density of towns, thereby preventing loss of farmland and natural environments. Growth was accommodated by establishment of new towns rather than by unregulated growth of individual towns. The plan also limited the amount of land that could be amassed by individuals, thereby preventing the system from evolving toward greater influence by fewer people.

A chief difference between the Oglethorpe Plan and modern planning paradigms is that the former placed physical design within the larger context of socioeconomic goals and objectives. Modern planning in the United

States, more than in other advanced nations, treads lightly and superficially in the areas of social planning. New Urbanism in particular has been disinclined to confront social and economic issues. Since it has demonstrated the potential to influence a generation of urban planners, a close look at this paradigm is warranted, and a comparison with the Oglethorpe Plan will show where it needs refinement.

Underlying New Urbanism and infusing its practice is an implicit belief in *design determinism,* the precept that the built environment shapes human behavior. Through this belief, New Urbanism avoids the complexity of sustainable development but also limits its further maturation as a paradigm. Ultimately, human behavior affects the physical environment more than design elements shape the human experience.

Critics of New Urbanism maintain that it is biased toward neoliberalism, the school of thought that advocates free-market solutions to even the most challenging social problems. Moreover, as a result of the influence of New Urbanism, "contemporary planning is adopting a language and practice allied to the ideals of neoliberal politics and material culture of postmodern society." The coupling of design determinism and neoliberalism undermines the ability of planners to understand cities and regions holistically and address the "complexity of metropolitan and regional systems, the interdependence of the social, cultural, political, economic, and environmental dimensions of places, and the indeterminacy of policy/design outcomes."[20]

An illustration of the weakness of a design-dominant model is found in the response to rebuilding the Miami area after Hurricane Andrew in 1992. The housing committee of the group that spearheaded the rebuilding effort concentrated its initial energy on locating inexpensive land for new affordable housing developments. Designers on the committee, chaired by a leading proponent of New Urbanism, saw the challenge as one of cost and design. It had to be pointed out to the designers that lower-income households have fewer transportation options, and many are reliant on public transit. Greenfield development, therefore, would create a mobility hardship for lower-income households and add to their transportation costs. Once this was pointed out, the committee, to its credit, responded by refocusing its attention on a major corridor. New Urbanism is far more sophisticated now; however, the lack of initial responsiveness to the complexity of human experience still suggests that design is a tactic that should involve a more comprehensive humanistic strategy.[21]

This critique of New Urbanism can be reformulated as the problem of "the ghost in the machine." Originally stated by the philosopher Gilbert Ryle, the problem is one of "category mistakes," that is, misapplications of concepts resulting from confusion about their use in language (somewhat like a mixed metaphor). The problem was first associated with the doctrine of mind-body dualism, but it is readily applied to other category mistakes. New Urbanists and other design professionals tend to mix physical categories (e.g., dimensions and proportions) with abstract categories (e.g., community and economic vitality). The confusion of these categories invokes a ghost into the machinery of urban design, which has led to a sense of accomplishing more than is actually possible through an arrangement of purely physical elements. Physical design is more appropriately placed within a larger, more conceptual category, such as "urban ecology," than the reverse.[22]

Ryle's critique is well worth exploring a little further because reductionist thinking is a serious, chronic affliction of planners, designers, and social scientists. The success of the physical sciences in reducing natural phenomena to laws and principles creates an illusion of transferability. The success enjoyed notably by New Urbanism in applying apparent physical laws leads adherents to organize their perception of problems and solutions exclusively in terms of that model. As Ryle puts it, "Whenever a new science achieves its first big successes, its enthusiastic acolytes always fancy that all questions are now soluble by extension of its methods of solving its questions."[23]

Ryle refers to this sort of ghost in the machine as the "bogey of mechanism." He illustrates the problem by describing a scientific spectator watching a game of chess without being able to see the players:

> After a time he begins to notice certain regularities. The pieces known to us as "pawns" normally move only one square at a time and then only forwards, save in certain circumstances when they move diagonally.... And so on. After much research this spectator will have worked out all the rules of chess, and he is then allowed to see that the moves of the pieces are made by people whom we know as "players." He commiserates with them upon their bondage. "Every move that you make", he says, "is governed by unbreakable rules.... The whole course of what you tragically dub your 'game' is remorselessly pre-ordained."

Ryles's players laugh and explain that every move is governed in some way by rules, but not ordained by those rules: "There is plenty of room for us to display cleverness and stupidity and to exercise deliberation and choice." In this example one can see an error often committed by planners and designers: the tendency to observe physical constraints on human behavior, to extrapolate those observations into principles, and then to organize them into a body of theory, which, if successful, becomes a paradigm. Everyone then wants to be on board the new vessel, having a sense that it is the theory that once and for all has reduced the full spectrum of human needs to a set of laws.[24]

The Oglethorpe Plan, admired but not well understood by New Urbanists, properly relegated design of the built environment to a subsidiary role in relation to its social and economic plan. Yet it placed great importance on site design, particularly ward (neighborhood unit) layout, as shown in chapter 2. The ward design continues to demonstrate adaptability and to support a diverse urban environment, but only when guided by a humanistic vision. The variety and arrangement of uses in each ward give it a unique life that contributes to the human ecology of the town as a whole.

The plan for the city of Tel Aviv illustrates the strength of a planning model that joins physical design with carefully conceived social theory. As with Oglethorpe's plan for Savannah, Patrick Geddes (1854–1932) conceived the 1925 plan for Tel Aviv as a supporting framework for larger social objectives. Geddes, a biologist and sociologist before becoming an urban designer, brought an appreciation of human ecology to the design of cities. The humanistic land-use plans for Savannah and Tel Aviv proved more enduring than their architecture, which in both cases was replaced with newer styles. In the case of Tel Aviv, multiple forms of modernist design (Bauhaus, art deco, international style) succeeded because of an underlying humanistic plan.[25]

In order to preserve a vibrant urban ecology, the City of Savannah has identified the need for several planning objectives that, as Oglethorpe intended, transcend pure design. Those objectives include workforce housing, entrepreneurship opportunities, and a certain amount of microregulation of land use. City policy makers recognize that, without such higher-level objectives, the historic district would ultimately benefit the few who attract the wealthy while ignoring the many who make up the citizenry.[26]

While only a few town planners and other development professionals may want to debate the efficacy of current and historical planning paradigms, many more are interested in specific practices that bring about tangible results. The following section concentrates on practical applications of the Oglethorpe Plan, in particular how its design elements, functioning artfully in the living laboratory of Savannah, might complement those of New Urbanism.

New Urbanism and the Savannah Plan

The urban design pioneers Andres Duany and Elizabeth Plater-Zyberk articulated and applied the first principles of neotraditional design in the early 1980s with a set of thirteen design elements. The emergent paradigm that later became New Urbanism quickly gained traction among academics, progressive local planners, and policy makers at various levels of government.

A broader foundation for the new planning paradigm was established in 1991 at a conference sponsored by the nonprofit Local Government Commission at the Ahwahnee Lodge in Yosemite National Park. The conference produced the Ahwahnee Principles, which united the Duany/Plater-Zyberk design elements and loosely connected "neotraditional" planning concepts into the cohesive body of doctrine that would become New Urbanism. The transformation became a fait accompli in 1993 with the establishment of the Congress for the New Urbanism. Subsequently, Duany, Plater-Zyberk, and others have refined the "rules" and practices of New Urbanism for general application up to the regional level.[27]

Planning conferences and other educational venues now routinely incorporate New Urbanism into their programs and curricula. With the launching of the Smart Growth initiative in 1996, principles of New Urbanism found wider distribution through a consortium of federal, state, and private organizations.

At least six of the thirteen neotraditional design elements articulated by Duany and Plater-Zyberk and quoted below are directly comparable with design elements found in the Oglethorpe Plan. Each of the six neotraditional analogs are discussed vis-à-vis Oglethorpe's design elements as they function today in Savannah.

1. The neighborhood has a discernible center. This is often a square or a green and sometimes a busy or memorable street corner. A transit stop would be located at this center. New Urbanism emphasizes the importance of a discernible center in neighborhoods and towns. The center provides community identity and becomes the nucleus of a pedestrian-oriented community. Centers of towns should ideally be no more than a half mile from any residence. Smaller centers within neighborhoods should be no more than a quarter-mile walk from any residence. The Oglethorpe Plan, by contrast, provides a multicentric alternative in the form of the ward. Designed with a one-acre central square and eight approaching streets, each twelve-acre ward creates a sense of place and produces a richly textured urban fabric within a larger framework of spatial regularity. Cumulatively the effect is to evenly decentralize commercial and civic activity, and the diversity associated with it, without necessarily eliminating a strong commercial core or main street. Uniformity of the ward design also facilitates efficient provision of public services and infrastructure.[28]

The advantage of the ward design over one that emphasizes a town center is its orchestration of organic, cellular growth that carries the "genetics" of the plan into each new ward. A community planned in this way is not dependent on larger town elements such as a central business district to establish character and identity. However, the ward design is capable of forming a "main street" on one of the linear arterials between wards when conditions arise to support it.[29]

2. Streets within the neighborhood form a connected network, which disperses traffic by providing a variety of pedestrian and vehicular routes to any destination. New Urbanism prescribes a geometric, often rectilinear, street grid. Streets within the grid should be continuous but visually interrupted by focal points to create context and a sense of place. Focal points are frequently created in conjunction with roundabouts (see subsequent discussion). Street widths, turning radii, and block length are among the devices used to control the speed of traffic. Traffic calming is vital in areas with heavy pedestrian traffic. Pedestrian facilities (such as sidewalks, arcades, and trails) offer attractive and efficient alternatives to vehicular travel.

The Oglethorpe ward plan, like the New Urban grid, allows for continuous vehicular movement. Traffic calming is induced by the central square, which creates short but continuous travel segments. Each ward is connected to other wards on the east and west (in the Savannah example) at three points, or five including alleys. Wards are connected by a single broad avenue on the north–south axis (again, in the Savannah example). Thus a ward connected to four other wards (one on each side) has twelve points of connectivity. The connectivity in the Savannah plan is contrasted below with that of a typical New Urban plan.

	Intersections	Segments	Focal points
Savannah plan	65	70	6
New Urban plan	12	31	1

Visual connectivity is maintained by broad avenues that are aligned with the squares. The juxtaposition of wards creates a dimorphic system of spatial orientation: the regular arrangement of squares provides a place, or geocentric orientation, and the linear pattern of streets provides a grid system, or geographic orientation. It has been shown that there are linguistic, cultural, and gender differences in way-finding that parallel these two systems. Thus the uniformity of the ward plan and the two systems of way-finding facilitate orientation by all people in a complex urban environment.[30]

The principal advantage of the Oglethorpe design rests in its ability to create an ideal environment for a mix of pedestrian and vehicular traffic. Vehicular speed in the interior of each ward, controlled by a combination of short travel segments and right-angle turns, is reduced to a level that falls within the comfort range of pedestrians. The effect is to create an enlarged civic space while allowing for continuous flow of traffic, similar to that provided by a roundabout. Additionally, the flow of vehicular and nonvehicular traffic between wards is enhanced by the wide avenues that connect them.

Additionally, the design allows for multiple-level enclaves formed by wards and groups of wards bounded by boulevards or axial streets, each with a different character. Moreover, economic disparities are minimized through spatial equality. That is, accessibility between neighborhoods remains high, while architectural and site differences are minimized. A similar form of spatial equality can be found in the plan for Tel Aviv discussed earlier.

3. The streets are relatively narrow and shaded by rows of trees. This slows traffic, creating an environment suitable for pedestrians and bicycles. New Urbanism takes advantage of the human tendency to drive slower on narrow streets and to turn corners slower where there is a short turning radius, design features that promote traffic calming. Trees add to the traffic-calming effect, causing drivers to instinctively slow down. At the same time, tree-lined narrow streets visually enhance the pedestrian experience. The result is a symbiotic environment in which vehicles and pedestrians safely and comfortably share the same space.

The Oglethorpe town plan achieves the same result with a somewhat different approach. In addition to the traffic-calming effect of the central square, each ward has a hierarchy of three street widths within its perimeter. The hierarchy provides for two additional street widths between wards. Street segments (lengths between intersections) within wards are shorter than in conventional grids, further contributing to traffic calming. An area smaller than sixty acres could have as many as five street widths, ranging from 22.5 feet to 145 feet, and 34 street segments, ranging from 90 to 300 feet. The practical effect on mobility is to create a variety of options for moving through the network while also allowing for circular movement within the network (e.g., when searching for parking or an unfamiliar destination). The aesthetic effect is to create visual diversity, to open a view corridor between squares, and to provide canopied, wide streets within and between wards.

In addition to allowing continuous movement of local and through traffic, providing multiple route options, and a pedestrian-friendly, humanistic environment, a notable advantage of the ward design is that variation in street width allows for proportionate variation in building height. The variation increases visual diversity and provides a wider range of development opportunities. The greater height appropriate on wider streets also gives local government an opportunity to structure one- or two-story height bonuses into the development (or zoning) code as a quid pro quo for achieving public policy objectives such as providing affordable housing. This contrasts sharply with New Urbanism, which has a more static approach to public policy objectives, where, in the example of affordable housing, merely permitting apartments above stores and garages is presumed to satisfy the need.

4. Buildings in the neighborhood center are placed close to the street, creating a well-defined outdoor room. New Urbanism has resurrected awareness of the third dimension, building height, in planning. Decades of two-dimensional, map-oriented thinking associated with land-use planning and zoning, relegating height to the legalist text in the zoning code, abetted the barrenness of suburbia. The influence of New Urbanism is now found even in conventional land-use plans and zoning codes, where ratio and proportion are often reunited with the district boundaries found on flat maps. It is understood now that ratios of building height to street width of at least 0.5 are required to create an outdoor-room effect. The Oglethorpe Plan in its original form was not concerned in the same way with outdoor rooms, but it easily adapted to the concept with Savannah's later architecture. The greater variation in street widths and segment lengths, repeated throughout a town or community by the ward template, creates a richly textured series of outdoor rooms (some of which might be called "foyers" and "halls"). The pattern can be described as a network of outdoor "suites" that make up the larger community.

The advantage of the Oglethorpe design is that by creating multiple outdoor "suites" it provides neighborhood identity ward by ward, seductively drawing them together in a holistic composition through a variety of attractive passages. Paul Zucker, in *Town and Square,* described these suites as "little islands of neighborliness and intimacy seldom found in a big city." The pattern of linked neighborhoods decentralizes commercial development without a loss of patrons, thereby encouraging local business investment and reducing the corporate investment found in more centralized commercial districts.

5. Certain prominent sites at the termination of street vistas or in the neighborhood center are reserved for civic buildings. These provide sites for community meetings, education, and religious or cultural activities. New Urbanism prescribes the use of prominent buildings and other visually significant features to define the larger context of a community, as outdoor rooms define the intimate spaces within it. They create a sense of place by featuring the civic institutions that represent the collective spirit of community residents. Such features define street segments and render them part of a community. This stands in stark contrast to undifferentiated suburban streets that all too often seem to be an independent phenomenon with a life of their own. Oglethorpe's ward design achieves a similar result by terminating all wide interior street segments at a square and placing sites for prominent buildings in a linear array between squares. The resulting consistency in form creates an eidetic effect that enhances familiarity, identity, and way-finding.

An advantage of the Oglethorpe design is that it also provides for continuous, context-sensitive streets without the use of roundabouts. Boulevards like Oglethorpe Avenue and Liberty Street in Savannah with extremely wide sidewalks, landscaped medians, and arching tree canopies create a rich visual experience that counters the effect of linearity. Other, narrower continuous streets, particularly those running through wards, are lined with architectural elements that also reduce the sense of linearity.

6. The neighborhood is organized to be self-governing. A formal association debates and decides matters of maintenance, security, and physical change. Taxation is the responsibility of the larger community. This element of New Urbanism might be interpreted as either high-minded democracy or the mere formality of forming a property owners' association. To the extent it is seen as the former, it may be another example of how New Urbanism presumes to address complex social matters through the magic of design determinism. This particular element, in any event, is not directly comparable to any aspect of the Oglethorpe ward plan. However, it is pertinent because civic functions such as local governance were central to the original Oglethorpe Plan. Oglethorpe's framework for local governance (especially in terms administrative authority) probably lacks relevance today, but the democratic element of spatial equality is woven into the design elements of his town plan. Equality is found in the size, placement, and distribution of residential (tything) lots, largely following the Roman model for socially level colonial cities (see chapter 2). The concept of spatial equality as a necessary condition for broader social equality is entirely missing in New Urbanism and most modern planning. The advantage of this element of the Oglethorpe design is that it infuses the entire community, ward by ward, with both physical access and economic opportunity. Decentralized commercial and civic uses in the ward plan for spatial equality are more accessible to lower-income residents. By extension, greater decentralization of commercial and civic uses is likely to produce more neighborhood (ward-level) participation in planning decisions.

The characteristics of the Savannah plan described above represent features that have evolved to promote a dynamic urban environment, in contrast to the steady-state design under the plan for agrarian equality. The neotraditional design analogs have remained central tenets of New Urbanism, even as the Congress for the New Urbanism created a new set of design principles with broader scope. In addition to the six Savannah design analogs described above (multicentric, dimorphic, humanistic, holistic, eidetic, and civic), three other elements warrant comparison with New Urban design. The Savannah design is *genetic* in the sense that the ward structure provides a genetic code for the physical development of the town while allowing environmental influences to spatially vary functions such as land use, design of structures, and character of public spaces. It is *organic* because the compact size and adaptability of ward units promote natural growth, unconstrained by larger-scale infrastructure projects or master plans. And it is *indeterministic*, as complexity within ward structure combined with organic growth allows the town to grow in a natural rather than preplanned manner.

Two other features of New Urban design, while not among the thirteen design elements, warrant discussion: the use of roundabouts and the preference for a well-defined edge. Both are prominent elements of New Urbanism with direct comparability to Oglethorpe's design characteristics.

Roundabouts are frequently incorporated into New Urban designs as a traffic-calming measure, to allow free flow of traffic, and to terminate vistas with community-defining features. New Urbanists differentiate between roundabouts and traffic circles. The former are more context-sensitive and may be used in pedestrian-friendly environments. The latter are larger and more oriented to vehicular mobility. Oglethorpe's ward offers another alternative to the conventional intersection. The central square in each ward creates a traffic circulation pattern that reduces vehicular speeds to less than twenty miles per hour, a demonstrated threshold up to which pedestrians and bicyclists comfortably share space with automobiles. Roundabouts, by contrast, often allow higher speeds while requiring a sight angle of more than ninety degrees for pedestrian safety (an uncomfortable turn of the neck). As a result, roundabouts and traffic circles are often devoid of pedestrian activity, in contrast to Savannah's squares, which are always in active use.[31]

For New Urbanists a well-defined edge is part of the progression of elements that contributes to a sense of community identity. Like outdoor rooms and prominent buildings that terminate vistas, a well-defined edge tells residents and visitors alike that they are in a distinct (and possibly distinctive) place. Oglethorpe's wards reduce the need for a distinct urban edge, particularly where, as in Savannah (in the decades after Oglethorpe), regularly spaced boulevards provide tiered edges. In other words, a pattern of wards and boulevards is sufficient to create spatial identification without the addition of perimeter roads, greenbelts, waterways, or similar edge-forming devices. The result is a nonstatic edge that enables a town or city to grow organically, producing neighborhood after neighborhood within the context of a physically uniform and socially diverse urban fabric.

The complexity of the urban fabric in Savannah, at the ward level, is readily apparent in the comparison below with a representative New Urban town plan. The comparison is based on a six-ward, seventy-six-acre area, equivalent to a twenty-block area in a New Urban town grid. Three measures of complexity provide a contrast in the two designs: the number of intersections, block segments, and focal points (the number of formal civic spaces). The complexity of the fabric in the Savannah plan increases connectivity, enhances the pedestrian environment, diversifies urban context, and produces visual interest.

Where New Urbanism creates a preplanned town center of sufficient size to accommodate future needs of the town, the Oglethorpe Plan creates linear corridors for development of primary streets, which may be more appropriate for slow growth, as the pattern of primary streets can grow organically with more intensive uses introduced gradually, displacing less intensive uses. Where New Urbanism offers corner stores and other options for mixed use throughout a community, the Oglethorpe Plan designates commercial areas within wards for multicentric commercial patterns and more effective support of local businesses (with lower rents because of ubiquity of location). Where New Urbanism predefines an architectural pattern, the Oglethorpe Plan's undefined architectural pattern may be more suitable for a variety of cultures and incomes, creating strong identity for a range of densities and development intensities. Where New Urbanism foci outside the town center are often recreational (e.g., parks) or visual (e.g., roundabouts), the Oglethorpe Plan foci are created at the center of each ward, where there is direct interaction among residential, commercial, and civic uses; more complexity attracts more use: the rich microenvironment at the center of a ward attracts pedestrians to its variety of uses.

A final point of comparison goes to the regional level. The transect model of urban form that transmuted New Urbanism into a viable planning paradigm contrasts sharply with the Savannah square-mile grid transect as described in chapter 2. The comparison highlights the more decentralized nature of the plan for Savannah, which envisioned a lower-density garden metropolis. It is not difficult to imagine a reconfiguration of the Savannah transect that would sustain a more contemporary urban environment with a less centralized design than that of New Urbanism. Such a redesign might effectively address the issues raised by resilience theory, which advocates redundancy, diversity, and modularity to achieve a resilient social-ecological system.[32]

Oglethorpe's ward-based design, therefore, is not merely a well-preserved vestige of a historic plan but a comprehensive town planning model with the potential for independent application or use as an adjunct to New Urbanism. Moreover, the emphasis on spatial equality and humanism built into Oglethorpe's Savannah plan represents a major initiative in moving town planning beyond the simplistic assumptions of design determinism.

Conclusion

The time is ripe for the Savannah plan to be better understood, fully appreciated, and reapplied in modern contexts. Largely protected from urban renewal bulldozers, modernist planners, and freeway advocates of the 1950s and 1960s, the plan has proven to be an effective model that supports a vibrant, organic, mixed-use urban environment. The underlying plan that makes it so is little understood, although sensed to be an ancestral spirit of New Urbanism. However, at the broadest level, the town plan, as part of the more comprehensive Oglethorpe Plan, also has much in common with ecological urbanism and sustainable development.

The vibrant urbanism found in Savannah today cannot be explained by design elements alone. The enduring success of Oglethorpe's town plan, as well as its restoration and expansion in Savannah, is due to the fact that it was part of a larger system, one that supported a vibrant human ecology but did not presume to create such an environment through design determinism.

Oglethorpe perceived that a plan to reduce inequality and poverty was one that altered human ecology. Today, planners are confronted with challenges of the same magnitude: moving beyond carbon dependence, reducing environmental footprints, and fostering economic opportunity to reduce income disparity. Such challenges require a more integrated, ecological approach to planning than currently exists. A new paradigm, more multidimensional in its approach to local planning, is a necessary advancement in meeting the challenge.

The principal surviving element of the Oglethorpe Plan, its network of interlocking wards, provides an excellent model for town planning, but only if taken in the larger context of human ecology. The ward layout is unique in its ability to support a complex human ecology because of its inward focus on the central square combined with its outward connectedness in a network of wards. Each square at the center of each ward is a focal point for people who live or work there, as well as those who visit or merely pass through. The design establishes a strong sense of neighborhood identity, while also creating a uniform point-grid pattern that enables people to locate places using landmarks or coordinates (the two principal mechanisms by which people find their way from place to place). Not only does each ward create an intimately human-scale environment, but adjacent wards can be seen from each central square. The result is a sense of connected, intimate urban neighborhoods, all of them inviting, attractive, and different in detail but fundamentally equal in form.

Figure 32 illustrates the multidirectional pedestrian connectivity built into the plan, where sixteen sidewalks (two for each street) tie into each public square. Figure 33 shows how pedestrian rights-of-way blend seamlessly with public streets to create an enlarged, shared public realm. While the public realm appears to dominate the cityscape, green space occupies only about 10 percent of the land area. The perception of open space is magnified by the melding of green space and rights-of-way into shared space. New towns adopting the plan would, therefore, sacrifice little valuable land to create high-value open space.

The complex hierarchy of rights-of-way also creates additional opportunities for both small- and large-scale development, as illustrated in figures 34 and 35. Redevelopment of Decker Ward, the design for which is discussed in chapter 4, was a model of public-private investment and coordination, enabled by the integrated nature of the ward layout. Small-scale development is facilitated through mixed-use zoning at every level of the street hierarchy, including alleys, or, as they are known in Savannah, lanes.

In modern Savannah, each square and each block within a ward relates in a unique way to the populations that inhabit or frequent them. In doing so, they form a vibrant human ecology. Town planners should strive to understand such rich urban microenvironments, much as Jane Jacobs did when she fought to preserve urban neighborhoods from urban renewal bulldozers in the 1950s and 1960s. By understanding the diversity of neighborhood patterns, town planners can recognize and reinforce the combination of attributes that makes a place uniquely successful.[33]

Jane Jacobs's work, like that of Oglethorpe, was notably prescient about the need for a new planning paradigm. Jacobs essentially prescribed a form of urban human ecology when she spoke of the importance of the "functional identity" of neighborhoods in city planning. She described the role of parks, squares, and public buildings in enhancing identity and knitting neighborhood fabric into the identity of larger districts, much as done by New Urbanists. Jacobs went on to say that there should be multiple functions (land uses) within districts, and they must ensure that those functions attract people into the public realm. A fine-grained mix of newer and older buildings adds to urban vitality and diversity by allowing for varying economic returns.[34]

FIGURE 32 Pedestrian connectivity. Savannah's squares have multiple pedestrian pathway alignments to connect with the street grid; interward connectivity promotes spatial equality, a component of the Oglethorpe Plan that remains relevant today.

FIGURE 33 Shared space. The Savannah plan provided an ideal environment to promote the modern concept of shared space; pedestrians move easily through the streets, even in dense business districts, without a sense of endangerment from vehicles. Bicycle riding through squares is prohibited to maintain an "island of serenity."

FIGURE 34　Focused redevelopment. The ward structure creates unique opportunities for urban redevelopment in manageable increments around a central focal point, the square, as occurred in Decker Ward between 2007 and 2010. Redevelopment at the periphery of the ward establishes an improved street wall with beneficial external effects.

FIGURE 35　Multiple opportunities for entrepreneurship. The richness of the ward structure, particularly the multilevel street hierarchy, promotes diversity and entrepreneurship; secondary streets and "lanes" (alleys) provide unique opportunities for small businesses and affordable housing, particularly in outlying wards.

Jacobs brought to light the "ballet" underlying creative human interaction on the city streetscape, and she set forth specific physical principles that set the stage for it to occur. Space, however, has become altered since Jacobs formulated those principles. Cyberspace and communities of choice are surpassing physical space and inherited communities as formative influences on human behavior. Pure physical design, therefore, is becoming less important than nonspatial connectivity on the stage of the human ballet. Oglethorpe's urban landscape, with its emphasis on garden towns and regional communications may be a better model for future human habitat than the physical design paradigms that currently grip urban planners.[35]

An area where modern planning is particularly adrift, and might find inspiration in the Oglethorpe Plan, is the extent to which it contributes to the humanistic ideals of equality and social justice. While Oglethorpe's quest for fundamental human equality might seem quaint but ingenuous to the modern planner, many of the physical elements of the plan that promoted equality remain feasible today. Egalitarian elements of Oglethorpe's plan, when taken together, constitute a system of spatial equality, the elements of which are as follows:

- A ward design that engenders a sense of equal ownership among ward residents
- A high degree of ward-to-ward accessibility that promotes familiarity and prevents formation of exclusionary neighborhoods
- A mixed-use design template that distributes civic, residential, and commercial space equitably throughout the larger community, thereby decentralizing economic activity and promoting local entrepreneurship
- Replication of wards with strict adherence to the town plan, thereby creating a network of equally accessible civic spaces and neighborhoods

Today, of course, it is neither practical nor legal to require equal allocations of land or to set limits on the amount of land that can be owned. The pursuit of spatial equality through town planning now takes the form of development regulations, usually within a zoning ordinance. Such regulations include minimum and maximum lot sizes, limits on building envelopes, prohibitions on "teardowns" to prevent mansions from towering over modest homes, "inclusionary" provisions for low- or moderate-income housing in new developments, and "linkage" provisions that require new commercial developments to contribute to workforce housing. New Urbanism advocates inclusionary affordable housing through community design that permits, for example, small house lots, small residential units above commercial uses, and accessory dwelling units such as garage apartments.

The City of Savannah contemplated and put in motion various measures that would renew and reinforce the system of spatial equality. Inclusionary economic development requirements would ensure relatively even distribution of small-capital businesses and entrepreneurship opportunities (perhaps a function of one or more of the trust lots). Inclusionary housing requirements would ensure that each ward has a percentage of units affordable to low-to-moderate-income and special-needs households.[36]

While inclusionary provisions are adopted to benefit lower-income populations (e.g., to provide workforce housing), a foundation of basic equality ultimately benefits everyone. A coupling of housing and economic inclusionary requirements could be particularly beneficial in creating unique and diverse ward environments. Such variation adds to identity, which in turn adds value. An enhancement of value occurs both from a highly desirable sense of ownership among ward residents and from the differentiation among wards that attracts visitors seeking a unique experience. Differentiation among wards and variation within them require certain limits to preserve a basic egalitarian framework, such as setting a maximum lot size to prevent a large portion of a ward from becoming disenfranchised.[37]

Modern planning paradigms address spatial equality only superficially or rhetorically, and only a few local governments have modified those paradigms to create a more level human environment. In doing so, Savannah and other locales are helping to build a bridge forward from current planning paradigms to one based on human ecology. Ultimately, the bridge forward needs to be built from a synthesis of New Urbanism and sustainable development and then maintained by a more horizontally integrated approach to comprehensive planning.

Leaders in the application of those planning paradigms would do well to study the Oglethorpe Plan and its enduring success. A new planning paradigm for the twenty-first century awaits a commitment by modern practitioners to reexamine their past and to forge a new way forward to a more egalitarian society. New paradigms, however, should inspire and not constrain, and individuality should be preserved from forces of uniformity.

The portion of the Oglethorpe Plan that survives today, the ward plan for Savannah, is acclaimed not only for its historic qualities but also as an example of high-quality urban design for a modern city. Lying dormant underneath this exceptional example of urban design is a more comprehensive plan, one that promotes a complex yet equitable human ecology. The Savannah ward plan, and its underlying planning paradigm, warrant further investigation by city planners and urban designers. Just as New Urbanism is a reinvention of traditional town planning, the broader practice of city and regional planning can begin reinventing itself by examining an inspired historic and humanistic plan.

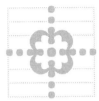

Enlightenment Legacy

The prologue provided a glimpse into the current of influences that channeled Oglethorpe toward social reform and the utopian plan for Georgia. The epilogue examines that current of influences as part of the Enlightenment, demonstrating that the colonial experiment was not a dead end but, rather, a contributing event in the progression toward modern ideas of humanism and democracy. In making that argument, the role of planning today may be seen in perspective as part of a continuous flow of events and as a mechanism to serve a greater purpose of human advancement.

Nearly every aspect of Oglethorpe's plan for the Georgia Colony conformed to the Enlightenment paradigm's emphasis on modern science and ancient knowledge. In taking the paradigm from theory to practice, Oglethorpe was positioned to play a vital, transformative role in the pivotal middle Enlightenment. When he set aside prison reform to establish the Georgia Colony, he redirected his energies from targeted reforms in England to systemic reform on the nation's frontier. He saw the frontier as a place to effect change on a blank slate and, in doing so, to create a model that would inspire change in the homeland.

Advancement of Enlightenment Ideals

The Oglethorpe Plan, in its formulation and its implementation, contributed bold thinking to the progression of ideas during the British Enlightenment. It was initiated at the midpoint between the Glorious Revolution and the American Revolution, a pivotal moment in history that flowed from the fertile milieu of 1720s London. The same milieu that produced Oglethorpe's revolutionary colonial experiment produced an array of actors who collectively steered the course of history toward humanism and democracy.

It was in that intellectual tradition that Oglethorpe synthesized a body of concepts consonant with tenets of the Enlightenment: Newton's harmonious universe, Harrington's balanced government, Locke's inalienable rights, and Shaftesbury's articulation of moral purpose. Like Bolingbroke, he wrote relatively little, but contributed at a critical time to the framing concepts of the century. Both men gave impetus to a reform movement, imparting momentum that would carry it to the end of the century.[1]

When John Burton delivered a sermon at the first anniversary meeting of the Trustees in 1733, declaring the colonists in Georgia would "in a literal sense begin the world again," he captured the essence of Enlightenment thinking. Thomas Paine would say it again in *Common Sense* in 1776: "We have it in our power to begin the world over again." It was a time when optimism reigned and there was a sense that reason could overcome centuries of backwardness. The Enlightenment "aimed to break the chains and forge a new future."[2]

Viewed in the context of the Enlightenment, the Oglethorpe Plan was a transitional step in the progression from liberal conceptualization to experimentation and finally to revolutionary change. Oglethorpe's unstated intent of facilitating *ridurre ai principii* and *translatio virtutis* was itself a form of revolution. His advocacy for the rights of common people, his opposition to slavery, and his agrarian principles were all seen recurring in the American Revolution. The Georgia Colony under the Trustees seen in that light was not a failed experiment but a step in a course of events leading to the world's first large democratic state.[3]

The American Founding Fathers were influenced by the same seventeenth-century philosophy that guided Oglethorpe, notably Harrington and Locke. The eighteenth-century British philosophers Shaftesbury and Hutcheson were widely read, as were the French philosophes Montesquieu and Voltaire, who were equally influential in Britain and America. Jefferson read and cited Bolingbroke extensively and adapted his republicanism to America. Nathanael Greene read Swift and Pope as well as Locke. The virtues extolled by those transformational figures—frugality, hard work, and honest living—were highly valued, and it was the responsibility of those in power to reinforce them. The Founding Fathers saw those virtues as an essential accompaniment to the balance of powers that preserved liberty.[4]

The progression from Oglethorpe's plan for a New World colony based on agrarian equality to Jefferson's vision of an agrarian republic is especially clear. Both were particularly tied to the views of Harrington and Locke that laboring, virtuous people have fundamental rights to use the earth to satisfy their wants. In Locke's words, God provided land for "the use of the industrious and rational—and labor was to be his title to it."[5]

Oglethorpe and Jefferson, however, faced profound economic change brought on by mercantilism, accelerated urbanization, and, in Jefferson's case, the Industrial Revolution. While Oglethorpe attacked the corrupting influences of urbanization through various reform initiatives, Jefferson addressed the issue more directly: "The mobs of great cities add just so much to the support of pure government, as sores do the strength of the human body. It is the manners and spirit of a people which preserve a republic in vigor." Both men believed that agricultural surpluses would be sufficient to obtain essential, but limited, manufactures, but not luxuries that would lead to social decay.[6]

Oglethorpe and Jefferson differed only in the details of their vision of an agrarian society. Oglethorpe was far more interested in the Roman model of town and regional planning as well as the restrictions they placed on land allocation and inheritance. Jefferson broke free of that classical model and sought an entirely new one. The two men also differed significantly in their attitude toward indigenous Americans. Oglethorpe admired their customs and respected their right to nationhood; Jefferson believed that they needed to abandon their traditions and assimilate into Euro-American society as it expanded westward.[7]

Contemporary economic thought consigns those agrarian models to the dustbin of history. Modern economists believe that nonfarm productivity is inherently greater than farm productivity, and cities thus drive a nation's prosperity. Agrarian economies such as those envisioned by Oglethorpe and Jefferson have limited potential for economic growth. Cities, by contrast, are a dynamic venue for new ideas and the "creative destruction" of obsolete institutions. However, signs of life remain in the fundamental concepts espoused by Oglethorpe and Jefferson, revived by the confluence of trends discussed in chapter 5.[8]

In one fundamental sense, Oglethorpe's vision for the New World proved more prescient than Jefferson's. He knew that Britain required, and would find, renewal in America, whereas Jefferson saw America as a new and independent national model. His view of America as a frontier that would build strength and virtue and create a colonial edenic garden contributed to an emerging antiurban political philosophy. The nation indeed

was renewed by its confrontation with revolutionary America and it ultimately accommodated the new nation as a young and more powerful ally.
America in turn found its own source of renewal in the western frontier, as
the historian Frederick Jackson Turner would later theorize.[9]

Following the revolutions of the later Enlightenment, the schools of
thought to which Oglethorpe contributed would endure another century. Rationalism, inductive reasoning, and the scientific method would
continue to gain momentum. The progression of philosophical thought
beginning with Locke, Berkeley, and Hume, later known as British empiricism, would continue to evolve into the early twentieth century as
logical positivism and continue to fuel the displacement of mysticism by
science. The simple dichotomy formulated in the Enlightenment that
contrasted experiential scientific knowledge with revealed religious knowledge would only gradually give way in the twentieth century to more a
complex dichotomy exemplified by Einstein's physics and Wittgenstein's
later philosophy. Einstein and Wittgenstein, in different ways, dismantled
the Enlightenment paradigm of direct correspondence between thought
and reality, finally overturning a paradigm that had reached its limit in
bettering the world.

The Revolution against Slavery

The Oglethorpe Plan was inspired principally by the emergent humanism
of the middle Enlightenment. While prohibition of slavery in Georgia was
initially a pragmatic step, opposition to slavery on moral grounds sprang
from the colony's founding principles, with the Carolina model acting as
a catalyst to speed up the process. Oglethorpe's reading of the Stoic philosophers, in particular, readily supported the virtuous agrarian life fostered
in Georgia while revealing slavery in Carolina to be inconsonant with a
harmonious universe.

Opposition to slavery on humanistic grounds is not frequently mentioned by Oglethorpe's biographers, probably because his early views on
slavery are unclear, but when he eventually addressed the matter, he did
so in the strongest possible language. In a letter to the Trustees written in
1739, quoted at length in chapter 3, he addressed the pragmatic case against
slavery and then raised the moral argument, saying that slavery "occasion[s]
the misery of thousands in Africa . . . who now live free there." The Georgia historian Phinizy Spalding, in tracing the origin of Amos Ettinger's
interest in Oglethorpe and the resulting definitive biography, found that he

began with William Wilberforce and traced the origin of his abolitionist movement back to the ban on slavery in Georgia.[10]

It appears likely that Oglethorpe's personal opposition to slavery emerged during the first years of planning and settling Georgia. He may have been moved first by the case of Job ben Jalla, an African prince enslaved in 1730. Permitted by his Maryland owner to write to his father, Job's letter (written in Arabic) found its way to Oglethorpe in 1732. Perceiving the injustice of enslaving someone so well educated (and perhaps having his first misgivings about the institution of slavery), he arranged to purchase Job's freedom before embarking for the colony. Soon after that he resigned as a director of the slave-trading Royal African Company and sold his stock in the enterprise.[11]

Oglethorpe's opposition to slavery crystallized when he witnessed conditions in South Carolina. Arriving there in January 1733, he saw firsthand the depravation of the slave-based plantation economy, a system that was antithetical to agrarian equality and Enlightenment humanism. The "Carolina way" impressed him as both unjust to those who were enslaved and character-debasing to those who perpetuated the system.

Oglethorpe soon became, in a sense, the first abolitionist. While there was no organized abolition movement until the later Enlightenment, the Georgia Colony aroused the first public debates over institutionalized slavery in Britain and produced the first extended debate on the inhumanity of slavery. The debate became particularly intense when Savannah Malcontents concertedly attacked Oglethorpe and the Trustees in 1740 and 1741 for prohibiting slavery and placing limitations on land tenure. Members of Parliament who were political opponents of many of the Trustees and opposed to funding the Georgia Colony seized upon the criticism. Considerable debate about slavery and whether it should be allowed in Georgia ensued.

As discussed in chapter 3, Oglethorpe responded to the Malcontents by encouraging opposition among other colonists and fighting any reconsideration of the prohibition on slavery among the Trustees. Most of the Trustees agreed with Oglethorpe, firmly and repeatedly rebuking efforts by the Malcontents to overturn the prohibition. The Trustees also repeatedly reprimanded William Stephens for not reporting transgressions where slaves were slipped into the colony and for not being firmer with violators. The prohibition remained in place until Oglethorpe ceased attending meetings of the Trust early in 1750.[12]

The antislavery movement in Britain would not emerge from this insipient state for another thirty years, during the later Enlightenment, when a high court ruled in 1772 that habeas corpus applied to slaves. It was at that time that Oglethorpe supported an incipient abolitionist movement by inspiring younger friends with stories of his earlier attempt to prohibit slavery and working with them to construct a potent case against the institution of slavery. His collaborations in later life, on slavery and in other areas, are discussed in the next section. The fact that Oglethorpe's humanitarian achievements and his efforts to abolish slavery began with a town and regional plan illustrates the vital connection between physical design and social evolution.

Oglethorpe's Later Agenda

The brief account of the life of James Edward Oglethorpe that follows reveals remarkable consistency and tenacity in his pursuit of a humanistic agenda. From the time of his return to England in 1743 until his death at age eighty-eight in 1785, he devoted himself equally to national service and public service. The last half of his life was, in that sense, a mirror image of the first half, a conclusion that reinforces the view that he added momentum to the Enlightenment and planted a time capsule of that age's ideals in the enduring plan of Savannah.

On September 15, 1744, a year after his return from Georgia, Oglethorpe married Elizabeth Wright, a wealthy heiress. He was forty-seven, and she was thirty-five. The couple elected to reside at her estate, Cranham Hall, in Essex, only nineteen miles from London. They divided their time between the relaxed atmosphere of the country and the stimulating intellectual environment of the city, where they maintained a town house.

Oglethorpe retained the Westbrook estate and continued to represent Haslemere in Parliament. He argued effectively for continued civil and military support to the Georgia Colony during the War of the Austrian Succession until the Treaty of Aix-la-Chapelle ended hostilities among European powers in 1748. Oglethorpe's Georgia regiment was only then finally disbanded.

Before the treaty ended conflict, France as well as Spain remained a threat to Britain. Fear of a French invasion required Britain to bolster its forces along England's southern coast, and in 1744 Oglethorpe, newly married, was ordered to raise a regiment for coastal defense. The following spring, while in defensive position on the southern coast, he was promoted to major general.[13]

An invasion soon came, but not by France directly nor on the southern coast. Jacobite forces led by the Young Pretender, Prince Charles Edward Stuart, landed in Scotland in August 1745. Oglethorpe was sent north to join other British army units. After raising volunteers to join his regulars, he was ordered to intercept the invaders, who were then in retreat. They escaped, however, before he reached them.[14]

The Duke of Cumberland, in commanded of the British army, accused Oglethorpe of intentionally allowing the getaway. Oglethorpe was brought before a court-martial in September 1746, but the charges were found frivolous or inconsequential. Nevertheless, Cumberland remained doubtful of Oglethorpe's loyalty and prevented him from returning to active duty. While there is evidence that Oglethorpe supported an English Jacobite faction out of loyalty to his family, it appears likely that his loyalty to the nation came before his family's long-standing commitment to the House of Stuart. Oglethorpe was sufficiently trusted to be promoted to lieutenant general in 1747.[15]

Oglethorpe remained an active Georgia Trustee to the extent that military duty, parliamentary service, and a new marriage allowed. He crafted refinements to the Georgia plan but argued strenuously against structural changes to the colony's founding principles. However, with the death of John Percival in May 1748, Oglethorpe's last staunch ally among the Trustees was gone, and it became clear that the remaining Trustees were losing their resolve to hold the line on the Georgia Colony's original principles. In view of the colony's altering course, Oglethorpe attended his last meeting in March 1749.

Oglethorpe turned his attention to business before Parliament. He argued for the right of soldiers to bring cases before Parliament and for a shorter period of required military service, taking up their cause as he had that of sailors. He argued against an oath of silence at courts-martial, rhetorically asking his fellow MPs, "What is it that makes the resentment of this House terrible to evil-doers? It is our being the grand inquest of the nation. Can we perform that function if men are tied up by oath from making any discovery?"[16]

Despite his leadership in these and other matters, Oglethorpe was defeated in his bid for reelection to Parliament in 1754, ending his political career. Still energetic and intent on serving humanity through his nation or through allied causes, he looked to America once again for duty. Britain was at war with France, and he offered to lead forces in the Canadian theater. His offer, however, was ignored. There is evidence that he returned to his Jacobite roots at this time, funding publication of material in support of the cause and even raising revenue for it through smuggling.[17]

In 1755, seeking an alternative, he began correspondence with an old friend, General James Keith, then in the service of Frederick II, king of Prussia. He expressed admiration for the visionary leadership of the king, who would become known as Frederick the Great, and offered his free-lance services as a senior officer. Oglethorpe and Keith agreed to rendez-vous in Rotterdam in December to discuss arrangements.[18]

Oglethorpe may have known when he contacted Keith that Britain and Prussia were on the verge of forming a new alliance, one that was formal-ized in January 1756. In a realignment of European powers, France and Austria, formerly enemies, became allies. The Seven Years' War ensued, in which Prussia sought to annex states held by Austria, and Britain went to war with France over territory in North America.

While Oglethorpe was intensely loyal to Britain and averse to over-throwing the established government, he nevertheless retained a high regard for the Stuart ideal of a strong and enlightened monarch. For that reason, he may have been attracted to Frederick, an inspired leader, a Patriot King, who sought to restore and improve German institutions. Devoted to the "humanitarian culture of the Enlightenment," Frederick modernized his government, abolished torture, allowed freedom of the press, supported the creative arts, and, although an agnostic influenced by English deism, he promoted religious tolerance. Frederick invited intellec-tuals such as Voltaire to advise on policy and to discuss science, philosophy, and the arts.[19]

Thus, acting upon a sense of duty and higher purpose, Oglethorpe trav-eled in secret from Rotterdam to Potsdam to join Frederick's army, visiting his sister Fanny in Piedmont en route. He adopted the name de Hurtmore to avoid detection, a name to which he was entitled through ownership of an estate by that name. Secrecy was necessary because he was acting without authorization by British authorities, and three of his sisters had married into prominent French families. Around the time of his arrival in Germany in July 1756, Oglethorpe adopted another alias, John Tebay.[20]

On September 11, 1756, Oglethorpe and Keith fought in the Battle of Pirna in the invasion of Saxony by Frederick's forces. After taking Sax-ony, Frederick's army moved deep into Austrian heartland. In April 1757, he began an assault on Prague as part of a plan to take Bohemia. Keith and Oglethorpe were sent to secure the west to cut off retreating Austrian forces, and Prague was taken in November. About this time Frederick,

Voltaire, Keith, and Oglethorpe met to discuss their prospects and their next objective, Bohemia.[21]

With Prague taken, Oglethorpe appears to have paid a visit to his sisters in January and February 1758. He reemerged in the service of Frederick in June, by then known by the alias Jacques Rosbif. Oglethorpe joined Keith during the invasion of Bohemia, where they fought side by side at the Battle of Hochkirch. On October 14, 1758, Keith died on the battlefield in Oglethorpe's arms. Oglethorpe remained in Prussia until Keith's body was secured for burial.[22]

Oglethorpe ended his service with Frederick after Keith's death. It was the end of an active military career during which he served under two inspired leaders, Eugene and Frederick, whom Napoleon ranked among the seven greatest generals in history. The war behind him, he relocated to Paris, where he resided with his sister Eleanor well into 1760, corresponding with his wife and friends in England through secret channels. He finally returned to England at age sixty-four following the death of George II in October 1760.[23]

Little is known about Oglethorpe's activities between 1761 and 1767. He was promoted in 1765 to full general, the highest rank in the army; however, the rank was ceremonial and his military career was over. Apparently he reentered the realm of politics during this period, and in 1768 he sought reelection to Parliament. He lost the election but seized the moment to reinvent himself to adapt to a new era, the dawn of the Industrial Revolution. Although his stoicism would be strained by the ensuing general affluence, he would thrive in the new milieu by engaging with London's intelligentsia and challenging them to pursue a humanistic agenda. It was a wise course to pursue, as he would become remarkably effective in the new role.

Oglethorpe remained mentally and physically vigorous to the very end of his long life. Horace Walpole, Robert Walpole's literary son, wrote that Oglethorpe "has the activity of a youth when compared to me. His eyes, ears, articulation, limbs, and memory would suit a boy, if a boy could recollect a century backwards." Jonathan Williams wrote to Benjamin Franklin that he "danced about the room with gaiety, kissed and said pretty things to all the ladies, and seemed to feel all he said as much as any young man could do. . . . This youthful old gentleman was General Oglethorpe whom I believe you know. He spoke of you with the strongest marks of esteem."[24]

A vigorous, well-read, and charming yet provocative Oglethorpe thus became a fixture of the London literati and formed close friendships with several of its greatest talents. James and Elizabeth Oglethorpe, both of whom were engaging figures, frequently entertained at their town house in London as well as their estate at Cranham. They hosted regular dinner parties for London's brightest talents and inaugurated an annual dinner party in April 1772.[25]

The first of Oglethorpe's friends among the literati was James Boswell (1740–1795), whom Oglethorpe called upon in April 1768 after the writer published his *Account of Corsica*. The work brought to light an independence movement founded on principles consistent with Oglethorpe's country party philosophy. Boswell wrote his account from first-hand knowledge obtained when he visited the island of Corsica, after a lengthy trek through Europe. He explored the island largely on foot under difficult physical circumstances, demonstrating a stoic determination that would have appealed greatly to Oglethorpe.

Boswell and Oglethorpe became close friends, frequently dining together and regularly corresponding when the former was at his home in Scotland. Boswell valued the friendship, writing that he "never failed to enjoy learned and animated conversation, seasoned with genuine sentiments of virtue and religion." He began work on a biography of Oglethorpe at the urging of Samuel Johnson, who in 1775 told him, "I know no man whose life would be more interesting." The work was not completed, but his notes have been preserved.[26]

Oliver Goldsmith (1730–1774) was the second literary talent after Boswell who became part of Oglethorpe's circle. Goldsmith, like Boswell, had explored Europe under great hardship for several years. He supported himself by playing the flute and living simply among common people, a manner of study that would have impressed Oglethorpe. Their meeting was occasioned with the publication of *The Deserted Village* in 1770. The famous poem describes the fate of an idyllic rural village, "Sweet Auburn! loveliest village of the plain." Goldsmith had previously authored the novel *The Vicar of Wakefield* (1766) and the play *The Good Natur'd Man* (1769) and was writing another play, *She Stoops to Conquer* (1771).

Oglethorpe was impressed with the depiction in *The Deserted Village* of rural depopulation and with its sense of hope that rural virtue can survive where there is a frontier—the concept of *translatio virtutis* that infused the plan for Georgia. Goldsmith's thesis was thus very close to Oglethorpe's agrarian philosophy.

Joshua Reynolds (1723–1792) entered Oglethorpe's circle soon after Goldsmith. Reynolds was among the most famous painters of the time and highly respected by his peers. Goldsmith dedicated *The Deserted Village* to him, and Boswell dedicated his *Life of Johnson* to him. Reynolds organized the first dinner for the group that became famously known as Johnson's Literary Club. He painted many of his friends' portraits, including Johnson's, Boswell's, Goldsmith's, and Oglethorpe's. The portrait of Oglethorpe, completed in 1780, was destroyed by fire in 1816.[27]

Johnson and Oglethorpe were finally introduced in March 1772 by Goldsmith. Oglethorpe knew of Johnson since subscribing to his poem *London* in 1738 and had looked forward to meeting him for some time. He wrote to Boswell: "I long to converse with the person of Mr. Sam Johnson, whose soul I am already acquainted with by his writings, and whose judgment I revere."[28]

Samuel Johnson, known as Dr. Johnson, was at the epicenter of creativity in London's literary Enlightenment. He wrote poetry, several acclaimed essays, and several biographies, most of poets. He was also a lexicographer, and his *Dictionary of the English Language* stood as a definitive reference until the position was taken by the *Oxford English Dictionary* a century and a half later.

Johnson's famed incisiveness and wit, delivered as often over dinner as in writing, contributed many quotable phrases to the English language, such as "Patriotism is the last refuge of a scoundrel." As a critic of slavery, he asked, rhetorically, "How is it that we hear the loudest yelps for liberty among the drivers of negroes?" He coined the phrase "pursuit of happiness," which was taken by Jefferson for the Declaration of Independence, modifying Locke's phrase "life, liberty, and the pursuit of property." Humor was a notable part of his repertoire; he described second marriages, for example, as "the triumph of hope over experience."

Johnson attended Oglethorpe's first annual dinner in 1772, shortly after the two met. Johnson and Oglethorpe often enlivened the dinner conversation during their numerous gatherings, the former making a provocative claim and the latter drawing a related lesson from his wealth of experience. It was at the first annual dinner that Johnson pursued the subject of duels, and Oglethorpe told the frequently repeated story of how one was avoided after the Siege of Belgrade when a prince of Wurttemberg splashed wine on him and he returned it with a full glass. Under the word *fillip*, the *Oxford English Dictionary* provides as an example of usage "The Prince, by a fillip, made some of the wine fly in Oglethorpe's face," a phrase recorded in Boswell's biography that arose from dinner conversation elicited by Johnson in discussing the custom of dueling.[29]

Horace Walpole was a member of Johnson's Literary Club as well as

Oglethorpe's circle of friends. The son of Robert Walpole, he overcame an animosity toward Oglethorpe, and the two became friends in their later years. Although they came from opposing political traditions, they found common ground in their interest in the creative arts, interests that placed both men on higher ground in later life.

Following a lengthy political career, Walpole became a respected writer and art historian. He anonymously wrote the gothic novel *The Castle of Otranto,* among other works, and produced voluminous commentary on Georgian society that later became a valuable resource for historians. He wrote skillfully and creatively; quips such as "This world is a comedy to those that think, a tragedy to those that feel" and "Every drop of ink in my pen ran cold" and the word *serendipity* are among many often-used words and phrases from his writing.

Culture and talent converge rarely but inevitably to create uniquely productive times in history. Such times occur when people of varied backgrounds and disciplines are drawn together in a dynamic where they influence each other in ways that influence a new paradigm of thought or even a new age. The overlapping intellectual circles of Oglethorpe and Johnson created that sort of dynamic during the later Enlightenment. In addition to Johnson, Boswell, Goldsmith, and Reynolds, there were many others who during this period would collectively influence creative arts, humanism, and political philosophy for generations.[30]

The Oglethorpe-Johnson milieu included Edmund Burke, the Irish author and political philosopher who became a leader of the conservative faction in the House of Commons and a proponent of classical liberalism (a foundation of modern libertarianism); David Hume, whose empiricism was central to the Scottish Enlightenment; Adam Smith, a colleague of Hume at Glasgow (but also well known in London), whose work in economics is considered a cornerstone of modern conservatism; David Garrick, the famed Shakespearean actor, playwright, and producer, who innovated a new style of acting; Charles Burney, composer and music historian, and his daughter, novelist and satirist Frances Burney; Edward Gibbon, author of the *History of the Decline and Fall of the Roman Empire,* whose depiction of religion and political institutions placed him at the center of thinking during the later Enlightenment; Hester Thrale, who writings became a vital source of information about the age; and Gen. Pasquale di Paoli, the central figure in Boswell's *Account of Corsica,* who was the soldier and visionary credited with writing the first national constitution based on Enlightenment humanism.[31]

These were among the many acquaintances that imbued Oglethorpe with the level of respect late in life that leveraged ideas he advocated throughout life: stoic personal discipline, hard work, civic duty, individual liberty. His advocacy of such ideals strengthened the current of Enlightenment thought as it flowed toward American independence, the abolition movement, and the more disciplined society that would emerge in the nineteenth century as the Victorian era.

Two other friends were particularly central to Oglethorpe's later life and essential to an understanding of his legacy, as they were vigorous implementers of his opposition to slavery. Hannah More (1745–1833) was a playwright, poet, and essayist from Bristol, who in her late twenties began regularly visiting London. In 1772 she was introduced to Garrick after seeing his portrayal of King Lear. Garrick then introduced her to Johnson. She met Burke at about the same time and was close to all of them for the remainder of their lives.[32]

More may have met Oglethorpe in the 1770s through one of their many mutual acquaintances; however, they did not become friends until 1784. She wrote glowingly and with considerable hyperbole of the new friendship:

> I have got a new admirer, and we flirt together prodigiously; it is the famous General Oglethorpe, perhaps the most remarkable man of his time. He was foster-brother to the Pretender . . . ; the finest figure you ever saw. He perfectly realizes all my ideas of Nestor. His literature is great, his knowledge of the world extensive, and his faculties as bright as ever; he is one of the three persons still living who were mentioned by Pope. . . . He was the intimate friend of Southern, the tragic poet, and of all the wits of that time. He is perhaps the oldest man of a gentlemen living. I went to see him the other day, and he would have entertained me by repeating passages from Sir Eldred. He is quite a preus chevalier, heroic, romantic, and full of old gallantry.[33]

More and Oglethorpe were part of another vibrant literary circle, that of Elizabeth Montagu. Montagu, a poet, editor, and translator, hosted many of those in Johnson's circle, while also building a network of female talent. Montagu's circle, which became known as the Blue Stocking Society, supplied mutual encouragement for intellectual and artistic pursuits by women at a time when they received little recognition for such achievements. Blue Stocking Society meetings also became a venue for discussing social and educational reform, creating an atmosphere supportive of More as she developed an interest in the abolition of slavery. Montagu's circle included the writer Anna Barbauld; the novelist Frances Burney; the poet Elizabeth Carter; the art collector Margaret Cavendish-Harley, Duchess of Portland; the artist Mary Delany; the writer Sarah Fielding (sister of writer Henry Fielding); and many other creative women.[34]

The Blue Stockings pressed the limit of feminine intellectualism in male-dominated society yet avoided exceeding it. In doing so, they raised the platform from which women spoke out on social issues and created a women's movement that arguably encouraged progressive feminist thinking at its periphery. Helen Maria Williams and Mary Wollstonecraft, radical feminists of the time, can be seen as contrasting with the Blue Stockings but were also participants in the advance of feminist expression engendered by the later Enlightenment.

More shared Oglethorpe's stoicism, sense of dedication to higher values, and appreciation of rural life. In the poem *Florio,* she describes the plight of a young man seduced by a life of ease but rescued from depravity by a rural maiden who leads him to realize that "the simplest pleasures are the best."

More's exposure to Oglethorpe's resolute views about slavery prepared her for a commitment to the emerging abolitionist movement. The commitment was complete by 1787, two years after Oglethorpe's death, when she attended a sermon by Rev. John Newton, the composer of "Amazing Grace." Afterward she received a visit from William Wilberforce, who enlisted her support for the cause with her pen. Her poem *Slavery,* written soon after that, attacked British inconsistency of thought about liberty.[35]

Oglethorpe was an active agent in the transition from intellectual opposition to slavery found in the Johnson and Montagu circles to the development of a formal abolitionist movement. Oglethorpe, seeking more than passive discussion, introduced himself to Granville Sharp (1735–1813) in 1776, beginning a productive dialogue on their mutual humanistic interests. Oglethorpe's association with Sharp led to active pursuit of freedom for slaves, as well as collaboration on the case against impressment and intervention on behalf of the rights of American colonists.

Sharp emerged as Oglethorpe's closest friend during his later years. He had little formal education but acquired a penetrating intellect through his years as an apprentice to tradesmen of various religious affiliations. Debating differing claims about the historical truth of religion led Sharp to study the Greek and Hebrew languages and classical history. Later he became a civil servant, working in the Ordinance Department until the beginning of the American Revolution, a position that allowed him time to continue his study of languages. It was during this period that he came to see the institution of slavery in the colonies as a national disgrace.[36]

Sharp's first action against slavery took place in September 1767, when he intervened in a court case in which a slave master attempted to retrieve a former slave, Jonathan Strong, whom the master had beaten nearly to death and abandoned two years earlier. Sharp was familiar with the case through his brother, a surgeon, who had treated the former slave after his beating. The judge declared Strong free, but an agent of the slave master immediately seized him. Sharp stepped forward, saying, "and I charge you for an assault." Sharp subsequently persevered through two years of legal wrangling that eventually resulted in Strong's emancipation.[37]

Sharp continued to work on behalf of individual slaves, and in so doing gradually built a legal framework against the institution of slavery. He also began writing extensively and eloquently against slavery. In February 1772, he published a tract that concluded, "It were better for the nation that their American dominions had never existed, or even that they had sunk into the sea, than that the kingdom of Great Britain should be loaded with the horrid guilt of tolerating such abominable wickedness."[38]

In 1776, Oglethorpe discovered that Sharp shared his views on slavery, American liberty, and the rights of seamen. Oglethorpe's initial letters to Sharp addressed the latter's law of retribution, a thesis that divine vengeance would be visited upon Britain for perpetuating the evil practice of slavery. Oglethorpe may have seen this in terms of *translatio virtutis*, the principle of migration of virtue, as it resonated with his own beliefs. The two men corresponded for several months, and after meeting they collaborated on a peace plan for the American colonies and a new edition of *The Sailor's Advocate*, Oglethorpe's tract initially published fifty years earlier.[39]

In 1783, Sharp began planning a settlement in Sierra Leone, for which "the majority of the settlers will probably be Africans returned from slavery to their own soil." A twenty-square-mile tract of land was purchased from King Tom. The site had a bay, navigable rivers, and springs with fresh water. The settlement was to become an egalitarian society named the Province of Freedom. The principal settlement was named Granville Town, later Cline Town, and then Freetown. During the early stages of planning, Oglethorpe shared his experience in designing the Georgia Colony with Sharp, and elements of the Oglethorpe Plan, particularly the settlement plan, were incorporated into the project. Sharp went on to publish a "General Plan" for colonial towns in 1794, a model that influenced the design of settlements in North America and Australia, where the squares in the city of Adelaide are similar to those in the Oglethorpe Plan. Sharp's plan sought a clear departure from the Grand Modell of Shaftesbury, one that had a strong component of spatial equality.[40]

In the years immediately after Oglethorpe's death in 1785, More and Sharp joined Wilberforce, Thomas Clarkson, and others in organizing a more focused attack on slavery. Their efforts resulted in the establishment of the Clapham Sect, also known as the Clapham Saints, a group that included a number of influential people, including government officials and business leaders as well as clergymen and intellectuals. The same year, Sharp joined a Quaker antislavery group to form the Society for the Abolition of the Slave Trade. From those initiatives, the formal abolitionist movement was born. Britain prohibited the slave trade in 1807 and abolished slavery in 1833, one hundred years after the founding of Georgia.

Oglethorpe articulated his opposition to slavery dating back to the Georgia Colony in his second letter to Sharp, excerpted below, on October 13, 1776. The letter blames the government rather than a loss of resolve by the Georgia Trustees for the legalization of slavery in Georgia. Nevertheless, his characterization of events appears to be a definitive statement about his long-standing commitment to humanistic philosophy:

> With great pleasure I received the favor of yours of 27th September, and since, several excellent tracts of your composing, which I have read with much satisfaction, as they all point to the great end of life,—the honor of God and the love of our neighbor. You have, with great judgment, showed the threats of the Prophets against the slave-owners and slave-sellers. . . .
>
> My friends and I settled the colony of Georgia, and by charter we were established trustees, to make laws, &c. We determined not to suffer slavery there; but the slave-merchants, and their adherents, occasioned us not only much trouble, but at last got the then government to favor them. We would not suffer slavery (which is against the Gospel as well as the fundamental law of England) to be authorized under our authority: we refused, as trustees, to make a law permitting such a horrid crime. The Government, finding the trustees resolved firmly not to concur with what they thought unjust, took away the charter by which no law could be passed without our consent. . . .
>
> This cruel custom of a private man's being supported in exercising more power over the man he affirms to have bought as a slave, than the magistrate has over him, the master, is a solecism in politics. This, I think, was taken

from the Romans. The horrid cruelty which that proud nation showed in all they did, gave such power to the masters of slaves, that they confused even the State. . . .

I find in Sir Walter Rawleigh's history of the Saracens, that *their* success, and the destruction of the Grecian and Persian empires, was chiefly owing to their having vast numbers of slaves, by whom all labor and husbandry were carried on. And, on the Mohametans giving freedom to all who professed their law, the multitude in every conquered province joined them.

You mention an argument urged by Hume, that the *Africans were incapable of liberty,* and that no man capable of government was ever produced by Africa. What a historian! He must never have heard of Shishak, the great Sesostris, of Hannibal, nor of *Tir-haka* king of Ethiopia, whose very name frightened the mighty Assyrian monarch (2 Kings xix.9). Is it possible he never should have seen Herodotus, where the mighty works of the pyramids, remaining to this day, are mentioned; and, in θαασĬα, the answer of the king of Ethiopia to Cambyses? In Leo, the African,'s [*sic*] geographical description of Africa, he would have found that Africa produced races of heroes.

The *Christian* Emperors would have qualified the laws for slavery; but the Senate of Rome, in whom the old leaven of idolatry still prevailed, stopped such designs. St. Austin [Augustine], in *"De Civitate Dei,"* mentions that idolatry was sunk into the marrow of the Romans;—that the destruction of Rome by the Goths seemed to be a necessary dispensation of Providence to root out idolatry. The Goths, and all the northern nations when converted, abolished slavery. The husbandry was performed by the men under the protection of the laws. Though some tenures of the villeyn [villein] were too severe, yet the villeyns [villeins] had the protection of the laws; and their lords could not exact more than by those laws was regulated (Bracton).

Spain and Portugal were subdued by the Moors: afterwards Portugal was recovered by the Christians. The Portuguese carried the war into Africa, discovered the sea-coast of Guinea, brought the unhappy natives away, and, looking on them as black heathens and hardly men, sold them for slaves.

The Spaniards imitated them, and declared that Moors and Turks, taken in war, might be held as slaves. But the French still hold the noble law of the Northern nations; they allow no slaves in France: but, alas! it is too true, in their plantations, where the King's will is the only law, Lewis the Fourteenth, by the *Code-Noir,* permits and regulates slavery.

I am exceedingly glad that you have entered the lists in opposition to these horrors. It is a proper time to bring these abominable abuses under consideration; and if those who have the power of legislation will be admonished, and correct them, it may save them and us from the justly menaced destruction.[41]

Oglethorpe was arguably the first modern philanthropist, and similarly one might cogently argue that he was also the first abolitionist. In formulating a slave-free colony at a time when few questioned the morality of slavery and many profited from it, he broke ranks and began a much-needed debate. He read extensively about the history of slavery, becoming an expert on the subject. Late in life, he held up the earlier achievement in Georgia, tenuous though it was, as a beacon of light for those who would follow, and he made it clear to all who would listen that slavery was demonstrably evil from both moral and historical perspectives. He ignited interest in abolition among those in Johnson's circle, and he framed new strategies for ending slavery that would be pursued by More and Sharp as they built the abolitionist movement in England.

In June 1785, Oglethorpe completed the handoff to the next generation of visionaries in two meetings with John Adams, who had arrived in London to assume the post of ambassador from the United States. Oglethorpe initiated the dialogue with a visit to Adams, in which he expressed a great admiration for the new United States of America. Adams returned the visit, and the two men conversed for more than two hours. Soon afterward Oglethorpe fell ill with a high fever, to which he succumbed on June 30. James Edward Oglethorpe was among the few products of the Enlightenment who, like Voltaire, ignited the era's early ideals and remained engaged with those ideals nearly to the end of the era.[42]

Oglethorpe and Bolingbroke: Divergent Outcomes

In the prologue it was observed that Oglethorpe and Bolingbroke shared the same basic political philosophy, but their methods differed greatly and produced divergent outcomes. Both men were woven into the fabric of the British Enlightenment, influencing it to the finish. And with the great accomplishments of the Enlightenment remaining a source of inspiration today, their respective contributions remain a valuable source of insight into that age.

Bolingbroke influenced the leaders of the American and French Revolutions by adding to Harrington's theory of a stable agrarian state and updating Machiavelli's thesis of *ridurre ai principii,* creating a basic structure on which to attach the newer ideas of advancement through reason and humanism, governance through social contract and a secular state, and balance of powers through a constitutional democratic republic.

Oglethorpe, by contrast, actively lived a life that pursued many of those principles, and in so doing influenced public discourse on many levels. The initiation of the Georgia Colony memorialized Oglethorpe as a philanthropist and humanist. Implementation of the colonial plan provoked debate over economic policies and slavery. Securing and holding the colony gave final form to the thirteen colonies that would unite into the first modern democracy. Oglethorpe's legacy in Georgia did not fade because he lived the remainder of his life with a constancy of purpose. The honor and stoic dedication with which he pursued his goals positioned him to influence the best minds of the later British Enlightenment at a stage of life when most people retire from public service and the war of ideas. In that position he was able to complete his life's work begun a half century earlier.

His story, however, did not end with the achievements of the later Enlightenment. The seed of humanistic idealism he planted in Georgia survived in the design of Savannah. That seed now grows, nourished with new ideals adopted by descendants of slaves in a city where African Americans are the majority.

A New Model for Town Planning

The Oglethorpe Plan is known to many people because of the Savannah National Historic Landmark District. The order and harmony of the town's wards and central squares are readily perceived and appreciated by visitors, who are seen everywhere contentedly strolling the town in outdoor rooms on floors of Enlightenment geometry, with walls of history and ceilings of urban forest. The experience stands in marked contrast to that in other historic towns where tourists bustle from one retail establishment to another without absorbing the genius loci—the spirit of the place.

Historic Savannah, many fail to realize, is not merely a preserve where one can take in the beauty of a bygone era. Nor is the more perceptive visitor entirely aware of the genius of the place in grasping that it is living history, both a historic town and a multifaceted urban environment where people live and work. The genius of the place resides deep in a design distilled from humanistic principles of the Enlightenment and in the ability of that design to accommodate a fundamental human need for spatial order.

Oglethorpe's enduring accomplishment was in conceiving a ward design that enabled subsequent generations to create entirely new built environments, expressions of a new era built on a transcendent plan. The two-dimensional ward layout for the town continues to inspire an evolving three-dimensional space of architecture and landscape.

Town planners often cite the Oglethorpe Plan, which they narrowly interpret to mean the Savannah town plan, and even its later architecture, as an exceptional model of urban design. In practice, however, they have ignored the potential use of the Savannah model in other contexts. Even New Urbanist designers, who employ a set of design elements similar to those used by Oglethorpe, have overlooked several principles of the Savannah plan that have enormous potential for application in a modern context.

The plan's unique attributes invite further study and wider application. The pattern of interlocking wards is especially compelling as a design strategy for encouraging neighborhood formation, creating safe spaces, and engendering community character. Each ward provides a blank slate for unique creative expression while retaining a high degree of connectivity and social equity with every other part of town. The Oglethorpe Plan left a permanent imprint on Savannah, yet its full potential awaits discovery.

Appendix A

Chronology of the British Enlightenment, Oglethorpe's Life, and the Planning and Founding of Georgia

1687 Isaac Newton publishes *Philosophiae Naturalis Principia Mathematica* (Mathematical Principles of Natural Philosophy)

1688 The Glorious Revolution takes place; James II flees to exile in France

1689 The reign of William and Mary begins; John Locke publishes *Two Treatises of Government*

1690 Locke publishes *An Essay Concerning Human Understanding*

1691 Theophilus Oglethorpe arrested for refusing to take an oath of allegiance to William and Mary

1694 Queen Mary dies; Voltaire born

1696 Arrest warrant issued for Theophilus Oglethorpe in February; James Edward Oglethorpe born in London on December 22; John Toland publishes *Christianity Not Mysterious*

1697 William Hogarth born on November 10

1698 Society for the Promotion of Christian Knowledge (SPCK) founded by Thomas Bray

1700 Toland edits and publishes Harrington's *Oceana*

1701 James II dies; Act of Settlement provides for Hanover succession

1702 King William dies, succeeded by Queen Anne; Theophilus Oglethorpe dies

1706 Oglethorpe enrolls in Queen Anne's First Regiment of Foot Guards at age nine

1709 Samuel Johnson born on September 18

1710 Eleanor Oglethorpe becomes a friend of Jonathan Swift and courtier of Queen Anne

1711 3rd Earl of Shaftesbury publishes *Characteristicks;* South Sea Company founded

1713 Oglethorpe commissioned lieutenant in Queen Anne's First Regiment of Foot Guards

1714 Oglethorpe enrolls in Corpus Christi College, Oxford, in July; Queen Anne dies in August

1715	Lord Bolingbroke becomes a Jacobite and fled to Paris; Jacobite uprising fails; Oglethorpe resigns his commission in the Foot Guards, takes leave from Oxford, relocates to Paris for military training
1716	Oglethorpe joins Prince Eugene's forces in the Balkans; following victories he briefly visits Turin, Venice, and Paris
1717	Oglethorpe returns to the Balkans and fights in Siege of Belgrade; he visits his brother in Turin
1718	Oglethorpe twice secretly visits James III in Urbino, then returns to Paris
1719	Oglethorpe reenrolls at Oxford in June; Defoe publishes *Robinson Crusoe*
1720	South Sea Bubble creates financial havoc in Britain; the Mississippi Bubble has similar effect in France
1721	Robert Walpole assumed office of first minister (considered Britain's first prime minister)
1722	Oglethorpe elected to Parliament; Bolingbroke pardoned; Toland dies
1723	Bolingbroke returns to London from exile in France
1724	Associates of Dr. Bray formally created
1725	Oglethorpe becomes an advocate for seamen; Francis Hutcheson publishes early works that would influence Thomas Jefferson
1726	Voltaire arrives in England; Swift publishes *Gulliver's Travels;* Bolingbroke begins publishing the *Craftsman*
1727	Isaac Newton dies; George I dies; Voltaire publishes *Essay on Epic Poetry* immortalizing Newton's apple; Augustan Age of English literature begins to flourish
1728	Oglethorpe publishes *The Sailor's Advocate;* Robert Castell publishes *Villas of the Ancients;* Castell dies in debtors' prison; Gay's *The Beggar's Opera* performed; Alexander Pope publishes *The Dunciad*
1729	Prison committee established and Oglethorpe appointed chair; Associates of Dr. Bray reorganized by Oglethorpe; Voltaire departs England
1730	Dr. Bray dies; Associates of the Late Dr. Bray petitions the king to establish the Georgia Colony in July; James Thomson publishes *The Seasons*
1731	Oglethorpe writes *Some Account of the Design of the Trustees for establishing Colonys in America;* Associates of the Late Dr. Bray meet with first prospective colonists
1732	Eleanor Oglethorpe dies; George II signs the charter in April creating the Trustees for Establishing the Colony of Georgia in America; the charter passes all offices in June; trust secretary Benjamin Martyn publishes *Some Account of the Designs of the Trustees for Establishing the Colony of Georgia in America;* the *Anne* sails for Georgia with Oglethorpe and the first colonists in November
1733	Colony of Georgia founded on February 1, 1732 O.S., February 12, 1733 N.S.; first anniversary meeting of the Trustees held in London on March 17; Oglethorpe establishes friendship with Chief Tomochichi of the Yamacraw people of the Lower Creek Nation; Pope publishes *An Essay on Man*

1734   Oglethorpe sails for England on May 7 after arranging for Chief Tomochichi to follow

1735   Oglethorpe departs for Georgia in November with the Wesley brothers; Bolingbroke retires to France

1736   Oglethorpe arrives at mouth of Savannah River with 257 colonists on February 5, leaves again for England on November 23

1737   Oglethorpe arrives in London on January 6; Oglethorpe named commander in chief of forces in South Carolina and Georgia; William Stephens, appointed secretary to the Trustees in Georgia, arrives in Savannah in November

1738   Stephens reports French preparing for war and Spain issues a proclamation of freedom to slaves fleeing Carolina; Oglethorpe arrives in Frederica in September and travels to Savannah in October; war with Spain begins

1739   Facing a petition for slaves and removal of land tenure restrictions from the Savannah Malcontents, Oglethorpe writes the Trustees on January 17 that "if we allow slaves we act against the very principles by which we associated together, which was to relieve the distressed"; Oglethorpe visits Charles Town to secure Carolina support in war against Spain; from July to September Oglethorpe travels upcountry to reaffirm treaties with Indian nations, returns to Savannah in September, then proceeds to Frederica; the Stono Rebellion (one of the largest slave rebellions in American history) begins on September 9; Tomochichi dies on October 5

1740   Oglethorpe leads British and Indian forces to Florida and initiates the Siege of St. Augustine in July; the siege fails to dislodge the Spanish, and British and Indian forces return to Frederica; William Stephens's son, Thomas, becomes a voice of the Malcontents

1741   William Stephens prepares *The State of the Province of Georgia* for the Trustees; Georgia divided along the Ogeechee River into Savannah and Frederica counties; William Stephens made president of Savannah County; Spanish reinforcements arrive in St. Augustine

1742   Walpole loses election, ending a twenty-year tenure as prime minister; the House of Commons finds Thomas Stephens's accusations against the Trustees to be "false, scandalous and malicious"; Spanish forces routed on St. Simons as they march on Fort Frederick in the Battle of Bloody Marsh; the Trustees ease regulation of land tenure and liquor

1743   Oglethorpe promoted to brigadier general and returns to England, departing Georgia on July 22

1744   Oglethorpe marries Elizabeth Wright while stationed on England's southern coast as threat of war with France increases; Bolingbroke returns permanently to England

1745   Oglethorpe promoted to major general; Prince Charles lands in Scotland, leading a new Jacobite Rebellion; Oglethorpe, ordered to pursue retreating Jacobite forces, accused of intentionally arriving late

1746   Court-martial finds charges against Oglethorpe frivolous and insubstantial; Oglethorpe again becomes busy with the work of Parliament

1747   The Trustees rescind inheritance regulations; Oglethorpe promoted to lieutenant general

1748   Trustees order President Stephens to strongly enforce restriction on slavery; John Percival, Earl of Egmont, first president of the Trustees, dies on May 1

1749   Last meeting of Trustees attended by Oglethorpe on March 16; President Stephens reports slaves being used in Georgia, and the prohibition of them cannot be effectively enforced; Bolingbroke publishes *The Patriot King*

1750   Oglethorpe becomes active with various reforms before Parliament; the Trustees rescind the prohibition on slavery and approve establishment of a Georgia assembly for future governance

1751   The Trustees approve the Constitution of an Annual Assembly of the People of Georgia

1752   The Trustees return administration of Georgia to the crown; the final meeting of the trust is held on June 28; the Gregorian calendar adopted in England

1753   George Berkeley dies

1754   Oglethorpe loses election to Parliament, ending his political career

1755   Oglethorpe meets his friend General Keith in Rotterdam in December and prepares to join forces of Frederick II of Prussia; Johnson publishes *A Dictionary of the English Language*

1756   Oglethorpe assumes various aliases while in Europe and takes part in the Battle of Pirna during the invasion of Saxony

1757   Oglethorpe and General Keith sent to secure the west and prevent retreat during the Battle of Prague; Prussian forces defeat the Austrians and begin an invasion of Bohemia

1758   General Keith dies in Oglethorpe's arms during the Battle of Hochkirch

1759   Oglethorpe remains in Berlin to receive Keith's body for burial, then proceeds to Paris to stay with his sisters until he can return to England

1760   George II dies; William Pitt arranges for Oglethorpe to return to England

1762   Rousseau publishes *The Social Contract;* Boswell moves to London

1764   Boswell visits Voltaire in France; Joshua Reynolds and Samuel Johnson form a literary club; Hogarth dies

1765   Oglethorpe promoted to general, the highest rank in the army

1766   James Francis Edward Stuart, the Old Pretender, dies in Rome; succeeded as monarch in exile by his son, Charles Edward Stuart, the Young Pretender, previously known as Bonnie Prince Charlie

1768   Boswell publishes *Account of Corsica;* Oglethorpe seeks reelection to Parliament and loses; Oglethorpe introduces himself to Boswell to discuss the *Account of Corsica,* and they become close friends

1769   Rousseau makes a permanent home in England; General Paoli of Corsica defeated by French forces, then exiled to England, where he becomes reacquainted with Boswell

1770   Oglethorpe and wife Elizabeth become social fixtures among London's reform-minded literati

1771   Oglethorpe and Oliver Goldsmith become friends following publication of *The Deserted Village* and *She Stoops to Conquer*

1772   The Oglethorpes begin hosting an annual dinner of the literati; Oglethorpe and Joshua Reynolds become friends (Reynolds later paints Oglethorpe's portrait)

1773   Annual dinner at the Oglethorpe's includes Boswell, Johnson, Reynolds, Goldsmith, Edmund Burke, and many others by this time

1774   Oliver Goldsmith dies; poet Hannah More arrives in London

1775   Edmund Burke addresses Parliament to appeal for reconciliation with America; British-American hostilities begin with the Battle of Lexington and Concord; James Watt patents the steam engine essential to the Industrial Revolution

1776   Thomas Paine publishes *Common Sense;* Second Continental Congress adopts the Declaration of Independence; Oglethorpe contacts Granville Sharp after reading his tract on slavery; Adam Smith publishes *The Wealth of Nations*

1777   Oglethorpe and Sharp advocate a peace plan for America and publish a new, enlarged version of *The Sailor's Advocate*

1778   Voltaire dies

1779   The Literary Club formally created; Boswell writes in his journal that he plans to write a biography of Oglethorpe

1780   Oglethorpe sits five times for his portrait by Reynolds

1781   Boswell takes notes for Oglethorpe's biography

1783   Horace Walpole, son of Robert, and Oglethorpe become friends; Treaty of Paris signed, British-American hostilities formally ended

1784   Hannah More meets and writes admiringly of Oglethorpe; Samuel Johnson dies on December 13

1785   John Adams received in London as the first United States Ambassador to Great Britain on June 1; Oglethorpe calls on Adams and expresses his admiration for the new nation; Adams reciprocates and visits Oglethorpe, and they talk for two hours; James Edward Oglethorpe dies at his country estate, Cranham Hall, on June 30 at age eighty-eight

Appendix B

Biographical Profiles

Information included in the following biographical sketches was drawn from the *Dictionary of National Biography*, biographical works cited in the bibliography, and the *Colonial Records of Georgia*.

Founding Trustees

ADAM ANDERSON (1692–1765). An official at the South Sea House and an historian of commerce who compiled extensive reference volumes on European trade and geography and advocated uniform currency and weights and measures throughout Europe. He served as a trustee for creating libraries at home and in the colonies under Queen Anne.

ARTHUR BEDFORD (1668–1745). A clergyman in the Church of England, moral reformer, oriental scholar, expert on ancient chronology, and mathematician at Oxford University. He served as chaplain to Prince Frederick.

WILLIAM BELITHA. A member of Oglethorpe's prison committee and of the Bray Associates.

RICHARD BUNDY (1693?-1739). Vicar of St. Bride's on Fleet Street, where Trustees sometimes met. He served as chaplain in ordinary to George II and accompanied the king to Hanover in 1732.

REV. JOHN BURTON (1696–1771). Theologian and classical scholar at Corpus Christi College, Oxford, elected to that position while Oglethorpe attended as a student. He brought the study of Locke's philosophy to the curriculum. He introduced Oglethorpe to Charles and John Wesley. He was likely a member of the inner circle that planned the Georgia Colony.

GEORGE LORD CARPENTER (1657–1732?). First Baron Carpenter of Killaghy and an army officer; a member of the Masonic Lodge at the Horn in Westminster. Briefly an MP from Westminster; earlier served as an MP in the Irish Parliament.

ANTHONY ASHLEY COOPER. See 4th Earl of Shaftesbury Anthony Ashley Cooper.

THOMAS CORAM (1668–1751). A noted philanthropist and parishioner of Dr. Bray. He was a successful merchant and shipbuilder who lived in New England from 1693 to 1704. He returned to England and became involved in charitable activities including those of the Bray Associates and the establishment of the Foundling Hospital. In 1717, he attempted to establish the colony of Georgeia (between New England and Nova Scotia) for disbanded soldiers and unemployed artisans, based on principles similar to those on which Georgia was later founded. He eventually broke with Oglethorpe and other Trustees on the issue of female inheritance; he and his wife lodged with Rev. Samuel Smith, a Trustee, for many years.

JAMES, 10TH EARL OF DERBY (1664–1736). Formerly James Stanley, the Earl, a British peer; became Baron Strange in 1732.

EDWARD DIGBY. A member of Irish nobility, in line to succeed his father as Baron Digby, but died before him.

FRANCIS EYLES (ca. 1650–1716). Possibly the son of Sir Francis Eyles, first baronet, merchant and financier. Served on the Board of Directors, Bank of England, 1707–1709; also a director of the South Seas Company.

THOMAS FREDERICK. A friend of Lady Walpole and perhaps a placeman of Robert Walpole in the trust. Appointed in 1733, by 1736 he offered to resign because of the conflict of interest posed by his relationship with the ministry.

SIR JOHN GONSON (?–1765). A magistrate and justice of the peace who was concerned about moral decay resulting from urbanization, led frequent raids of illegal vice establishments, which Hogarth depicted twice in *A Harlot's Progress* and Alexander Pope wrote of in his *Essay on Man*. Gonson was known as "the scourge of Gin Lane." He was a founding governor of the Foundling Hospital; the hospital took in the children of prostitutes among other needy children.

STEPHEN HALES (1677–1761). A respected scientist awarded the Royal Society's Copley Medal in 1739 and an Associate of Dr. Bray. Hales attended Corpus Christi College at Oxford before Oglethorpe and became a fellow of that institution. Attended Oxford and Cambridge; described by Charles Wesley as "a truly pious, humble Christian, full of zeal for God, and love to man."

GEORGE HEATHCOTE. Served as treasurer for the Trustees. Nephew of Sir Gilbert Heathcote, governor of the Bank of England, he served as a city alderman and was elected lord mayor of London in 1740. He was known as the wealthiest commoner in England when he died. Alexander Pope lampooned him for being a miser. His brother Caleb was mayor of New York. He was one of the young Trustees whom Vernon complained about to Percival as having too little regard for the religious part of the colonial design. A member of the Masonic Lodge at the Rummer Tavern, Charing Cross. He was a Jacobite follower of Wyndham.

SIR WILLIAM HEATHCOTE (1693–1751). Served on the Common Council until 1739. He was a London banker. As a patron of Hogarth he purchased *Morning and Night*. He served in Parliament 1722–27 and 1729–41. Cousin of Sir John Heathcote; he was a merchant until he inherited a fortune and then retired.

ROGERS HOLLAND. A member of the prison committee who was involved in the prosecution of wardens Bambridge and Huggins. Noted in Percival's diary as being chief justice of North Wales.

ROBERT HUCKS. A wealthy brewer and one of the young Trustees whom Vernon complained about to Percival as having too little regard for the religious part of the colonial design.

WILLIAM HUCKS (?–1740). A member of Oglethorpe's prison committee who represented Wallingford in Parliament.

ROBERT KENDALL. Alderman of Cheapside, London; became Sir Robert Cater.

HENRY L'APOSTRE. Most likely a private philanthropist; strongly supported Oglethorpe and Percival on the issues of land tenure and slavery.

JOHN LAROCHE. A member of Oglethorpe's prison committee and of the Masonic Lodge at the Prince Eugene's Head Coffee House, St. Alban's Street. He was of Huguenot extraction.

JAMES LORD VISCOUNT LIMERICK. An Irish MP who served on Oglethorpe's prison committee.

ROBERT MORE. One of the young Trustees whom Vernon complained about to Percival as having too little regard for the religious part of the colonial design.

JOHN PERCIVAL (often spelled Perceval), 1st Earl of Egmont (1682–1748). A member of Oglethorpe's prison committee, became the closest associate of Oglethorpe in conceiving and planning the colony. Percival, from Cork, Ireland, later became the Earl of Egmont. He was a close friend of George Berkeley, who had long planned to build a Christian college in the New World. He was a political independent but sympathized with country party philosophy.

SIR ERASMUS PHILLIPPS (1699–1743). Fifth baronet; politician; named in Thomas Bray's feoffment but did not serve as an Associate.

4TH EARL OF SHAFTESBURY ANTHONY ASHLEY COOPER. Son of the 3rd earl, who influenced Enlightenment thinking, and great grandson of the 1st earl. He was editing the 1732 edition of his father's principal work when he became a Trustee. Younger and less experienced than the other Trustees, he represented a link to a highly respected intellectual tradition.

REV. SAMUEL SMITH. An assistant to Dr. Bray, became a member and secretary in 1730. He wrote an account of Dr. Bray, published in 1746; active with the Associates over his career, he was a frequent correspondent with ministers, missionaries, and catechists who worked with Indians and slaves in America.

JAMES STANLEY. See James, Earl of Derby.

THOMAS TOWER. An attorney, drafted a town court system for the town of Savannah. One of the young Trustees whom Vernon complained about to Percival as having too little regard for the religious part of the colonial design. The name is also spelled "Towers."

JOHN LORD VISCOUNT TYRCONNEL (1690–1754). A member of Irish peerage from County Cork and of the British Parliament.

JAMES VERNON. Held various government posts beginning in 1701, including clerk and later secretary of the Privy Council. He participated in many of the same endeavors as Oglethorpe, including the prison committee, the Associates of Dr. Bray, and the Freemasons, but he became increasingly at odds with Oglethorpe over the governing principles for the colony. His brother was Admiral Vernon. He was a member of the Masonic Lodge at the Bedford Head, Covent Garden.

JOHN WHITE. One of the young Trustees whom Vernon complained about to Percival as having too little regard for the religious part of the colonial design and an established church. He was described as a "dissenter" by Percival.

OTHER TRUSTEES. Little biographical information is available on the following Trustees: James Lord D'Arcy, William Hanbury, John Page, William Sloper, Christopher Tower (brother of Thomas Tower), and George Tyrer (alderman of Liverpool).

Staff to the Trust

BENJAMIN MARTYN (1699–1763), Secretary. Served the trust from October 1732 until the charter was surrendered in June 1752; then served as agent for the Crown from February 1753 until 1763. Martyn authored several publications on the colony for the Trustees. Before he was retained by the Trustees, he authored a well-received tragedy, *Timolean*, in 1730, an effort supported by Pope; he and Pope also collaborated on an effort to erect a monument to Shakespeare. Martyn helped to found the Society for the Encouragement of Learning in 1736.

HARMAN VERELST, Accountant. Served the trust from August 1732 until the charter was surrendered in June 1752. He also served as secretary and accountant to the Bray Associates from 1735 to 1754 and was a frequent visitor to Percival and other trustees, often acting as a liaison and mediator.

WILLIAM STEPHENS (1671–1753), Secretary to the Trust in Georgia, later President of Trustee Georgia. Employed by the Trust from 1737 to 1750, when he retired to his estate near Savannah. Stephens was a dedicated employee, committed to the Trustees' plan for Georgia, although his son, Thomas, became a voice for the Malcontents. His journal provides a detailed record of daily life in the colony as well as the challenges of implementing the Oglethorpe Plan.

Advisors to the Trust

SIR JOSEPH JEKYLL (1663–1738). Master of the rolls in the House of Commons, advocate and financial supporter of the Georgia Colony, and political advisor to Oglethorpe and the Trustees. As master of the rolls he gave a final decree to the authority of the Bray

Associates. Oglethorpe named Jekyll Island for him. Jekyll shared a number of philosophical beliefs with Oglethorpe, including belief in freedom of religion, basic separation of church and state (without challenging the primacy of the Anglican Church), and the Tory value of a strong gentry.

JOHN PINE (1690–1756). An accomplished engraver who may have become involved with Oglethorpe and the Trustees through his friend William Hogarth, who painted the prison committee. He prepared the first conceptual map of the colony, illustrating many of its design principles; he may have prepared the more detailed plan for Savannah. Pine, like Hogarth, Oglethorpe, and several Trustees, was a Freemason. He studied his craft under Bernard Picart, who was associated with radical intellectuals in Holland. After his involvement with the Trustees, he prepared an update of the maps of London. Pine is believed by some researchers to have been of African ancestry. His son, Robert Pine, painted George II and Garrick before emigrating to America, where he painted Washington and other notable figures of the time.

SIR HANS SLOANE (1660–1753). Sloane, who succeeded Sir Isaac Newton as president of the Royal Society in 1727, was science advisor to Oglethorpe and the trustees as well as a benefactor. Like Newton, Oglethorpe, and several Trustees, he was a Freemason. Sloane was responsible for the innovation of the Trustees' Garden and retaining a botanist to acquire plants from various parts of the world to experiment on their viability in Georgia. While noted for his contributions to medicine and botany, he was also a dedicated humanitarian, rising early to treat the poor at no charge and others for fees affordable to their level of income. He served as president of the College of Physicians in London and as physician to Queen Anne and George II. He was founder of the British Museum, the Natural History Museum, and the British Library.

Notes

Abbreviations

CRG   Allen D. Candler et al., eds. *The Colonial Records of the State of Georgia.* Atlanta: Franklin, 1904–16 (vols. 1–19, 21–26); Athens: University of Georgia Press, 1976– (vols. 20, 27–).

DVP   *Manuscripts of the Earl of Egmont: Diary of Viscount Percival, Afterwards First Earl of Egmont,* 3 vols. (London: Historical Manuscripts Commission, 1920–23)

JEO   James Edward Oglethorpe

SCD   Savannah, City of, and Chatham County Documents

Prologue

1. Spalding, *Oglethorpe in America,* 72, 152, 156; Baine, *Creating Georgia,* xxiv.

2. This characterization of humanism is based on the definition in the *Oxford English Dictionary,* U.S. English online edition; the related concept of "civic humanism," emphasizes empowerment of citizens under a republican government.

3. Ettinger, *Imperial Idealist,* 10, identifies five generations of Oglethorpe family members loyally serving the crown through the mid-seventeenth century.

4. Ibid., 10–12.

5. Hill, *Oglethorpe Ladies,* 1–2; Ettinger, *Imperial Idealist,* 15–20.

6. Hill, *Oglethorpe Ladies,* 2; Ettinger, *Imperial Idealist,* 17–19.

7. Ettinger, *Imperial Idealist,* 22–23. Charles died before the rite of extreme unction was completed, remaining eternally in the Church of England.

8. Ibid., 23–28, 31–32.

9. Hill, *Oglethorpe Ladies,* 4.

10. William and Mary were thus first cousins.

11. Ettinger, *Imperial Idealist,* 31–32.

12. Dickson, *Financial Revolution,* 9.

13. James III relocated from Paris, as required by the pan-European Treaty of Utrecht of 1713, to Bar-le-Duc in Lorraine, then Avignon, Urbino in Italy, and finally Rome.

14. Hill, *Oglethorpe Ladies,* 8; Ettinger, *Imperial Idealist,* 32.

15. Ettinger, *Imperial Idealist,* 51, 53–54.

16. Hill, *Oglethorpe Ladies,* 16, 44; Lang, "Queen Oglethorpe." William Thackeray's novel *Henry Esmond* portrays Fanny Oglethorpe as "her Oglethorpean Majesty," mistress to James III.

17. Ettinger, *Imperial Idealist,* 52, 70, 72.

18. Ibid., 50, 70–71.

19. Hill, *Oglethorpe Ladies,* 32. Hill notes that Eleanor owned another residence in Paris, rented for a time by the British government, in which she found a letter from Lord Bolingbroke revealing complicity with the Whig oligarchy (58). See Kramnick, *Bolingbroke,* 1–2, for historians' views of Bolingbroke and ibid., 14–15, for his associates in Paris.

20. See Thomas, lecture, 2, on Oglethorpe's absence from Oxford.

21. Ettinger, *Brief Biography,* 8–9.

22. Thomas, lecture, 3. Oglethorpe joined Prince Eugene's forces as they took Petrovaradin and Timisoara in October 1716. He may have taken an interest in Roman ruins near those towns, and he had the opportunity to discuss Roman colonial planning and defenses with Eugene's sophisticated entourage of advisors.

23. Ettinger, *Imperial Idealist,* 73–74, quotation of correspondence from the Duke of Mar to Fanny Oglethorpe, February 19, 1718, on 74. For other information placing Oglethorpe in the area, see Rand, *Berkeley and Percival,* 130. Oglethorpe's defense of Bishop Francis Atterbury in the House of Commons, as discussed elsewhere, described Jacobitism as a failed cause.

24. Quoted in Ettinger, *Brief Biography,* 6. Victor Amadeus II was the Duke of Savoy and the King of Sicily when Oglethorpe was in Europe.

25. Ettinger, *Brief Biography,* 7–8. Also see Thomas, lecture, for an overview of Oglethorpe's history at Oxford; and Jacob, *Radical Enlightenment,* for Prince Eugene's impact on what she terms the "Radical Enlightenment."

26. Hill, *Oglethorpe Ladies,* 112.

27. The description of the incidents are based primarily on the assessment and cited materials in Ettinger, *Brief Biography,* 81–83.

28. Ettinger, *Imperial Idealist,* 86; Hill, *Oglethorpe Ladies,* 73; Doyle, *English in America,* 416. Doyle describes Oglethorpe as a "free lance" within Wyndham's country party.

29. Church, *Oglethorpe,* 5–8, 25–28; Ettinger, *Imperial Idealist,* 86–89.

30. Church, *Oglethorpe,* 12; see ibid., 12n18, for a list of committee members.

31. See Dickson, *Financial Revolution,* esp. 42, for an assessment of the era.

32. Ibid., 4–6, 41, 46, 52.

33. Ibid., 7n4.

34. Ibid., 26.

35. Ibid., 192.

36. Hill, *Oglethorpe Ladies,* 59–62.

37. Walpole and other ministers were appointed by the king, rather than by Parliament, to run the government; British political philosophy generally opposed concentration of power, and the concept of a "prime minister" was resisted until the twentieth century. Walpole was the first minister housed at 10 Downing Street, a reward provided by George I.

38. Richetti, *Cambridge History*, 5–6; Dowling, "Augustan England," 502. Robert Harley initiated the country party alliance ten years before the South Sea Bubble (see Fouke, *Philosophy and Theology*, 44), but the political realignment hardened in the 1720s.

39. Pocock, "Machiavelli," 122–24.

40. Porter, *Creation*, 188–89; Fries, *Urban Idea*, 144, 145–46.

41. See Thomas, lecture; JEO, "Library." Oglethorpe's lengthier writings were compiled by Baine in JEO, *Publications*.

42. Kramnick, *Bolingbroke*, 14–17, 19, 32–33, 261.

43. Quoted in Hill, *Oglethorpe Ladies*, 80. Percival's diary describes Oglethorpe's visits with Walpole in a way that suggests the two men were comfortable with each other, even after Percival had a falling out with the first minister (see *DVP*, 2:339–41 [February 6, 1737]).

44. Leapman, *Book of London*, 23.

45. Ibid., 22, 167.

46. *DVP*, 1:264 (April 29, 1732).

47. See Porter, *Creation*, for an account of the British Enlightenment and the vibrant scene in London in the 1720s.

48. Rand, *Shaftesbury*, xii; Douglas J. Den Uyl, foreword to Shaftesbury, *Characteristicks*, 1:vii.

49. Jacob, *Radical Enlightenment*, 109; Diane Clements, director of the Library and Museum of Freemasonry, London, e-mail message to author, March 9, 2005.

50. Hammond, *Pope and Bolingbroke*, 151.

51. Porter, *Creation*, 6, 24; Kramnick, *Bolingbroke*, 14.

52. Duddy, *Irish Thought*, 186.

53. Rand, *Shaftesbury*, 13, 19–20; Shaftesbury, *Characteristicks*, 1:23.

54. Fouke, *Philosophy and Theology*, 44–45.

55. See Jacob, *Radical Enlightenment*, 60–61, 118, 148, 164–66, 170, on the interrelationships among Pine, Toland, Prince Eugene's advisors, and others associated with the Radical Enlightenment; see Kramnick, *Bolingbroke*, 257–60, for the ideological relationship linking Harrington, Toland, and Bolingbroke.

56. Rivers, "Religion and Literature," 467; Krieger, *Kings and Philosophers*, 150.

57. Marissen, "Unsettling History," 24–30.

58. Jacob, *Radical Enlightenment*, 164–66; R. Stewart, *Robert Edge Pine*, 7; see "John Pine" on Pine's ancestry.

59. JEO, *Publications*, 362n26; JEO, *Some Account*, 33; Hunt, *Garden and Grove*, 195.

60. Paulson, *Hogarth*, 75. While the Augustan period is most closely associated with Pope and the middle Enlightenment, it is broadly defined to include the Age of Johnson, a span of time that corresponds closely to Oglethorpe's adult lifetime.

61. Kramnick, *Bolingbroke*, 206–7.

62. Pope, *Major Works*, 245.

63. Kramnick, *Bolingbroke*, 230.

64. Sichel, *Bolingbroke*, 247–54; Hammond, *Pope and Bolingbroke*, 41, 54–55; Kramnick, *Bolingbroke*, 163–69.

65. Rivers, "Religion and Literature," 467; C. Moore, "Shaftesbury," 281–85.

66. Kramnick, *Bolingbroke*, 195, quoting Defoe's *The True-Born Englishman*.

1. The Plan for a Model Colony

1. Oglethorpe estimated that ten thousand prisoners had been released as a result of his prison reform initiative. *DVP,* 1:90 (April 1, 1730). See Saye, "Genesis of Georgia," 198, for more on the estimated debtor population; also see Saye, "Was Georgia a Debtor Colony?" for an examination of the multipurpose nature of the colony.

2. Zurbuchen, "Republicanism and Toleration," 48, maintains that republicans (the principal component of the country party) after the Glorious Revolution became adept at cloaking themselves in conventional politics to gain broad public acceptance and government support. Oglethorpe appears to have adopted this practice.

3. Pitofsky, "Warden's Court Martial," 92–93.

4. Church, *Oglethorpe,* 17.

5. Baine, *Creating Georgia,* xv, xvii. Oglethorpe met with Thomas Bray in December 1729 to discuss the colonial venture and then formally approached Percival with the concept in February 1730.

6. Laugher, *Bray's Grand Design,* ix, 6.

7. Baine, *Creating Georgia,* xv.

8. See ibid. for comprehensive information on the chronology and minutes of the of the Bray Associates.

9. P. Taylor, *Georgia Plan,* 8.

10. *DVP,* 1:45–46 (February 13, 1730). Saye provides a conclusive analysis of the broadened scope of purposes behind the colony in "Was Georgia a Debtor Colony?"

11. *DVP,* 1:214 (January 12, 1732); Rand, *Berkeley and Percival,* 31.

12. *DVP,* 1:45, 214, 236 (February 13, 1730, January 12 and March 14, 1732); Reps, "Searching"; Berkeley and Wright, *Works,* 5. See Rand, *Berkeley and Percival,* for text of extensive correspondence. Berkeley met either Theophilus Oglethorpe or James Oglethorpe (see ibid., 130).

13. The present city of Berkeley acquired the name as it grew up around the Berkeley campus. The pronunciation differs from that of George Berkeley, where the first *e* is pronounced as a long *a.*

14. *DVP,* 1:90 (April 1, 1730).

15. Baine, *Creating Georgia,* 12, 15. The master of the rolls and records of the Chancery of England is the senior judge after the lord chief justice.

16. *DVP,* 1:227 (February 25, 1732); Ettinger, *Imperial Idealist,* 118.

17. Doyle, *English in America,* 5:417–18.

18. *CRG,* 1:65 (July 20, 1732).

19. Ibid., 1:11.

20. Ibid., 1:12.

21. Ibid., 1:18.

22. Ibid., 1:21.

23. JEO, *Publications,* 159, 167, 200–201. Baine, the editor of *Publications,* substantiated JEO's authorship after a review of an original found in the Tampa-Hillsborough Public Library in Tampa, Florida. Also see Baine and Spalding's introduction to JEO, *Some Account,* especially xx–xxii, for discussion of early Trustee publications.

24. *DVP,* 1:301 (December 1, 1732).

25. Ibid., 1:293 (October 18, 1732). The Trustees were presumed to govern the colony

in lieu of a royal governor; thus Oglethorpe did not hold that position in a formal capacity.

26. JEO, *Publications*, 174–83.

27. *DVP*, 1:45–46 (February 13, 1730).

28. JEO, *Some Account*, 11.

29. JEO, *Publications*, 164–65.

30. Ibid., 167–68.

31. Ibid., 219.

32. Lane, *Colonial Letters*, 2:414 (July 4, 1739); F. Moore, *Voyage*, 22; Bearcroft quoted in Fries, *Urban Idea*, 143.

33. Shaftesbury, *Characteristicks*.

34. Pine's cartographic skills were put to work again soon after his work on the Georgia plan in his collaboration with cartographer Jean Roque to produce the most detailed map of London of the time, a project begun in 1735.

35. Martyn, *Some Account*.

36. *DVP*, 2:41 (March 3, 1734). James Vernon complained to Percival that several younger members had a scheme for the colony that took precedence over the "religious part of our designs." They included George Heathcote, Robert Hucks, Robert More, Thomas Towers, and John White; Vernon was also concerned that Benjamin Martyn, their secretary, was among the group.

37. Ibid., 2:41–43, 200 (March 3, 1734, October 7, 1735).

38. Ibid., 2:233 (February 11, 1736); *CRG*, 1:252 (May 5, 1736), 276 (March 17, 1737).

39. *DVP* 2:235, 237–38, 252, 268–69 (February 19–May 4, 1736).

40. Burton, "Duty and Reward," 30. Kramnick discusses *ritorno ai principii* in *Bolingbroke*, 147. John Najemy, in a personal communication to the author, suggested *ridurre* in place of *ritorno*.

41. JEO, *Publications*, 165.

42. Pocock, in "Machiavelli," 130, refers to Harrington's theory as the "doctrine of the agrarian."

43. JEO, *Publications*, 174–75, 180, 182.

44. The Turner thesis maintains that American national character was forged in its westward expansion. Machiavelli's concepts of *ridurre ai principii* and *translatio virtutis*, the restoration of original principles and the geographic migration of virtue, likely would have made an impression on Oglethorpe, as did Machiavelli's principles of settlement cited in Oglethorpe's promotional materials. See JEO, "Library," for related holdings in his library. Bolingbroke began publishing initial ideas about *ridurre ai principii* and a Patriot King who would bring it about in *The Craftsman* in the late 1720s. See Fries, *Urban Idea*, 138, for an analysis of the Trustees' intention to "cleanse the city of economic dislocations and political corruption by reintegrating the city with the country into a social whole."

45. *DVP*, 1:303, 370 (December 1, 1732, April 30, 1733).

46. *CRG*, 1:292 (July 13, 1737).

47. JEO, *Publications*, 178–79, 180.

48. Stephens, *Journal*, 1:308 (October 22, 1738).

49. Tail-male inheritance, where property passes to the son or sons, is found in

traditional English law; it was official policy of the Trustees as a means of preventing amassing of land. However, the Trustees made it clear that they would consider female inheritance on a case-by-case basis where it could be shown that property holdings would not be increased beyond the maximum allowed through marriage.

50. See Sweet, "Thirteenth Colony," on the views of historians (a subject taken up further in chapter 3).

2. The Plan for an Ideal City

1. Pope, *Essay on Man,* epistle 1, in *Major Works,* 280.

2. Such a rendering is also termed a "bird's-eye view" map.

3. F. Moore, *Voyage,* 22.

4. Ibid., 22–23.

5. The map was published by Tobias Conrad Lotter (1717–1777), a German cartographer. Various sources date the map between 1735 and 1740. Joseph Avery, a colonist who arrived in Georgia in 1737, has been named by several sources as having prepared the original sketch. See De Vorsey's discussion in Spalding and Jackson, 41–42, on its origin. Stephens recorded in his journal on February 20, 1737 (O.S.), 1:115, that the surveyor Noble Jones was directed to modify the plan by creating half-mile grid sections near rivers.

6. Home, *Of Planting and Planning,* 9.

7. JEO, *Some Account,* 24, 33–36; JEO, *Publications,* 174–82.

8. Burton, "Duty and Reward," 26.

9. *DVP,* 2:36–38 (February 27, 1734); F. Moore, *Voyage,* 22.

10. *CRG,* 31:58 (March 16, 1747); Garrison, *Oglethorpe's Folly,* 75; *DVP,* 1:264 (April 29, 1732), see prologue to the present volume for the complete passage; Porter, *Creation,* 306. Also see Ettinger, *Imperial Idealist,* 142–43, regarding earlier correspondence envisioning a metropolis. Burton's "Duty and Reward," sermon speaks of a "change of an uncultivated desert into a fruitful garden" (27).

11. For a discussion of the Savannah plan's genesis, see Bacon, *Design,* 217; Bannister, "Oglethorpe's Sources"; Bell, "New Theory"; Reps, *Urban America;* Reps, "$C^2 + L^2 = S^2$."

12. Home, *Of Planting and Planning,* 9; Reps, "$C^2 + L^2 = S^2$," 116.

13. JEO, *Publications,* 362n26; Thomas, lecture, 11.

14. Malgrave, *Architectural Theory,* 98–102, 232–41.

15. Bacon, *Design,* 217; Zucker, *Town and Square,* 99–108.

16. Kostof, *City Shaped,* 128. Also see Avalon Project, "Agrarian Law."

17. Kostof, *City Shaped,* 165–66; Zucker, *Town and Square,* 46–48.

18. Reps, "$C^2 + L^2 = S^2$," 113–15; Zucker, *Town and Square,* 250. Oglethorpe may have also seen remnants of Roman castra in Britain.

19. JEO, *Some Account,* 38.

20. Ibid., 40.

21. Reps, *Urban America,* 187.

22. JEO, *Some Account,* 36. Also see F. Moore, *Voyage,* 19–20; Lawrence, "Greening," 100.

23. For a discussion of these plans see Sears, *First One Hundred Years.*

24. Reps, "$C^2 + L^2 = S^2$," 101–51; Reps, "Searching." For Oglethorpe's visits to Turin see Ettinger, *Imperial Idealist,* 73–74, 77; and Bruce, *General Oglethorpe,* 15, 19.

25. Martyn, *Some Account.* See Avalon Project, "Agrarian Law," and Avalon Project, "Julian Law," for Roman law on common land and right-of-way.

26. Reps, "$C^2 + L^2 = S^2$," 114–20.

27. See Sweet, "Misguided Mistake."

28. Bell, "New Theory," 149.

29. JEO, *Some Account,* 39.

30. F. Moore, *Voyage,* 25; Leapman, *Book of London,* 165.

31. JEO, *Some Account,* 38. The source of the radial plan remains uncertain; it may have been adapted the from an ancient Saxon settlement pattern.

32. Ibid., 30, 38.

33. P. Taylor, "Statistical Note."

34. Ibid. See P. Taylor, *Georgia Plan,* for further analysis.

35. See Reinberger, "Oglethorpe's Plan," citing Reps, *Urban America;* Newton, *A Dissertation.*

36. Reinberger, "Oglethorpe's Plan," 850; Fries, *Urban Idea,* 28; Anderson, "Savannah and the Issue of Precedent," 115; Reps, "$C^2 + L^2 = S^2$," 138; Bacon, *Design,* 220. Also see Anderson, "The Plan of Savannah," 63, 65; Lawrence, "Greening," 112; and Kostof, *City Shaped,* 96.

37. See Anderson, "Ecological Model."

3. Implementation of the Plan

1. "Peter Gordon's Journal," in Cashin, *Setting Out,* 34–35.

2. Burton, "Duty and Reward," 26.

3. Lane, *Colonial Letters,* 1:16–17 (June 9, 1733); "Peter Gordon's Journal," in Cashin, *Setting Out,* 34.

4. Lane, *Colonial Letters,* 1:7 (March 12, 1733).

5. Ibid., 1:19 (August 12, 1733). See Sweet, "Evil Rum," for a thorough discussion of the consumption and regulation of rum in the colony.

6. Reiss, *Jews in Colonial America,* 77–79; Church, *Oglethorpe,* 234–35; Levy, "Early History," 166–67; Bruce, *General Oglethorpe,* 126–27; Ettinger, *Imperial Idealist,* 137.

7. Lane, *Colonial Letters,* 1:27, 29–30 (December 1733).

8. *DVP,* 2:111–12 (June 19, 1734).

9. Ettinger, *Imperial Idealist,* 144–45.

10. Lane, *Colonial Letters,* 1:48 (September 3, 1734).

11. *CRG,* 2:96 (April 23, 1735).

12. Sweet, *Negotiating for Georgia,* 87–90; Ettinger, *Imperial Idealist,* 161–64; McConnell, 41–43.

13. Lane, *Colonial Letters,* 1:275–76 (June 1736).

14. Ibid., 1:256 (March 24, 1736).

15. *DVP,* 2:252–53, 281–83 (March 31 and June 16, 1736).

16. Lane, *Colonial Letters,* 1:285 (November 26, 1736).

17. *DVP,* 2:326–27 (January 9, 1737).

18. Ibid.

19. Ibid., 2:460–61, 465–66 (January 11 and February 8, 1738).

20. Stephens, *Journal,* 2:410, 388. Also see ibid., 1::17–8, 26, 57, 134–35, 346–47, 383, 401, 424, 443–44, 2:217, 326, 378–79, 416–17, 474–75, 476–78, 491, 498.

21. Lane, *Colonial Letters,* 2:350 (October 3, 1738).

22. Stephens, *Journal,* 1:304–12 (October 10–24, 1738).

23. Lane, *Colonial Letters,* 2:374 (December 9, 1738).

24. *DVP,* 3:53–56 (April 29, 1739).

25. *CRG,* 1:367 (March 5, 1740); Reese, *Clamorous Malcontents,* 23–121.

26. *DVP,* 3:105 (January 30, 1740).

27. Ibid., 3:252 (June 24, 1742).

28. Lane, *Colonial Letters,* 2:389–90 (January 17, 1739); Stephens, *Journal,* 1:380 (January 13, 1738); *CRG,* 1:431–32 (October 12, 1743).

29. Stephens, *Journal,* 1:61 (December 15, 1737), 152 (March 15, 1738), 2:380 (May 21, 1740), 388 (May 29, 1740); Lane, *Colonial Letters,* 2:477 (September 18, 1740).

30. Mereness, *Travels,* 215–36; Stephens, *Journal,* 1:67, 142–43.

31. *CRG,* vol. 2:367 (April 15, 1741).

32. Mellon, "Christian Priber's Cherokee 'Kingdom,'" 319–23.

33. Stephens, *Journal,* 2:474–75 (August 14, 1740).

34. *CRG,* 31:41 (July 18, 1746).

35. Ibid., 2:497 (May 29, 1749).

36. Ibid., 2:504 (April 11, 1750), and 2:56–57 (May 6, 1751).

37. Ibid., 1:531–32 (May 17, 1749).

38. Lane, *Colonial Letters,* 1:292 (February 10, 1737).

39. Ibid., 1:119 (January 27, 1735), 83 (January 1, 1735).

40. P. Taylor, *Georgia Plan,* 108–9.

41. See ibid., esp. 89–98, for a detailed analysis of the labor issue.

42. See *DVP,* 1:309 (January 17, 1733).

43. Lane, *Colonial Letters,* 1:249 (March 6, 1736).

44. Ibid., 1:275 (June 1736).

45. Ibid., 1:161 (April 25, 1735).

46. Ibid., 1:164–65 (May 7, 1735).

47. Stephens, *Journal,* 1:304–12 (October 10–24, 1738), 325–27 (November 11, 1738), 346–47 (December 5, 1738), 413 February 21, 1739), 428–35 (March 5–10, 1739), 2:141–82 (September 21–November 5, 1739).

48. Ettinger, *Imperial Idealist,* 131; Spalding, "Oglethorpe's Quest," 7; *DVP,* 1:304 (December 28, 1732).

49. See, for example, Stephens, *Journal,* 1:132–33 (March 7, 1738), 263–64 (August 15, 1738), 2:48, 54, 56, 58 (June 21–July 4, 1739)23 (November 15, 1737). The National Oceanic and Atmospheric Administration's National Climatic Data Center maintains historical records for temperature and rainfall. A review of the data suggests greater variability in coastal Georgia and South Carolina than in more northern areas that were formerly colonies.

50. Ibid., 1:221–24 (June 5–20, 1738), 310–11 (October 23–24, 1738), 2:141 (September 21, 1739).

51. Ibid., 1:253–54 (August 2, 1738), 263–64 (August 15, 1738), 2:23 (May 25–26, 1739), 75 (July 27, 1739), 494–95 (September 2, 1740), 505 (October 1, 1740).

52. M. Stewart, *What Nature Suffers*, 140; Russell, "United States and Malaria," 624, 647; G. M. Jeffery, Sc.D., U.S. Public Health Service, retired, personal communication with the author, January 21, 2011.

53. M. Stewart, *What Nature Suffers*, 21, 28.

54. Ibid., 72–77, 80. See JEO, *Some Account*, 15–22, for a discussion of environment.

55. See Sweet, *Negotiating Georgia*, for a thorough assessment of relations between the Trustees and the Indian nations.

56. See Stephens, *Journal*, 2:107, 219 (August 26 and December 19, 1739) on alarm over the French.

57. Morgan, *Slave Counterpoint*, 95–96, 386; Sweet, *Stephens*, 100.

58. *CRG*, 21:184 (October 26, 1749).

59. Lane, *Colonial Letters*, 1:225 (August 27, 1735). Morgan, *Slave Counterpoint*, 134–38, shows that slaves were actually dependent on plantation owners for meager allocations of grains and vegetables but were able to hunt abundant fish and game.

60. Stephens, *Journal*, 2:416–17 (July 7, 1740).

61. Lane, *Colonial Letters*, 2:477–78 (September 18, 1740). See Reese, *Colonial Georgia*, and Lannen, "Liberty and Authority," for alternative assessments of the Malcontents.

62. Lane, *Colonial Letters*, 1:225–26 (August 27, 1735).

63. Ibid., 2:555 (February 19, 1741).

64. Ibid., 2:397–99 (March 13, 1739); *CRG*, 25:288–89 (May 3, 1748).

65. See *DVP*, 3:55–70 (April 29–June 19, 1739), for discussion of opposition.

66. Lane, *Colonial Letters*, 2:389 (January 17, 1739).

67. *CRG*, 31:56–57 (March 16, 1747); see also ibid., 1:506–7 (March 17, 1747).

68. Ibid., 1:530–31 (May 16, 1749).

69. Sweet, "Misguided Mistake," 28–29; Sweet, "Thirteenth Colony," 29. See Sweet, "Thirteenth Colony," for an overview of historians' conclusions.

70. Reese, *Colonial Georgia*, 43; M. Stewart, *What Nature Suffers*, 86; Lannen, "Liberty and Authority," 190.

71. P. Taylor, *Georgia Plan*, 296.

72. Fries, *Urban Idea*, 139.

73. P. Taylor, *Georgia Plan*, 207, citing *CRG*, 5:636–37. Taylor's chapter 6 provides a detailed discussion of the parliamentary debate.

4. The Plan Today

1. SCD, *Tricentennial Plan*, vol. 2, *Community Assessment*, 8.3, and vol. 3, *Community Agenda*, 5.5.

2. SCD, *Tricentennial Plan*, vol. 2, *Community Assessment*, 8.3.5.

3. In 2009 there were 4,135 hotel rooms. Joseph Marinelli, president, Savannah Area Convention and Visitors Bureau, e-mail to the author, December 14, 2009.

4. The City of Savannah continued to designate areas as wards as it expanded in a grid pattern. The term "subdivision" replaced "ward" with suburban development.

5. Sieg, *Squares*, 29.

6. SCD, *Tricentennial Plan*, vol. 3, *Community Agenda*, 2.2, 5.5, and vol. 2, *Community Assessment*, 5.4.

7. *Savannah Morning News*, editorial, February 6, 1956.

8. SCD, Golden Heritage Plan; Polster, "Golden Heritage Plan."

9. Christian Sottile, personal communication with the author, August 28, 2010.

10. SCD, Historic District Ordinance.

11. SCD, *Tricentennial Plan*, vol. 3, *Community Agenda*, 2.2 (F).

12. SCD, Civic Master Plan.

13. SCD, Historic District Ordinance.

14. Two "gated community" plans submitted to the Metropolitan Planning Commission in 2006 were reviewed by the author.

15. SCD, *Tricentennial Plan*, vol. 3, *Community Agenda*, 4.1.1, and vol. 2, *Community Assessment*, 5.6.1.

16. Johnson, "Two Savannahs."

17. The 330-foot width is based on reverse engineering described in chapter 2.

18. The acquisition was recommended by a transportation planning initiative called Connecting Savannah.

19. Sears, *First One Hundred Years*, 39–40.

20. Ibid., 14–17, 160.

21. Lane, *Colonial Letters*, 1:238 (February 1, 1736).

22. Ibid., 1:252 (March 16, 1736), 254 (March 24, 1736).

23. *DVP*, 3:91 (November 16, 1739); Stephens, *Journal*, 1:3 (October 21, 1737).

24. Sears, *First One Hundred Years*, 44–49.

25. Home, *Of Planting and Planning*, 25–29.

5. The Future of the Plan

1. See the epilogue to Spalding, *Oglethorpe in America*, for a view of how the Georgia Colony might have flourished under a modified form of the Oglethorpe Plan.

2. Zucker, *Town and Square*, 242; Bacon, *Design*, 219; A. Jacobs, *Great Streets*, 255–56; Reps, "C² + L² = S²," 101. See Bell, "New Theory," for more quotes.

3. The term "paradigm" was introduced by Thomas Kuhn in *The Structure of Scientific Revolutions* (originally published in 1962) and defined as "universally recognized scientific achievements that for a time provide model problems and solutions to a community of practitioners" (x).

4. Nelson, "Leadership," 393; Aoki, "Race, Space, and Place," 16.

5. Aoki, "Race, Space, and Place," 2–16.

6. SCD, "Golden Heritage Plan"; SCD, *Tricentennial Plan*, vol. 2, *Community Assessment*, chapter 5. The terms "overcrowding" and "blight" remain in use to justify urban renewal projects in many state planning, zoning, and redevelopment enabling laws.

7. Aoki, "Race, Space, and Place," 53–55.

8. See DeGrove, *Planning Policy and Politics*, for a comprehensive analysis.

9. United Nations, *Our Common Future*; United Nations, "Rio Declaration."

10. Montenegro, "Urban Resilience," 1, 3.

11. New practices include the form-based code (including the Duany Plater-Zyberk SmartCode), the transect model, the LEED-ND (Leadership in Energy and Environmental Design for Neighborhood Development) system, and the Light Imprint Initiative for resource stewardship.

12. Kuhn, *Structure*, 79.

13. American Institute of Certified Planners Code of Ethics, http://www.planning
.org/ethics/ethicscode.htm; Briggs, *Democracy,* 50–56, 314.

14. The author was planning director for Beaufort County and supervised adoption of its first comprehensive plan and implementing zoning ordinance in 1997 and 1998, respectively.

15. Daufuskie Island Code, http://www.bcgov.net/about-beaufort-county/public
-service/planning/Daufuskie-Island-Code.php.

16. Lindsay, "New Urbanism"; Sherman, "GSD Throwdown"; Langdon, review of *Urbanism;* Montenegro, "Urban Resilience," 1.

17. Kimble, "Suburban Living"; Bundoran Farm website, http://www.bundoranfarm
.com; Moffat, "New Ruralism," 73.

18. The widely cited Kyoto Protocol, for example, calls for international recognition of human effects on global warming and prescribes a set of national and local actions to prevent global catastrophe. A national protocol for energy independence is emerging in the United States, based on a new consensus that petroleum dependence is a threat to national security. This incipient national protocol is mirrored at the local level in recent support (viewed as patriotic) for efficient land-use planning, development of public transit, and energy-efficient construction (notably the Leadership in Energy and Environmental Design program).

19. See Levitt, "Landscape Scale Conservation," for an interdisciplinary perspective.

20. Schweitzer and Knox, "Determinism Redux," 15.

21. The author served as an advisor to the committee.

22. Ryle, *Concept of Mind,* 15–23.

23. Ibid., 76.

24. Ibid., 77.

25. Mehaffy et al., "Urban Nuclei," 41–43.

26. See the *Chatham County–Savannah Tricentennial Plan* Land Use and Housing elements; the Savannah Downtown Master Plan; and Mayor Otis Johnson's issue paper "Two Savannahs."

27. Duany, Plater-Zyberk, and Speck, *Suburban Nation,* 15–17 and chapter 6; Calthorpe, *Next American Metropolis,* 62–71; Duany and Plater-Zyberk, SmartCode.

28. The half-mile rule of thumb is often associated with transit-oriented development, a form of New Urbanism. The central area in a ward is two acres, with half forming the square and half used for right-of-way.

29. As discussed in chapter 2, Oglethorpe did not intend for Savannah (or other towns in the Georgia Colony) to grow beyond six wards; the discussion here refers to the modern context of the plan.

30. Deutscher, "You Are What You Speak," 45. Also see earlier work on geographic orientation by Yi-Fu Tuan.

31. Baker, "Why Don't We?" 4; Garrick, "Care to Share?" 1; Hamilton-Baillie, "Toward Shared Space," 133.

32. Montenegro, "Urban Resilience," 1–3.

33. See J. Jacobs, *Death and Life,* for an analysis of neighborhood attributes.

34. Ibid., 128–29, 150–51.

35. Ibid., 50–54; Lehrer, "Physicist," 50. Oglethorpe wrote to Percival, "And there is

no true way of civilizing a country without communications." Lane, *Colonial Letters,* 1:238 (February 1, 1736).

36. SCD, *Tricentennial Plan,* vol. 3, *Community Agenda;* SCD, Thomas Square Streetcar Historic District Neighborhood Plan and implementing zoning regulations.

37. The point is made quite effectively in Mayor Otis Johnson's "Two Savannahs" position paper and reiterated in the 2006 *Tricentennial Plan.*

Epilogue

1. C. Moore, "Shaftesbury," 319, discusses the influence of Shaftesbury and Bolingbroke in the context of the ethical poets of the century.

2. Porter, *Creation,* 48; Paine's quote is found in the "appendix" to the third edition of *Common Sense,* available at http://www.ushistory.org/paine/commonsense/sense6.htm.

3. Becker, in *Heavenly City,* 83–88, describes the Enlightenment as advancing from a theoretical to a practical orientation.

4. Wills, *Inventing America,* 172–73, 175; McCullough, *1776,* 22; Middlekauff, *Glorious Cause,* 52, 137.

5. Quoted in Krall, "Jefferson's Agrarian Vision," 134.

6. Quoted in ibid., 139.

7. Ibid., 136. Sweet in *Negotiating for Georgia* provides a portrait of Oglethorpe's honorable relationship with indigenous Americans.

8. Greenspan, *Age of Turbulence,* 470–72; Katz, Muro, and Bradley, "Miracle Mets," 34–35.

9. Fries, *Urban Idea,* xiv. Wills, *Inventing America,* 365–68, describes Jefferson's vision for America as a Newtonian model. Turner published *The Frontier in American History* for presentation to the American Historical Association in 1893.

10. Lane, *Colonial Letters,* 2:389–90 (January 17, 1739); Ettinger, *Brief Biography,* xviii.

11. Bruce, *General Oglethorpe,* 132–37. See Bluett, *Life of Job,* and F. Moore, *Travels,* for accounts of Job's life.

12. Benjamin Martyn to the President and Assistants, March 16, 1747, Martyn to William Stephens, July 17, 1747, Harman Verelst to the President and Assistants, May 28, 1748, and Martyn to the President and Assistants, May 19, 1749, in *CRG,* 31:62, 79, 94, 134.

13. Ettinger, *Imperial Idealist,* 258–59.

14. Ibid., 263.

15. Church, *Oglethorpe,* 295–98; Ettinger, *Imperial Idealist,* 269–70; Baine and Williams, "Oglethorpe in Europe," 116–17. See Monod, *Jacobitism,* 34, 83–84, 231 on Jacobite ties.

16. Quoted in Bruce, *General Oglethorpe,* 242.

17. Monod, "Dangerous Merchandise," 158, 178; Monod, *Jacobitism,* 34, 231.

18. Baine and Williams, "Oglethorpe in Europe," 117.

19. Krieger, *Kings and Philosophers,* 251; Gay, *Enlightenment,* 490; Durant and Durant, *Age of Voltaire,* 402, 442–46.

20. Baine and Williams, "Oglethorpe in Europe," 117–18.

21. Ibid., 119, 121.

22. Ibid., 119–21.

23. Henderson, *Eugen,* ix (the other five were Alexander the Great, Hannibal, Caesar, Gustavus Adolphus, and Turenne); Williams, "Oglethorpe's Literary Friendships," 109; Boswell, "Fables."

24. Quoted in Ettinger, *Imperial Idealist,* 318, 324–25.

25. Ibid., 296, 302, 306.

26. Williams, "Oglethorpe's Literary Friendships," 101; Boswell, *Life,* 2:350n2, 586.

27. W. Roberts, *Hannah More,* 22.

28. Boswell Collection, M 208:1, M 208:2; Williams, "Oglethorpe's Literary Friendships," 52.

29. Boswell, *Life;* Williams, "Oglethorpe's Literary Friendships," 39; *OED,* online edition, http://www.oed.com/.

30. Janek and Toulmin, *Wittgenstein's Vienna,* 9, 32; Ettinger, *Imperial Idealist,* 291.

31. Kendall, *David Garrick,* 31, 35.

32. W. Roberts, *Hannah More,* 18–19.

33. Ibid., 130–31.

34. Ettinger, *Imperial Idealist,* 311, 321–22; W. Roberts, *Hannah More,* 22.

35. T. Taylor, *Hannah More,* 78–80.

36. Stuart, *Granville Sharp,* 5–6.

37. Ibid., 7–8.

38. Ibid., 14.

39. Hoare, *Granville Sharp,* 2:231–45, 267.

40. Stuart, *Granville Sharp,* 35–38, 42; Home, *Of Planting and Planning,* 23–26.

41. Hoare, *Granville Sharp,* 1:234–37.

42. Ettinger, *Imperial Idealist,* 326.

Bibliography

Anderson, Stanford. "The Plan of Savannah and Changes of Occupancy during Its Early Years: City Plan as Resource." *Harvard Architecture Review* 2 (1981): 60–67.

———. "Savannah and the Issue of Precedent: City Plan as Resource." In *Settlements in the Americas: Cross-Cultural Perspectives,* edited by Ralph Bennett, 110–44. Newark: University of Delaware Press; London: Associated University Presses, 1993.

———. "Studies toward an Ecological Model of the Urban Environment." In *On Streets,* edited by Stanford Anderson, 267–307. Cambridge: MIT Press, 1978.

Aoki, Keith. "Race, Space, and Place: The Relation between Architectural Modernism, Post-Modernism, Urban Planning, and Gentrification." 20 *Fordham Urban Law Journal* 699 (1993).

Avalon Project. "Agrarian Law; 111 b.c.." Yale Law School, Lillian Goldman Law Library. http://avalon.law.yale.edu/ancient/agrarian_law.asp.

———. "Julian Law on Agrarian Matters, 58(?) b.c.." Yale Law School, Lillian Goldman Law Library. http://avalon.law.yale.edu/ancient/Julian_agrarian.asp.

Bacon, Edmund N. *Design of Cities.* New York: Penguin Books, 1974.

Baine, Rodney M., ed. *Creating Georgia: Minutes of the Bray Associates & Supplementary Documents, 1730–1732.* Athens: University of Georgia Press, 1995.

Baine, Rodney M., and Mary E. Williams. "James Oglethorpe in Europe: Recent Findings in His Military Life." In *Oglethorpe in Perspective: Georgia's Founder after Two Hundred Years,* edited by Phinizy Spalding and Harvey H. Jackson, 112–21. Tuscaloosa: University of Alabama Press, 1989.

Baker, Linda. "Why Don't We Do It in the Road?" Salon.com, May 20, 2004. http://entertainment.salon.com/2004/05/20/traffic_design/.

Bannister, Turpin C. "Oglethorpe's Sources for the Savannah Plan." *Journal of the Society of Architectural Historians* 20, no. 2 (May 1961): 47–62.

Becker, Carl L. *The Declaration of Independence: A Study in the History of Political Ideas.* New York: Vintage Books, 1958.

———. *The Heavenly City of the Eighteenth-Century Philosophers.* New Haven, CT: Yale University Press, 1932.

Bell, Laura Palmer. "A New Theory on the Plan of Savannah." *Georgia Historical Quarterly* 48, no. 2 (June 1964): 147–65.

Berkeley, George, and G. N. Wright. *The Works of George Berkeley, D.D.* Vol. 1. London: Thomas Tegg, 1843. Reprint, Whitefish, MT: Kessinger, n.d.

Bluett, Thomas. *Some Memoirs of the Life of Job, the Son of Solomon the High Priest of Boonda in Africa.* London: Printed for R. Ford, 1734.

Boswell, James. *Boswell's Life of Johnson.* 2 vols. London: Henry Frowde, 1904.

———. "Oglethorpe's Fables." Boswell Collection, Yale University. M 208:1 and M 208:2.

Briggs, Xavier de Souza. *Democracy as Problem Solving: Civic Capacity in Communities across the Globe.* Cambridge, MA: MIT Press, 2008.

Brooks, E. St. John. *Sir Hans Sloane: The Great Collector and His Circle.* London: Batchworth, 1954.

Bruce, Henry. *Life of General Oglethorpe.* New York: Dodd, Mead, 1890.

Burton, John. "The Duty and Reward of Propagating Principles of Religion and Virtue exemplified in the History of Abraham: A Sermon Preach'd before the Trustees for Establishing the Colony of Georgia in America." Sermon delivered at the first anniversary meeting of the Trustees. March 15, 1732 (O.S.). Gale Digital Collections, Eighteenth Century Collections Online. Originally published London: Mount and Page, 1733.

Calthorpe, Peter. *The Next American Metropolis: Ecology, Community, and the American Dream.* New York: Princeton Architectural Press, 1993.

———. *Urbanism in the Age of Climate Change.* Washington, DC: Island, 2011.

Candler, Allen D., et al., eds. *The Colonial Records of the State of Georgia.* Atlanta: Franklin, 1904–16 (vols. 1–19, 21–26); Athens: University of Georgia Press, 1976–89 (vols. 20, 27–32).

Cashin, Edward J. "Glimpses of Oglethorpe in Boswell's Life of Johnson." *Georgia Historical Quarterly* 88, no. 3 (Fall 2004): 398–405.

———, ed. *Setting Out to Begin a New World: Colonial Georgia, a Documentary History.* Savannah: Beehive, 1995.

Church, Leslie F. *Oglethorpe: A Study of Philanthropy in England and Georgia.* London: Epworth, 1932.

Coleman, Kenneth. *Colonial Georgia: A History.* New York: Charles Scribner's Sons, 1976.

Coulter, E. Merton, ed. *The Journal of William Stephens.* 2 vols. Athens: University of Georgia Press, 1958.

Crane, Verner W. "Dr. Thomas Bray and the Charitable Colony Project, 1730." *William and Mary Quarterly*, 3rd ser., 19 (January 1962): 49–63.

———. "The Philanthropists and the Genesis of Georgia." *American Historical Review* 27, no. 1 (October 1921): 63–69.

DeGrove, John. *Planning Policy and Politics: Smart Growth and the States.* Cambridge, MA: Lincoln Institute of Land Policy, 2005.

Deutscher, Guy. "You Are What You Speak." *New York Times Magazine*, August 29, 2010, 42–47.

De Vorsey, Louis, Jr. *The Georgia–South Carolina Boundary: A Problem in Historical Geography.* Athens: University of Georgia Press, 1982.

———. "Oglethorpe and the Earliest Maps of Georgia." In *Oglethorpe in Perspective: Georgia's Founder after Two Hundred Years,* edited by Phinizy Spalding and Harvey H. Jackson, 22–43. Tuscaloosa: University of Alabama Press, 1989.

Dickson, P. G. M. *The Financial Revolution in England: A Study in the Development of Public Credit, 1688–1756.* New York: St. Martin's, 1967.

Dowling, William C. "Augustan England and British America." In *The Cambridge History of English Literature, 1660–1780,* edited by John Richetti, 498–523. Cambridge: Cambridge University Press, 2005.

Doyle, John A. *The Colonies under the House of Hanover.* Vol. 5 of *The English in America.* New York: AMS Press, 1969.

Duany, Andres, and Elizabeth Plater-Zyberk. SmartCode. Miami: Duany Plater-Zyberk, 2003.

Duany, Andres, Elizabeth Plater-Zyberk, and Jeff Speck. *Suburban Nation: The Rise of Sprawl and the Decline of the American Dream.* New York: North Point, 2000.

Duddy, Thomas. *A History of Irish Thought.* London: Routledge, 2002.

Dunn, Richard S. "The Trustees of Georgia and the House of Commons, 1732–1752." *William and Mary Quarterly,* 3rd ser., 11 (October 1954): 551–65.

Durant, Will, and Ariel Durant. *The Age of Voltaire.* New York: Simon & Schuster, 1965.

Ettinger, Amos Aschbach. *James Edward Oglethorpe: Imperial Idealist.* Oxford: Clarendon, 1936. Reprint, Hamden, CT: Archon Books, 1968.

———. *Oglethorpe: A Brief Biography.* Edited by Phinizy Spalding. Macon, GA: Mercer University Press, 1984.

Force, Peter. *Tracts and Other Papers Relating to the Origin, Settlement, and Progress of the Colonies in North America from the Discovery of the Country to the Year 1776.* Vol. 2. Washington: printed by author, 1838.

Fouke, Daniel C. *Philosophy and Theology in a Burlesque Mode: John Toland and "The Way of Paradox."* New York: Humanity Books, 2007.

Fries, Sylvia Doughty. *The Urban Idea in Colonial America.* Philadelphia: Temple University Press, 1977.

Garrick, Norman W. "Care to Share?" *Roads & Bridges* 42, no. 9 (August 2005). http://www.roadsbridges.com/Care-to-Share-article6270August.

Garrison, Webb. *Oglethorpe's Folly: The Birth of Georgia.* Lakemont, GA: Copple House Books, 1982.

Gay, Peter. *The Enlightenment: An Interpretation.* Vol. 2, *The Science of Freedom.* New York: W. W. Norton, 1969.

Greenspan, Alan. *The Age of Turbulence: Adventures in a New World.* New York: Penguin, 2007.

Hamilton-Baillie, Ben. "Shared Space: Reconciling People, Places and Traffic." *Built Environment* 34 (2): 161–81.

———. "Towards Shared Space." *Urban Design International* 13 (2008): 130–38.

Hammond, Brean S. *Pope and Bolingbroke: A Study of Friendship and Influence.* Columbia: University of Missouri Press, 1984.

Harrington, James. *The Commonwealth of Oceana.* 1656. Reprint, Tutis Digital, 2008.

Harris, Thaddeus Mason. *Biographical Memorials of James Oglethorpe, Founder of the Colony of Georgia, in North America.* 1841. Reprint, Whitefish, MT: Kessinger, n.d.

Harvey, David. "The New Urbanism and the Communitarian Trap." *Harvard Design Magazine,* Winter/Spring 1997, 68–69.

Henderson, Nicholas. *Prince Eugen of Savoy.* New York: Frederick A. Praeger, 1965.

Hertzler, James R. "Slavery in the Yearly Sermons before the Georgia Trustees." *Georgia Historical Quarterly* 59 (Supp. 1975): 119–26.

Hill, Patricia Kneas. *The Oglethorpe Ladies.* Atlanta: Cherokee, 1977.

Hoare, Prince. *Memoirs of Granville Sharp, Esq.* 2nd ed. 2 vols. London: Henry Colburn, 1828.

Home, Robert. *Of Planting and Planning: The Making of British Colonial Cities.* London: E & FN Spon, 1997.

Hunt, John Dixon. *Garden and Grove: The Italian Renaissance Garden in the English Imagination, 1600–1750.* Princeton, NJ: Princeton University Press, 1986.

Hunt, John Dixon, and Peter Willis. *The Genius of Place.* Cambridge, MA: MIT Press, 1997.

Jackson, Harvey H. "Parson and Squire: James Oglethorpe and the Role of the Anglican Church in Georgia, 1733–1736." In *Oglethorpe in Perspective: Georgia's Founder after Two Hundred Years,* edited by Phinizy Spalding and Harvey H. Jackson, 44–65. Tuscaloosa: University of Alabama Press, 1989.

Jacob, Margaret C. *The Radical Enlightenment: Pantheists, Freemasons, and Republicans.* London: George Allen & Unwin, 1981.

Jacobs, Allan B. *Great Streets.* Cambridge, MA: MIT Press, 1993.

Jacobs, Jane. *The Death and Life of Great American Cities.* New York: Vintage Books, 1961.

Janek, Allan, and Stephen Toulmin. *Wittgenstein's Vienna.* New York: Simon & Schuster, 1973.

"John Pine: A Sociable Craftsman." *MQ Magazine* 10 (July 2004): 2–5.

Johnson, Otis. "Two Savannahs." Issue paper, 2004.

Katz, Bruce, Mark Muro, and Jennifer Bradley. "Miracle Mets: Our Fifty States Matter a Lot Less Than Our 100 Largest Metro Areas." *Democracy: A Journal of Ideas,* Spring 2009, 14–35.

Kendall, Alan. *David Garrick: A Biography.* New York: St. Martin's, 1985.

Kimble, Megan. "Suburban Living, Down on the Farm." *Los Angeles Times* (latimes. com), November 29, 2010.

Kirk, Rudolf. "A Latin Poem by James Edward Oglethorpe." *Georgia Historical Quarterly* 32, no. 1 (March 1948): 29–31.

Kostof, Spiro. *The City Shaped: Urban Patterns and Meanings through History.* New York: Little, Brown, 1999.

Krall, Lisi. "Thomas Jefferson's Agrarian Vision and the Changing Nature of Property." *Journal of Economic Issues* 36, no. 1 (March 2002): 135–66.

Kramnick, Isaac. *Bolingbroke and His Circle: The Politics of Nostalgia in the Age of Walpole.* Cambridge, MA: Harvard University Press, 1968.

Krieger, Leonard. *Kings and Philosophers, 1689–1789.* New York: W. W. Norton, 1970.

Kuhn, Thomas. *The Structure of Scientific Revolutions.* 3rd ed. Chicago: University of Chicago Press, 1996.

Lane, Mills, ed. *General Oglethorpe's Georgia: Colonial Letters, 1733–1743.* 2 vols. Savannah: Beehive, 1990.

———. *Our First Visit in America: Early Reports from the Colony of Georgia, 1732–1740.* Savannah: Beehive, 1974.

Lang, Andrew, with Alice Shield. "Queen Oglethorpe." In *Historical Mysteries,* 2nd ed. London: Smith, Elder, 1905. Project Guttenberg, EBook 18679.

Langdon, Philip. Review of *Urbanism in the Age of Climate Change,* by Peter Calthorpe. *New Urban News,* December 2010. http://newurbannetwork.com/article/urbanism -age-climate-change-13619.

Lannen, A. C. "Liberty and Authority in Colonial Georgia, 1716–1776." Ph.D. diss., Louisiana State University, 2002.

Laugher, Charles T. *Thomas Bray's Grand Design: Libraries of the Church of England in America, 1695–1785.* Chicago: American Library Association, 1973.

Lawrence, Henry W. "The Greening of the Squares of London: Transformation of Urban Landscapes and Ideals." *Annals of the Association of American Geographers* 83, no. 1 (March 1993): 90–118.

Leapman, Michael, ed. *The Book of London: The Evolution of a Great City.* New York: Weidenfeld & Nicolson, 1989.

Lehrer, Jonah. "A Physicist [Solves] the City." *New York Times Magazine,* December 19, 2010: MM46.

Levitt, James N. "Landscape-Scale Conservation: Grappling with the Green Matrix." *Land Lines* 16, no. 1 (January 2004): 1–5.

Levy, B. H. "The Early History of Georgia's Jews." In *Forty Years of Diversity: Essays on Colonial Georgia,* edited by Harvey H. Jackson and Phinizy Spalding, 163–78. Athens: University of Georgia Press, 1984.

Liebner, Judy. "New Street Grids Blend Old Designs: Residents Want Connectivity Pattern Inspired by Savannah." *Toronto Star,* September 20, 2003.

Lindsay, Greg. "New Urbanism for the Apocalypse." May 24, 2010. http://www.fast company.com/1651619/the-new-urbanism-meets-the-end-of-the-world.

Lund, Roger D., ed. *The Margins of Orthodoxy: Heterodox Writing and Cultural Response, 1660–1750.* Cambridge: Cambridge University Press, 1995.

MacGregor, Arthur. *Sir Hans Sloane: Collector, Scientist, Antiquary, Founding Father of the British Museum.* London: British Museum, 1994.

Malgrave, Harry Francis, ed. *Architectural Theory.* Vol. 1, *An Anthology from Vitruvius to 1870.* Oxford: Blackwell, 2006.

Manuscripts of the Earl of Egmont: Diary of Viscount Percival, afterwards First Earl of Egmont. 3 vols. London: Historical Manuscripts Commission, 1920–23.

Marissen, Michael. "Unsettling History of That Joyous 'Hallelujah.'" *New York Times,* April 8, 2007, 24–30.

Martyn, Benjamin. *Some Account of the Trustees Design for the Establishment of the Colony of Georgia in America.* London, 1732.

McConnell, Francis John. *Evangelicals, Revolutionists and Idealists: Six English Contributors to American Thought and Action.* New York: Abbingdon-Cokesbury, 1942.

McCullough, David. *1776.* New York: Simon & Schuster, 2005.

Mehaffy, Michael, et al. "Urban Nuclei and the Geometry of Streets: The 'Emergent Neighborhoods' Model." *Urban Design International* 15, no. 1 (2010): 22–46.

Mellon, Knox. "Christian Priber's Cherokee 'Kingdom of Paradise.'" *Georgia Historical Quarterly* 57, no. 3 (Fall 1973): 319–26.

Mereness, Newton. *Mereness's Travels in the American Colonies.* New York: Macmillan, 1916. Reprint, Carlisle, MA: Applewood Books, 2007.

Meroney, Geraldine. "The London Entrepot Merchants and the Georgia Colony." *William and Mary Quarterly,* 3rd ser., 25 (April 1968): 230–44.

Middlekauff, Robert. *The Glorious Cause: The American Revolution, 1763–1789.* Oxford: Oxford University Press, 1982.

Moffat, David. "New Ruralism: Agriculture at the Metropolitan Edge." *Places* 18, no. 2 (2006): 71–74.

Monod, Paul Kleber. "Dangerous Merchandise: Smuggling, Jacobitism, and Commercial Culture in Southeast England, 1690–1760." *Journal of British Studies* 30, no. 2 (1991): 150–82.

———. *Jacobitism and the English People, 1688–1788.* Cambridge: Cambridge University Press, 1989.

Montenegro, Maywa. "Urban Resilience." *Seed,* February 16, 2010. http://seedmagazine .com/content/article/urban_resilience/.

Moore, C. A. "Shaftesbury and the Ethical Poets in England, 1700–1760." *PMLA* 31, no. 2 (1916): 264–325.

Moore, Francis. *Travels into the Inland Parts of Africa.* London: Edward Cave, 1738.

———. *A Voyage to Georgia.* 1774. Reprint, St. Simons Island, GA: Fort Frederica Association, 2002.

More, Hannah. *Slavery: A Poem.* London: T. Cadell, 1788.

Morgan, Philip D. *Slave Counterpoint: Black Culture in the Eighteenth-Century Chesapeake and Lowcountry.* Chapel Hill: University of North Carolina Press, 1998.

Najemy, John M. "Machiavelli between East and West." In *From Florence to the Mediterranean and Beyond: Essays in Honour of Anthony Molho,* 2 vols., edited by D. Ramada Curto et al., 2:127–45. Florence: Olschki, 2009.

Nelson, Arthur C. "Leadership in a New Era." *Journal of the American Planning Association* 72, no. 4 (Autumn 2006): 393–407.

Newton, Isaac. "A Dissertation upon the Sacred Cubit of the Jews and the Cubits of the Several Nations; in which, from the Dimensions of the Great Egyptian Pyramid, as taken by Mr. John Greaves, the Antient Cubit of Memphis is Determined." London, 1737. Online at the Newton Project, http://www.newtonproject.sussex .ac.uk/view/texts/normalized/THEM00276.

Oglethorpe, James Edward. "The Library of Oglethorpe." Rodney M. Baine Papers, MS 3029, box 7, folder 7. Hargrett Rare Documents Library, University of Georgia, Athens.

———. *The Publications of James Edward Oglethorpe.* Edited by Rodney M. Baine. Athens: University of Georgia Press, 1994.

———. *Some Account of the Design of the Trustees for Establishing Colonys in America.* Edited by Rodney M. Baine and Phinizy Spalding. Athens: University of Georgia Press, 1990.

Oxford Dictionary of National Biography. Sir Leslie Stephens and Sir Sidney Lee, eds. Oxford: Oxford University Press, 1968.

Paulson, Ronald. *Hogarth: His Life, Art, and Times.* Abridged ed. New Haven, CT: Yale University Press, 1974.

Pitofsky, Alex. "The Warden's Court Martial: James Oglethorpe and the Politics of Eighteenth-Century Prison Reform." *Eighteenth-Century Life* 24, no. 1 (Winter 2000): 88–102.

Pocock, J. G. A. "Civic Humanism and Its Role in Anglo-American Thought." In *Politics, Language and Time: Essays on Political Thought and History,* 80–103. New York: Atheneum, 1971.

———. "Machiavelli, Harrington, and English Political Ideologies in the Eighteenth Century." In *Politics, Language and Time: Essays on Political Thought and History,* 104–47. New York: Atheneum, 1971.

Polster, Nathaniel. "The Golden Heritage Plan." *Savannah Morning News,* October 12, 1958, 1C.

Pope, Alexander. *The Major Works.* Edited by Pat Rogers. New York: Oxford University Press, 1993.

Porter, Roy. *The Creation of the Modern World: The Untold Story of the British Enlightenment.* New York: W. W. Norton, 2000.

Rand, Benjamin. *Berkeley and Percival.* Cambridge: University Press, 1914.

———. *The Life, Unpublished Letters, and Philosophical Regimen of Anthony, Earl of Shaftesbury.* New York: MacMillan, 1900.

Ready, Milton L. "Land Tenure in Trusteeship Georgia." *Agricultural History* 48, no. 3 (1974): 353–68.

———. "Philanthropy and the Origins of Georgia." In *Forty Years of Diversity: Essays on Colonial Georgia,* edited by Harvey H. Jackson and Phinizy Spalding, 46–59. Athens: University of Georgia Press, 1984.

Reese, Trevor R. "Benjamin Martyn, Secretary to the Trustees of Georgia." *Georgia Historical Quarterly* 38, no. 2 (June 1954): 142–47.

———, ed. *The Clamorous Malcontents: Criticisms and Defenses of the Colony of Georgia, 1741–1743.* Savannah: Beehive, 1973.

———. *Colonial Georgia: A Study in British Imperial Policy in the Eighteenth Century.* Athens: University of Georgia Press, 1963.

Reinberger, Mark. "Oglethorpe's Plan of Savannah: Urban Design, Speculative Freemasonry, and Enlightenment Charity." *Georgia Historical Quarterly* 81, no. 4 (Winter 1997): 839–62.

Reiss, Oscar. *The Jews in Colonial America.* Jefferson, NC: MacFarland, 2004.

Reps, John W. "C^2 + L^2 = S^2? Another Look at the Origins of Savannah's Town Plan." In *Forty Years of Diversity: Essays on Colonial Georgia,* edited by Harvey H. Jackson and Phinizy Spalding, 101–51. Athens: University of Georgia Press, 1984.

———. *The Making of Urban America: A History of City Planning in the United States.* Princeton, NJ: Princeton University Press, 1965.

———. "Searching for the Sources of a Unique City Plan: A New Theory of the Origins of Savannah's Urban Design." Lecture delivered at Wesley Monumental Church, Savannah, September 14, 2006.

Review of *Inductive Metrology; or, The Recovery of Ancient Measures from the Monuments*, by W. M. Flinders Petrie. *Nature* 17 (March 7, 1878): 357–59.

Richetti, John, ed. *The Cambridge History of English Literature, 1660–1780*. Cambridge: Cambridge University Press, 2005.

———. Introduction to *The Cambridge History of English Literature, 1660–1780*, edited by John Richetti, 1–9. Cambridge: Cambridge University Press, 2005.

Rivers, Isabel. "Religion and Literature." In *The Cambridge History of English Literature, 1660–1780*, edited by John Richetti, 445–70. Cambridge: Cambridge University Press, 2005.

Roberts, Gary Boyd. "Notable Kin—Surprising Connections, #5: James Edward Oglethorpe, Henry Sampson of the Mayflower, Other Colonial Immigrants, and Kings of Italy." American Ancestors. New England Historic Genealogical Society, April–May 1992. http://www.americanancestors.org/james-edward-oglethorpe-henry-sampson-of-the-mayflower/.

Roberts, William. *Memoirs of the Life of Mrs. Hannah More*. Vol. 1. London, 1836.

Rogal, Samuel J. "William Stephens and John Wesley: 'I Cannot Pretend to Judge.'" *Georgia Historical Quarterly* 90, no. 2 (Summer 2006): 260–90.

Russell, Paul F. "The United States and Malaria: Debits and Credits." *Bulletin of the New York Academy of Medicine* 44, no. 6 (1968): 623–53.

Ryle, Gilbert. *The Concept of Mind*. 1949. Reprint, New York: Barnes & Noble, 1959.

Sambrook, James. "Club (*act.* 1764–1784)." *Oxford Dictionary of National Biography*, online ed., May 2006, February 2009. Oxford University Press. http://www.oxforddnb.com/view/theme/49211.

Savannah, City of. *Chatham County–Savannah Tricentennial Plan*. 3 vols. 2006. Prepared and maintained by the Chatham County–Savannah Metropolitan Planning Commission for the City of Savannah and Chatham County.

———. Civic Master Plan. Prepared by Sottile & Sottile, 2006.

———. Downtown Master Plan. Draft. 2010.

———. Golden Heritage Plan. Chatham County–Savannah Metropolitan Planning Commission. 1958.

———. Historic District Ordinance (amendments). City of Savannah, 2009 (prepared by Sottile & Sottile).

———. McKinnon Map of 1798. City Hall Archives. XA-37.

———. Thomas Square Streetcar Historic District Neighborhood Plan. 2005.

Savannah Morning News. Editorial. February 6, 1956.

Saye, Albert B. "Genesis of Georgia: Merchants as Well as Ministers." *Georgia Historical Quarterly* 24, no. 3 (September 1940): 191–201.

———. "Was Georgia a Debtor Colony?" *Georgia Historical Quarterly* 24, no. 5 (December 1940): 323–41.

Schumacher, E. F. *Small Is Beautiful: Economics as If People Mattered*. London: Blond & Briggs, 1973.

Schweitzer, Lisa, and Paul Knox. "Determinism Redux: Planners, Design, and the Struggle for Professional Relevance." Draft paper posted online, 2009. Published as Knox and Schweitzer, "Design Determinism, Post-Meltdown: Urban Planners and the Search for Policy Relevance," *Housing Policy Debate* 20, no. 2 (2010): 317–27.

Sears, Joan Niles. *The First One Hundred Years of Town Planning in Georgia.* Atlanta: Cherokee, 1979.

Shaftesbury, 3rd Earl of (Anthony Ashley Cooper). *Characteristicks of Men, Manners, Opinions, Times.* 3 vols. Indianapolis: Liberty Fund, 2001. Originally published in 1711. The Liberty Fund publication is a reprinting of the 1732 edition, with a foreword by Douglas J. Den Uyl.

Sherman, Genevieve. "GSD Throwdown: Battle for the Intellectual Territory of a Sustainable Urbanism." *Urban Omnibus,* November 17, 2010. http://urbanomnibus .net/author/genevieve/.

Sichel, Walter. *Bolingbroke and His Times: The Sequel.* New York: Longmans, Green, 1902.

Sieg, Chan. *The Squares: An Introduction to Savannah.* Virginia Beach, VA: Donning, 1996.

Spalding, Phinizy. "James Edward Oglethorpe's Quest for the American Zion." In *Forty Years of Diversity: Essays on Colonial Georgia,* edited by Harvey H. Jackson and Phinizy Spalding, 60–79. Athens: University of Georgia Press, 1984.

———. *Oglethorpe in America.* Chicago: University of Chicago Press, 1977. Reprint, Athens: University of Georgia Press, 1984.

———. "Oglethorpe, William Stephens, and the Origin of Georgia Politics." In *Oglethorpe in Perspective: Georgia's Founder after Two Hundred Years,* edited by Phinizy Spalding and Harvey H. Jackson, 80–98. Tuscaloosa: University of Alabama Press, 1989.

———. "Some Sermons before the Trustees of Colonial Georgia." *Georgia Historical Quarterly* 57, no. 3 (1973): 332–46.

Spalding, Phinizy, and Harvey H. Jackson, eds. *Oglethorpe in Perspective: Georgia's Founder after Two Hundred Years.* Tuscaloosa: University of Alabama Press, 1989.

Stephens, William. *A Journal of the Proceedings in Georgia.* 2 vols. London: W. Meadows, 1742. Reprinted by the Readex Microprint Corporation, 1966.

Stewart, Mart A. *What Nature Suffers to Groe: Life, Labor, and Landscape on the Georgia Coast, 1680–1920.* Athens: University of Georgia Press, 1996.

Stewart, Robert G. *Robert Edge Pine: A British Portrait Painter in America, 1784–1788.* Washington, DC: Smithsonian Institution Press, 1979.

Stuart, Charles. *Memoir of Granville Sharp.* New York: American Anti-Slavery Society, 1836.

Sweet, Julie Anne. "The British Sailors' Advocate: James Oglethorpe's First Philanthropic Venture." *Georgia Historical Quarterly* 91, no. 1 (Spring 2007): 1–27.

———. "'The Excellency and Advantage of Doing Good': Thoughts on the Anniversary Sermons Preached before the Trustees of Georgia, 1731–1752." *Georgia Historical Quarterly* 90, no. 1 (Spring 2006): 1–36.

———. "'A Misguided Mistake': The Trustees' Public Garden in Savannah, Georgia." *Georgia Historical Quarterly* 93, no. 1 (Spring 2009): 1–29.

———. *Negotiating for Georgia: British-Creek Relations in the Trustee Era, 1733–1752.* Athens: University of Georgia Press, 2005.

———. "'That Cursed Evil Rum': The Trustees' Prohibition Policy in Colonial Georgia." *Georgia Historical Quarterly* 94, no. 4 (Spring 2010): 1–29.

———. "The Thirteenth Colony in Perspective: Historians' Views on Early Georgia." *Georgia Historical Quarterly* 85, no. 3 (Fall 2001): 435–60.

———. *William Stephens: Georgia's Forgotten Founder.* Baton Rouge: Louisiana State University Press, 2010.

Swift, Jonathan. *Gulliver's Travels.* 1776. Reprint, London: Puffin Books, 1997. Tachieva, Galina. *Sprawl Repair Manual.* Washington, DC: Island, 2010.

Taylor, Paul S. "Colonizing Georgia, 1732–1752: A Statistical Note." *William and Mary Quarterly,* 3rd series, 22, no. 1 (January 1965): 119–27.

———. *Georgia Plan: 1732–1752.* Berkeley: Institute of Business and Economic Research, University of California, 1972.

Taylor, Thomas. *Memoir of Mrs. Hannah More.* London: Joseph Rickerby, 1838.

Thomas, Sir Keith. Lecture given to the Georgia Tercentenary Commission at Oxford University, October 5, 1996.

Toland, John. *The Oceana and Other Works of James Harrington, with an Account of his Life by John Toland.*

Tuan, Yi-Fu. *Topophilia: A study of Environmental Perception, Attitudes, and Values.* Englewood Cliffs, NJ: Prentice-Hall, 1974.

Uglow, Jenny. *Hogarth: A Life and a World.* New York: Farrar, Straus, & Giroux, 1997.

United Nations. *Our Common Future/World Commission on Environment and Development* New York: Oxford University Press, 1987.

———. "Rio Declaration on Environment and Development." The United Nations Conference on Environment and Development, Rio de Janeiro, June 1992.

Van Gelderen, Martin, and Quentin Skinner. *Republicanism: A Shared European Heritage.* Vol. 2. Cambridge: Cambridge University Press, 2002.

Van Horne, John C. *Religious Philanthropy and Colonial Slavery: The American Correspondence of the Associates of Dr. Bray, 1717–1777.* Urbana: University of Illinois Press, 1985.

Wilkins, Thomas Hart. "James Edward Oglethorpe: South Carolina Slaveholder?" *Georgia Historical Quarterly* 88, no. 1 (Spring 2004): 85–94.

———. "Sir Joseph Jekyll and His Impact on Oglethorpe's Georgia." *Georgia Historical Quarterly* 91, no. 2 (Summer 2007): 119–34.

Williams, Mary E. "Oglethorpe's Literary Friendships." Ph.D. diss., University of Georgia, 1980.

Wills, Garry. *Inventing America: Jefferson's Declaration of Independence.* Garden City, NY: Doubleday Books, 1978.

Wood, Betty. "James Edward Oglethorpe, Race, and Slavery: A Reassessment." In *Oglethorpe in Perspective: Georgia's Founder after Two Hundred Years,* edited by Phinizy Spalding and Harvey H. Jackson, 66–79. Tuscaloosa: University of Alabama Press, 1989.

———. *Slavery in Colonial America, 1619–1776.* Lanham, MD: Rowman & Littlefield, 2005.

———. *Slavery in Colonial Georgia, 1730–1775.* Athens: University of Georgia Press, 1984.

Young, Percy. "A Study in Handelian Thought." *Proceedings of the Royal Musical Association,* 75th sess. (1948–49): 53–63.

Zucker, Paul. *Town and Square: From the Agora to the Village Green.* New York: Columbia University Press, 1959.

Zurbuchen, Simone. "Republicanism and Toleration." In *Republicanism: A Shared European Heritage,* vol. 2, edited by Martin van Gelderen and Quentin Skinner, 2:47–72. Cambridge: Cambridge University Press, 2002.

Index

Italicized page numbers refer to figures, a "t" following a page number denotes a table, and the abbreviation "JEO" is used for James Edward Oglethorpe.

Abercorn village, *67*, 104, *110*, 117
abolition movement. *See* Oglethorpe, James Edward: on slavery; slavery
Account of Corsica (Boswell), 198, 200, 212
Acton, William (warden), 39
Acton village, 95, 117
Adams, John, 206, 213
Adelaide, Australia, 157, 204
agrarian democracy, 159, 190–91
agrarian equality, 50, 57–59, 70–71, 86, 96, 110–12, 114, 116, 119–22, 124, 128, 131, 133, 159, 167, 178, 187–92
Ahwahnee Principles, 173
Aix-la-Chapelle, Treaty of, 194
Alberti, Leon Battista, 74, 98
Altamaha River, 44, 88, 108–9, *110*, 118, 156
"Amazing Grace" (Newton), 202
American Institute of Certified Planners, 165
American Revolution, 2, 23, 26, 190, 203
Anderson, Adam (Georgia Trustee), 214
Anderson, Stanford, 99
Anne, Queen, *6*, 10–11, 25, 209

appropriate technology, 163
Aristotle, 74
Assembly of the People of Georgia, Annual, 116, 212
Associates of Dr. Thomas Bray (later Associates of the late Dr. Bray), 40, 43, 51–52, 61, 210
Atlanta, Ga., 156, 167
Atterbury, Bishop Francis, 14, 220n23
Augusta, Ga., 89, *110*, 131, 153, 156
Augustan Age, 30–31, 33, 35, 210
Augustus Caesar, 30
Avery, Joseph, 224n5

Bacon, Edmund N., 160
Bacon, Sir Francis, 49
Baine, Rodney, 222n23
Bambridge, Thomas (warden), 38–39
Bambridge on Trial for Murder by a Committee of the House of Commons (Hogarth), 38, *39*
Bank of England, 15–17, *18*, 45
Barbauld, Anna, 202

Bateman, William, 107–8

Bavaria, 106

Bearcroft, Rev. Phillip, 50

Beaufort County, S.C., 166, 229n14

Bedford, Rev. Arthur (Georgia Trustee), 55, 214

Beggar's Opera, The (Gay), 32, 210; painting by Hogarth, *33*

Belgrade, Siege of, 12, 210

Belitha, William (Georgia Trustee), 214

Berkeley, George (bishop), 26–27, 42–43, 50, 75, 120, 192, 212, 222n13

Bethany village, 117

Bloody Marsh, Battle of, 115, 211

Blue Stocking Society, 201–2

Bohemians, 105

Bolingbroke, Lord (Henry St. John), 10–11, 18–22, 25–26, 28, 31–33, 35, 41, 55, 60, 190, 206–7, 210, 211, 212, 220n19, 223n44

Bolzius (Boltzius), Rev. Johann Martin, 121, 130

Boswell, James, 198–200, 212, 213

Bray, Rev. Thomas, 40–44, 209, 210

Bray Associates. *See* Associates of Dr. Thomas Bray (later Associates of the late Dr. Bray)

Briggs, Xavier, 165

Broughton, Thomas, 140

Broughton Street, 140

Brownfield, John, 121, 123

Brunswick, Ga., 157

Bull, Col. William, 102, 139

Bull Street, 139–40

Bundoram Farm, 167

Bundy, Rev. Richard (Georgia Trustee), 214

Burke, Edmund, 200–201, 213

Burlington, 3rd Earl of, 30–31

Burney, Charles, 200

Burney, Frances, 200, 202

Burton, Rev. John, 50, 59, 69, 102, 190, 214

Campbell, Colen, 74

Cape Bluff (settlement), 104, 117

cardo maximus, 76–77

Caroline, Queen, 23, 72

Carpenter, George Lord (Georgia Trustee), 214

Carte, Thomas, 21

Carter, Elizabeth, 202

Castell, Robert, 22, 30, 38, 72, 74, 76, 91, 210

Castle of Otranto, The (Walpole), 200

castrum, 76–77

Cataneo, Pietro di Giacomo, 74–75

Causton, Thomas, 123, 129

Cavendish-Harley, Margaret, Duchess of Portland, 202

chain. *See* measurement, units of

Characteristics of Men, Manners, Opinions, Times (3rd Earl of Shaftesbury), 51, 74, 209

Charles Town (later Charleston), S.C., 101, 103, 106–7, *110,* 123, 128, 211

Charles I, King, 4, *6,* 8

Charles II, King, 4, *6,* 7, 219n7

Charlottesville, Va., 167

Chatham County, *67, 80,* 144, 150

Chatham County–Savannah Metropolitan Planning Commission (MPC), 161

Cherokee, 102, 115

Choctaw, 102, 127

Christie, Thomas, 123

Church of England, 4, 8, 16, 37, 219n7

civic center (Savannah), 144, 149

Civic Master Plan. *See under* Savannah, city of (post-colonial era)

civic virtue, 3

Clapham Sect (or Clapham Saints), 204

Clarkson, Thomas, 204

Coastal Georgia Comprehensive Plan, 163

Committee of the House of Commons, A (Hogarth). See *Bambridge on Trial for*

Murder by a Committee of the House of Commons (Hogarth)

common (town common). *See under* Savannah plan

Common Sense (Paine), 190, 213

commonwealthmen, *18*

Commonwealth of England, *6*

Commonwealth of Oceana, The (Harrington), 47, 209

comprehensive planning. *See under* planning paradigms

Congress for the New Urbanism, 173, 178

Conroy, Pat, 166

Cooper, Anthony Ashley. *See* 1st, 3rd, and 4th Earls *under* Shaftesbury

Coosaponakeesa. *See* Musgrove, Mary

Coram, Thomas (Georgia Trustee), 41, 47, 50–51, 215

Corpus Christi College, Oxford, 11–13, 50, 209

Corsica, 198, 200, 212, 213

Costa Rica, 162

country party, *18,* 19–20, 25, 30, 32, 37, 41, 47, 54–56, 58, 68–69, 72, 119, 198, 222n2

court party, *18,* 19–20, 25, 30, 32, 55

Craftsman, The (magazine), 32, 34, 210

Cranham Hall, 194, 198, 213

Creeks. *See* Lower Creeks; Upper Creeks

Cromwell, Oliver, 4

cubit. *See* measurement, units of

Cumberland, Duke of, 195

D'Arcy, Lord (Georgia Trustee), 217

Darien, Ga., 88–89, 105, *110,* 112–13, 118, 125, 130, 153–55, *155*

Daufuskie Island, S.C., *67, 110,* 166–67

da Vinci, Leonardo, 74

debtors' prisons, 38. *See also* prison committee, Oglethorpe's

Decker, Matthew, 137

Decker Ward, 142, 144–45, *146,* 182, *184;* restoration of, *145*

Declaration of Independence, 26, 199, 213

decumanus maximus, 76–77

Defoe, Daniel, 25, 33–34, 210

deism, 27–29

dengue fever. *See* environmental conditions (Georgia Colony): disease

Derby, Earl of (James Stanley; Georgia Trustee), 137, 215

Desaguliers, John, 25, 97

Deserted Village, The (Goldsmith), 34, 198, 213

design determinism, 170, 181

Digby, Edward (Georgia Trustee), 215

dimorphic spatial orientation, 175

divine right, 4, *18*

Dobree, Elisha, 121

Doyle, John, 44

Duany, Andres, 173

dysentery. *See* environmental conditions (Georgia Colony): disease

Earth Charter Initiative, 162

East India Company, 15, 137

Ebenezer, Ga., *67,* 88, 105, *110,* 112–13, 117, 153–54, *154,* 156

ecological urbanism. *See under* planning paradigms

economic revolution (of England, 1688–1756), 15–19

Egmont, Earl of. *See* Percival, John, Earl of Egmont (Georgia Trustee)

eidetic effect, 177

Einstein, Albert, 192

Elizabeth, Queen, 4

ell. *See* measurement, units of

Ellis Square, 144–45, *146*

empiricism, 26, 192

English Civil War, 4

Enlightenment: Age of, 2–4, 11, 22–36, 40, 52–55, 60, 62, 72, 89–90, 98, 119, 133, 165, 168, 189–208; feminism, 202; humanism, 2, 23, 52, 62, 73, 133, 200, 219n2; radical, 28–29, 220n25, 221n55; Scottish, 200
entrepreneurship (multiple opportunities), 182, *184*
environmental conditions (Georgia Colony), 124–26; climate and weather, 125–26, 226n49; disease, 125–26; terrain, 124; water quality, 125; wildlife and insects, 125
Essay on Man, An (Pope) 31, 65, 210
estates. *See* Savannah plan: estates and manors of
Ettinger, Amos Aschbach, 192
Eugene, Prince of Savoy, 12–13, 28, 75–77, 197, 210
evangelicalism, 113
Eveleigh, Samuel, 109
Eyles, Francis (Georgia Trustee), 215

farm district. *See under* Savannah plan
Fielding, Henry, 202
Florida Planning Act, 161
focused redevelopment, 182, *184*
Forsythe Park, 157
Fort Argyle, *67, 110,* 117, 155–56
Fort Frederica. *See* Frederica: town and fort
Fort King George, *110,* 118
France, 8–12, 17, 26, 42, 45, 56, 58, 108, 111, 114, 118, 127, 194–96, 205, 210, 211, 212. *See also* French Mississippi Company; French Revolution
Franklin, Benjamin, 197
Frederica: County, created, 115, 118, 211; town and fort, 88–89, *110,* 112, 115, 118, 130, 153, 157, 211
Frederick, Prince of Wales, 55, 108, 157, 214
Frederick, Thomas (Georgia Trustee), 215

Frederick II (Frederick the Great), 196–97, 212
Freemasonry, 25, 29–30, 51, 64–65, 97
Freetown, Sierra Leone, 157
French Mississippi Company, 17, 210
French Revolution, 23, 26, 206
Fries, Sylvia, 20, 132, 223n44
functional identity, 182
furlong. *See* measurement, units of

Galeshewe, South Africa, 158
Gandhi, Mahatma, 163
Garden Cities movement, 161
garden district. *See under* Savannah plan
Garrick, David, 200–201
Gay, John, 25, 32, 210
Geddes, Patrick, 172
genius loci (genius of the place), 31, 207
Gentleman's Magazine, The, 34
gentry, 34, 68, 70, 78–79, 81, 88, 96, 105
George I, King, *6,* 11–12, 30, 43
George II, King, *6,* 44, 197, 212
George III, King, *6*
Georgeia (proposed colony), 41
Georgia Colony: agriculture in, 117–18, 132 (*see also* agrarian equality; slavery); borders of, 44–45; chronology of settlement of, 103*t*; demographics of settlers in, 103–6; end of Trustee period of, 116–17; enemies of, 126–28; environment of, 124–26; founded, 101–2; freedom of religion in, 45, 54–55, 58, 61; idealized depiction of, *64;* map of, *110;* settlements of, 117–18; timeline of, 210–12. *See also* environmental conditions (Georgia Colony)
Georgia Trustees. *See* Trustees for the Establishment of the Colony of Georgia in America *and specific Trustees by name*
Ghost in the Machine, The (Ryle), 171
Gibbon, Edward, 200

Glorious Revolution, 3, 7–8, 15–16, *18,* 23, 32, 209

Golden Heritage Plan, 143

Goldsmith, Oliver, 34, 198–200, 213

Gonson, Sir John (Georgia Trustee), 215

Gordon, Peter, 65, 72, 123; map of Savannah, 65, *66,* 73, 79, 85, 88, 139

Grand Modell (*or* Model), 24, 69, 73–74, 88, 204

Granville Town (later Freetown, Sierra Leone), 157, 203

Great Fire of 1666, 15, 74–75

Great Plague of 1665–66, 15, 90

Greene, Nathanael, 190

Gulliver's Travels (Swift), 31, 210

Hales, Stephen (Georgia Trustee), 25, 51, 90, 107, 215

Hampstead village, *67,* 79, *80,* 94–95, 104, 117

Hanbury, William (Georgia Trustee), 217

Handel, George Frederick, 28–29

Hanover, House of, *6,* 11

Hardwick, Ga., 157

Harley, Robert, 10–11, 25, 28, 221n38

Harlot's Progress, A (Hogarth), 34, *35*

Harrington, James, 20, 28, 47, 50, 57, 190–91, 206, 209

Haslemere, 9, 13, 194

Heathcote, George (Georgia Trustee), 25, 51, 54–55, 137, 215

Heathcote, Sir William (Georgia Trustee), 215–16

Highgate village, *67,* 94–95, 104, 117

Hilton Head Island, S.C., *69, 110,* 166–67

Hippodamus, 74, 76

Historic District Ordinance. *See under* Savannah, city of (post-colonial era)

Historic Savannah Foundation, 135, 137

Hochkirch, Battle of, 197, 212

Hogarth, William, 29–30, 34, 38–40, 209, 212; paintings/plates by, *33, 35, 39*

Holland, Rogers (Georgia Trustee), 51, 55, 216

Holland, 7–8, 15–16, 28–29

Holling, C. S., 163

Holy Roman Empire, 106

Horton, Lt. William, 130

Housing Act of 1954, 182; Section 701 planning grants, 160; urban renewal program, 160. *See also* Savannah, city of (post-colonial era): urban renewal of

Hucks, Robert (Georgia Trustee), 51, 54–55, 216

Hucks, William (Georgia Trustee), 216

human ecology, 98, 172, 181–82, 186–87

Hume, David, 26, 192, 200

Hunter Army Airfield, 151

Hurricane Andrew, 170

Hutcheson, Francis, 26, 190, 210

Hutchinson Island, *67,* 104, *110,* 149

immaterialism, theory of, 26

impressment of sailors, 36. See also *Sailor's Advocate, The* (Oglethorpe)

inalienable rights, *18,* 26

indentured servants, 105

Industrial Revolution, 191, 197, 213

Irene village, 117

Jacob, Margaret, 25, 220n25, 221n55

Jacobites, 9–15, *18,* 21, 31, 210; Rising of 1715, 12, 210; Rising of 1745, 211

Jacobs, Allan, 160

Jacobs, Jane, 182, 185

James I, King, 4–9, *6*

James II, King, 4, *6,* 7–8, 209

James III ("The Old Pretender"), *6,* 9–14, 210, 212, 219n13

Jefferson, Thomas, 2, 159, 161, 190–91, 199, 210, 230n9

Jekyll, Sir Joseph, 43, 51, 157, 217–18
Jekyll Island, *110, 118*, 157
Jews (Georgia colonists), 104, 106
Job ben Jalla, 193
Johnson, Arthur, 121
Johnson, Mayor Otis (Savannah), 150
Johnson, Robert, governor of S.C., 90, 124
Johnson, Samuel (Dr. Johnson), 198–202, 209, 212, 213; Age of, 31; Literary Club, 199, 212; More enters circle of, 201; overlap of Johnson and Oglethorpe circles, 200, 206; urges Boswell to write biography of Oglethorpe, 198
Jones, Inigo, 74
Jones, Noble, 121, 224n5
Jones, Thomas, 114, 128–29
Joseph's Town, *67, 110,* 117
Judaism, 29. *See also* Jews (Georgia colonists)

Keith, James, Field Marshal, 196–97, 212
Kendall, Robert (Georgia Trustee), 216
Kent, William, 30
Kingdom of Paradise, 115
King's Bench Prison, 39
Kuhn, Thomas, 165, 228n3

landscape urbanism. *See under* planning paradigms
L'Apostre, Henry (Georgia Trustee), 216
Laroche, John (Georgia Trustee), 51, 216
Legacy Square, 157
Liberty: A Poem (Thomson), 33
Liberty Ward, 144
Life of Johnson (Boswell), 199
Limerick, Lord Viscount (Georgia Trustee), 216
Locke, John, 24, 26–27, 30, 35, 51, 120, 191–92, 199, 209
London Magazine, 34

Lotter, Conrad, 224n5
Louis XIV, King, 9, 13
Lower Creeks, 101–2, 104, 127, 210
Lutherans, 106

Machiavelli, Niccolò, 47, 49, 55–57, 60, 206, 223n44
MacKay, Hugh, 113
malaria. *See* environmental conditions (Georgia Colony): disease
Malcontents, 106, 108, 111–14, 115, 118, 128–31, 132, 193, 211
manors. *See* Savannah plan: estates and manors of
Mar, Duke of, 13, 22n23
Marcer, Samuel, 123
Marlborough, Duke of, 13
Marshalsea Prison, 39
Martyn, Benjamin, 45–46, 51, 54, 68, 96, 131, 210, 217
Mary, Queen of Scots, 4
Mary II, Queen, *6,* 8–9, 209
McIntosh, Lachlan, 157
McIntosh County, 153, 157
McKinnon, John, 84; map of Savannah, 84, *85,* 91, 93–94, *94,* 150
measurement, units of, 81
Messiah (Handel), 28–29
Miami, Fla., *170*
Mikve Israel, 106
Mississippi Bubble. *See* French Mississippi Company
modernism, 161–62
Montagu, Elizabeth, 201–2
Montesquieu, Charles-Louis de Secondat, Baron de La Brède et de, 12, 26, 190
Moore, Francis, 50, 65–66, 72–73, 95
Morando, Bernardo, 75
Moravians, 105, 108
More, Hannah, 201–2, 204, 206, 213

More, Robert (Georgia Trustee), 51, 54–55, 216

Mostafavi, Moshen, 165

Musgrove, John, 102, 106

Musgrove, Mary, 102, 156

Napoleon Bonaparte, 197

neoliberalism, 170

Newcourt, Richard, 74–75

New Ebenezer, Ga. *See* Ebenezer, Ga.

Newgate Prison, 32

Newington village, 117

new ruralism. *See under* planning paradigms

Newton, Sir Isaac, 24–25, 27, 51, 60, 65, 77, 84, 96–98, 120, 190, 209, 210, 230n9

Newton, Rev. John, 202

New Urbanism. *See under* planning paradigms

New Windsor village, 117

Oceana. See Commonwealth of Oceana, The (Harrington)

Ockstead estate, 117

Ogeechee (or Ogetie; settlement), 104

Ogeechee River, *67*, 109, *110*, 115, 155

Oglethorpe, Anne Henrietta (JEO's sister), *5*, 7, 9, 28, 220n19

Oglethorpe, Eleanor (JEO's mother), 4–12, *5, 6*, 25, 209, 210

Oglethorpe, Eleanor (JEO's sister), *5*, 7, 17

Oglethorpe, Frances Charlotte (Fanny; JEO's sister), *5*, 7, 220n16

Oglethorpe, James (JEO's infant brother), *5*, 10

Oglethorpe, James Edward: in the age of Boswell and Johnson, 198–202; on agrarian equality, 50; aids Job ben Jalla, 193; aliases used in Europe, 196–97; attains rank of full general, 197; attends Corpus Christi College, Oxford University, 11–13; Atterbury speech of, 14; in the Battle of Bloody Marsh, 115; birth and childhood of, 9–11; and Bolingbroke, 11, 19–23, 41, 55, 60, 190, 206–7; ceases attending meetings of Georgia Trustees, 181; circle of associates of, 40, 50–55; conceives plan for New World colony, 37, 42; death of, 204, 206; elected to Parliament, 13–14; family ancestry of, 4–7, *5, 6;* Georgia plan of, 55–62; —, influences on, 73–79; Jacobite family of, 4–7; and Jacobite Rising of 1715, 12; and Jacobite Rising of 1745, 195; joins Bray Associates and expands its mission, 40–41; later military career of, 194–97; later years in Parliament, 194–95, 197; lays out Savannah, 64–66; leads first colonists, 47, 101; leads Siege of St. Augustine, 115; library of, 13; as a man of the Enlightenment, 1–3, 189–92; marriage of, 194; meets with John Adams, 206; and Native Americans, 127, 156; places named after, 156–57; political philosophy of, 20–21, 53, 57; religious views of, 27–29; in Royal African Company, 193; selects site for Savannah, 101–2; serves as prison committee chair, 1, 15, 38–40; serves under Frederick the Great, 196–97; serves under Prince Eugene, 12–13, 220n22; on slavery, 61, 130, 192, 204–6; timeline of life of, 209–13; travels upcountry to reaffirm Indian treaties, 114; voyages between England and Georgia, 47, 111–12, 174, 210, 211

Oglethorpe, Lewis (JEO's brother), *5*, 7, 9

Oglethorpe, Luisa Mary (Molly; JEO's sister), *5*

Oglethorpe, Sutton (JEO's grandfather), 4, *6*

Oglethorpe, Sutton (JEO's infant brother), *5*

Oglethorpe, Theophilus (JEO's father), 4–9, *5, 6,* 209

Oglethorpe, Theophilus, Jr. (JEO's brother), *5,* 7, 9–10, 13, 75

Oglethorpe County, 156

Oglethorpe Plan: assessment of, 118–31; component purposes of, 37, 53*t,* 55–62; comprehensiveness and integrated structure of, 37–38, 55, 58–59, 100, 159–60, 163, 168–69, 181–82; conceived, 42–43; conceptual plan of Savannah region, *85;* defined, 68; described in *Some Account* and promotional materials, 69; evolution of, 140–46; genesis of, 38, 48; grid of, 66–67, *72,* 124, 150–51, 169; and humanism, 2; implemented, 64; inspired by the Enlightenment ideals, 3–4; Masonic influence on, 64–65; in modern context (historic Savannah), 134–50; in modern context (Savannah region), 150–52; original plan lost, 63; as a planning paradigm, 72–73; purposes of, 37; regional form, components, and specifications of, 37–38, 60, 65–66, 68–73, 70*t,* 71*t,* 83*t, 84, 85;* relevance today, 1, 168–69, 181–82, 207–8; secularism of, 51, 61; spacing of towns in, 156; successes and failures summarized, 62; terminology of, 67–68, 73; vision of, 47; visual rendering of (Pine), 63, *64. See also* Savannah plan

Oglethorpe University, 156

Old Pretender. *See* James III ("The Old Pretender")

original principles (founding principles), 55–56, 60, 192, 195

Ormonde, Duke of, 11

outdoor rooms, 177

out-villages. *See* Savannah plan: village district of; villages ("out-villages")

Page, John (Georgia Trustee), 217

Paine, Thomas, 190, 213

Palatine Germans, 106

Pallachacolas (Palachacolas, Parachucla), S.C., *67, 110,* 156

Palladio, Andrea, 30, 76, 98

Paoli, General Pasquale de, 200, 213

paradigms. *See* planning paradigms

Parliament: debate over founding principles and administration of Georgia, 114, 129, 132, 227n73; grants to the Georgia Trustees, 45, 47, 102–3, 108. *See also* prison committee, Oglethorpe's

patriot king (Bolingbroke concept), *18,* 31–32, 223n44

pedestrian connectivity, 182, *183*

Penn, William, 49

Percival, John, Earl of Egmont (Georgia Trustee), 22, 26, 42–44, 47–48, 50, 52–54, 60–61, 72, 96, 111, 113–14, 122, 131, 137, 154, 195, 212, 216

Petrovaradan, 12

Phillips, Sir Erasmus (Georgia Trustee), 216

Piazza San Carlo (Piazza Carlina), 42, 75, 89

Picart, Bernard, 29, 218

Pine, John, 25, 29–30, 51, 63, 68, 78, 95, 97, 218, 223n34; frontispiece to *Some Account* by, *64*

Pirna, Battle of, 196, 212

Pitt, William, 1st Earl of Chatham, 212

planning paradigms, 160–73; comprehensive planning, 160–62, 186; ecological urbanism, 164; landscape urbanism, 164; new ruralism, 167; New Urbanism, 158, 164–65, 167, 228n11 (*see also* design determinism; Savannah plan: and New Urbanism [design analogs]); Oglethorpe Plan as, 72–73, 160; scientific paradigms, 165,

228n3; Smart Growth, 165, 173; sustainable development, 162–63; urban design, 164–65

Plater-Zyberk, Elizabeth, 165, 173

pole. *See* measurement, units of

Pope, Alexander, 25, 30–31, 34, 65, 76, 190, 210

population density, 57, 59

Port Royal, S.C., 101

Pretender, Old. *See* James III ("The Old Pretender")

Pretender, Young. *See* Stuart, Charles ("Bonnie Prince Charlie, The Young Pretender")

Priber, Christian, 115

prison committee, Oglethorpe's, 15, *18*, 38–40, *39*, 222n1

protocols, 168, 229n18

Province of Freedom, 203

Pulteney, William, 20, 32

Purysburg (Purrysburg), S.C., *67*, 90, 104, 108, *110*, 118

Reinberger, Mark, 97

Renaissance ideal city, 74–76

Reps, John, 42, 75, 89–90, 97, 160

republicanism. *See* country party

resilience theory, 163, 167

Restoration, the, 4

Reynolds, Joshua, 198, 200, 212, 213

Ribeiro, Dr. Samuel Nunes, 104

ridurre ai principii, 55, 57, 59, 100, 190, 206, 223n40, 223n44

Robinson Crusoe (Defoe), 33, 210

Roman colonies and town planning, 47, 49, 57, 60, 69, 74, 76–77, *77*, 112, 178, 191

roundabouts, 179

Rousseau, Jean Jacques, 212, 213

Royal African Company, 15, 193

Royal Society for the Improvement of Natural Knowledge (Royal Society), 16, 27, 51, 77, 126

rum (and spirits), 103–4, 107–8, 120, 123, 127, 132–33

Ryle, Gilbert, 171–72

Sailor's Advocate, The (Oglethorpe), 15, 203, 210, 213

St. Augustine, Fla. (Spanish town and citadel), 109, *110;* preparations for war with British, 114–15; Siege of, 115, 211

St. Helena Island, S.C., *110*, 166–67

St. Joe Company, 167

St. John, Henry. *See* Bolingbroke, Lord (Henry St. John)

St. Simon's Island, *110*, 115, 118

Salzburgers, 88, 103–5, 113, 121, 129–30, 153–54, 156

Savannah, city of (post-colonial era): African American neighborhoods of, 141; architectural character of, *135*, 137, 147–48; Chatham County–Savannah Tricentennial Plan (comprehensive plan), 146; civic center of, 149; Civic Master Plan of, 147–48; Decker Ward, 144–46; design standards of, 143; Downtown Expansion areas, 146–47; Downtown Master Plan of, 147, 149; East Riverfront, *147*, 148; Ellis Square, 144–46, *145*, *146;* founded, 64; as "gated" development, 149; Golden Heritage Plan of, 143; historic character of, 136; Historic District Ordinance, 147; historic districts of, *136*, *138;* Housing Authority of, 148; Metropolitan Planning Commission of, 161, 228n14; National Historic Landmark District, 1, 134–49, *138*, 207; pedestrian connectivity in, 148–49, 174–75, *183;* policy of reciprocity in, 149; shared space in, 175, *183;* squares of, *139*, 144, 146–47, 149, 183; street grid of, 137,

Savannah, city of (*continued*)
140–41, 150–51, *152*, 156; suburbanization
of, 135, 143–44, 151, 157; Thomas Square
neighborhood plan of, 157, 230n36; and
tourism, 137; as urban forest, 135; as an
urban laboratory, 159; urban renewal of,
143–44, 157, 161, 181; urban residential and
commercial character of, *136;* visual connectivity of, 175; ward design in modern,
134, 137–50; zoning of, 145–47, 149. *See also*
Savannah plan
Savannah, town of (Trustee period): founding of, 101–3; as garden metropolis, 135;
maps of, *66, 67, 80, 82, 85, 94, 138, 110,
139, 142, 152;* population of, 104–6, 111;
planned population of, 71–72
Savannah College of Art and Design
(SCAD), 135
Savannah County (Trustee period): created, 115; maps of, *66, 67;* settlements in,
117–18, 211
Savannah Morning News, 143
Savannah plan: agrarian character of,
68–73, 99, 140; common, 69–71, 79,
89–90, 140; as conceptual regional plan,
84; defined, 68; estates and manors of,
96; farm district of, 92–93, 150; as garden
metropolis, 72, 134–35, 180, 224n10; garden district of, 91–92; genesis of, 73–79,
134; land grants and survey methods in,
79–85; mechanics of, 96–98; and New
Urbanism (design analogs), 173–81;
original copy lost, 63; the plan today,
135–40; regional plan, 68–73, 83*t,* 134;
replication of wards, 72, 98–99; revered
for exceptional design, ix, 1, 98, 148, 150,
159–60, 208; six-ward plan, 65–66, 72, *82,*
86, 104, 134, 140; spatial equity or equality of, 100; squares (*see* ward design and
specifications of, *below*); survey map of,

85; after Trustee period, 140–50; village
district of, 88, 93–95, 143, 150, 153; ward
design and specifications of, 1, *85,* 85–89,
87, 87t, 180
Savannah River, 44, 95, 101–2, 107, 109, *110,*
124, 148, 156
Savannah Town (settlement near Augusta),
117
Savoy, Duchy of, 106
Scamozzi, Vincenzo, 74
Schumacher, E. F., 163
Scots (settlers and soldiers), 108
Scottish Enlightenment, 200
Scriblerus Club, 25
Sea Islands, 166
Seasons, The (Thomson), 32–33, 210
Serenbe Farms, 167
Seven Years' War, 196
Shaftesbury: 1st Earl of (politician and
statesman), 19, 24, 28, 69, 204; 3rd Earl
of (philosopher), 24, 27–28, 32, 35, 60, 97,
190, 209; 4th Earl of (Georgia Trustee),
24, 51, 54, 131, 216
shared space, 175, *183*
Sharp, Granville, 157, 202–6, 213
Sierra Leone, 203
Skidaway Island (settlement), *67,* 95, 104,
118
slavery, 3, 23, 36, 52, 60–61, 69–70, 108–9, 116,
128–33, 190, 192–94, 201–6, 212, 213, 227n59
Slavery (More), 202
Sloane, Hans, 25, 51, 61, 90, 218
Sloper, William (Georgia Trustee), 217
Smart Growth. *See under* planning
paradigms
Smith, Adam, 26, 200, 213
Smith, Samuel Rev. (Georgia Trustee), 216
social equity, 1–3, 159–60, 162–63, 165, 169
Society for the Promotion of Christian
Knowledge (SPCK), 41, 43, 52, 209

Society for the Propagation of the Gospel in Foreign Parts (SPG), 41, 43, 52

Some Account of the Design of the Trustees for establishing Colonys in America (Oglethorpe tract), 45, 49, 63, 66, 69, 74, 76, 78–79, 86, 94–96, 98, 210, 222n23

Some Account of the Trustees Design for the Establishment of the Colony of Georgia in America (Martyn tract), 45, 48, 51, 63–64, 68, 89–90, 96, 210

Sottile, Christian, 144

Sottile & Sottile (urban designers), 145, 147

South Carolina: assistance in settling Georgia, 101–4; and the "Carolina way," 193; embrace of and dependence on slavery, 107, 128–31; Indian trade in, 104, 106, 127–28, 132–33; and Malcontents, 115–16, 128–31; relations with Georgia, 115–16, 123, 128–31, 159

South Sea Bubble, 17, 210

South Sea Company, 15, 209

Spain, 9, 17, 44, 56, 58, 108–9, 111, 114–15, 118, 127, 194, 205, 211. *See also* St. Augustine, Fla. (Spanish town and citadel)

Spalding, Phinizy, 1, 192, 228n1

spatial equity (spatial equality), 100, 140, 175, 178, 183, 186, 204

squares, 174–77, 179, 181–82, *183. See also* Savannah plan: ward design and specifications of

Stephens, Thomas, 111, 113–14, 125, 129

Stephens, William, 61, 111–16, 123–25, 128, 130–31, 193, 211, 212, 217

stock market, 15–17, *18*

Stoicism, 25

Stono Rebellion, 211

Strong, Jonathan, 203

Structure of Scientific Revolutions, The (Kuhn), 228n3

Stuart, Charles Edward ("Bonnie Prince Charlie, The Young Pretender"), 6, 195, 212

Stuart, James Francis Edward ("The Old Pretender"). *See* James III ("The Old Pretender")

Stuart, House of, 4, *6, 7*

suburbanization, 161. *See also under* Savannah, city of (post-colonial era)

survey units of measurement. *See* measurement, units of

sustainable development. *See under* planning paradigms

Swabians, 106

Swift, Jonathan, 25, 30–31, 190, 209, 210

Tailfer, Patrick, 113, 129

tail-male inheritance, 62, 108, 223–24n49

Taylor, Paul, 132

Tel Aviv, Israel, 172, 175

Thomas Square, 157

Thomson, James, 32–34, 210

Thorpe village, 117

Thrale, Hester, 200

Thunderbolt village, *67,* 95, 104, 117

Timgad, plan of, *76, 77,* 112

Timisoara, 12, 76–77

Toland, John, 28, 209

Tomochichi, Chief, 102, 106–7, 127, 210–11

Tory party, 17–19, 55

Tower, Christopher (Georgia Trustee), 217

Tower, Thomas (Georgia Trustee), 51, 54, 217

Town and Square (Zucker), 177

town plan (within the Oglethorpe Plan), defined, 68

towns (in the Georgia Colony), *110;* list of, 117–18

traffic-calming, 176, 179

translatio virtutis, 57, 59, 61, 190, 198, 203, 223n44

Tricentennial Plan. *See* Savannah, city of (post-colonial era): Chatham County–Savannah Tricentennial Plan (comprehensive plan)

trust blocks, *82,* 86–88, 139, 141–42, 144, 146, 148

Trustees for the Establishment of the Colony of Georgia in America: amendments to the plan for agrarian equality, 62; appoint William Stephens as secretary, 111; approve constitution for Georgia Assembly, 116; attorneys banned, 31; charter of, 43–45; and colonist recruitment, 45–47; colonists, 103*t;* and colonist demographics, 103–16; counties of Savannah and Frederica established by, 115; crops envisioned by, 62; and design of the colony, 55–58; division among, 54, 223n36; end of Trustee period, 117; genesis as the Bray Associates, 40–44; guiding principles of, 58–59; land allocation by, 60; Native American policy of, 103; painting of (Verelst), 106, *107;* and parliamentary grants, 103; prohibition of slavery by, 60–61, 108, 116; purposes in forming, 52–56; relations with South Carolina, 107–8; vision for Georgia, 58

Trustees' Garden, 90, 112

trust farm lots, 92, 98

Turin, Italy, 12, 26, 75, 89, 210

Turner, Frederick Jackson, 59, 192

Turner thesis, 223n44

Tybee Island, *67,* 104, *110,* 118

Tyrconnel, Lord Viscount (Georgia Trustee), 217

Tyrer, George (Georgia Trustee), 217

tything blocks (and lots), *82,* 83*t,* 86–88, 139, 141–42, 144, 146, 148–49, 166

Uchee, 102

Unitas Fratrum, 105

United Nations, 163; Agenda, 21, 162; Brundtland Commission, 162; UNESCO World Heritage Sites, 75–76

University of Virginia, 137

Upper Creeks, 102

urban design. *See under* planning paradigms

urban ecology, 171

urban renewal. *See under* Housing Act of 1954 *and* Savannah, city of (post-colonial era)

Utrecht, Treaty of, 106

Vasari, Georgio, 74

Vaudois, 106

Verelst, Harman, 54, 217

Verelst, William, 106–7

Vernon, James (Georgia Trustee), 54, 123, 131, 217

Vernonburg village, 95, 117

Victorian era, 201

villages ("out-villages"), *110;* list of, 117–18. *See also* Savannah plan: village district of

Villas of the Ancients (Castell), 22, 38, 72, 74, 91, 210

Vitruvian Man (da Vinci), 74

Vitruvius, 30, 74, 98

Vitruvius Britannicus (Campbell), 74

Voltaire (François-Marie Arouet), 12, 23, 26, 35, 190, 197, 206, 209, 210, 212, 213

Wall, Eleanor. *See* Oglethorpe, Eleanor (JEO's mother)

Walpole, Horace, 197, 199–200, 213

Walpole, Robert, *18,* 19, 21, 30–32, 43, 52, 54, 197, 200, 211, 213, 220n37

War of Austrian Succession, 194

Water is Wide, The (Conroy), 166

way-finding, 175, 177

Wealth of Nations, The (Smith), 213

Wesley, Charles, 108–9

Wesley, John, 108–9, 111, 113

Westbrook Manor, 9, 13, 194

Westbrook village, 104, 118

Whig party, 11, 14, *18,* 19, 27, 30

White, John (Georgia Trustee), 51, 54–55, 217

Whitefield, George, 113

Wilberforce, William, 193, 202, 204

William III (William of Orange), King, *6,* 8–10, 209

William and Mary, *6,* 8–9, 15, 209. *See also* Mary II, Queen; William III (William of Orange), King

Williams, Helen Maria, 202

Williams, Jonathan, 197

Williams, Robert, 129

Wittgenstein, Ludwig, 192

Wollstonecrft, Mary, 202

Wright, Elizabeth (JEO's wife), 194, 197, 211, 213

Wrightsborough, Ga., 157

Wyndham, William, 14, 20, 55

Yale University, 42–43

Yamacraw, 101–2, *110,* 127, 210

yellow fever. *See* environmental conditions (Georgia Colony): disease

yeomen, 3, 68, 70, 78–79, 81, 88, 96, 105

Zamosc, plan of, *75*

Zinzendorf, Count Nikolaus Ludwig von, 105

Zucker, Paul, 159–60, 177